Nineteenth-Century Lives

Essays presented to
JEROME HAMILTON BUCKLEY

Edited by
Laurence S. Lockridge,
John Maynard, and
Donald D. Stone

Bibliography compiled by
David M. Staines

The right of the
University of Cambridge
to print and sell
all manner of books
was granted by
Henry VIII in 1534.
The University has printed
and published continuously
since 1584.

CAMBRIDGE UNIVERSITY PRESS

Cambridge
New York   New Rochelle
Melbourne   Sydney

Published by the Press Syndicate of the University of Cambridge
The Pitt Building, Trumpington Street, Cambridge CB2 1RP
32 East 57th Street, New York, NY 10022, USA
10 Stamford Road, Oakleigh, Melbourne 3166, Australia

First published 1989

Printed in Great Britain at
the University Press, Cambridge

British Library cataloguing in publication data

Nineteenth-century lives: essays presented to Jerome Hamilton Buckley
1. English biographical literature, *1837–* – Critical studies
I. Lockridge, Laurence S.   II. Maynard, John, *1941–*
III. Stone, Donald D. (Donald David)   IV. Buckley, Jerome Hamilton
820.9'351

Library of Congress cataloguing in publication data

Nineteenth-century lives: essays presented to Jerome Hamilton Buckley
/ edited by Laurence S. Lockridge, John Maynard, and Donald D. Stone:
bibliography compiled by David Staines.
p.   cm.
Bibliography.
Includes index.
1. English literature – 19th century – History and criticism.
2. Authors, English – 19th century – Biography – History and criticism.
3. Great Britain – Biography – History and criticism.   4. Narration (Rhetoric)
5. Autobiography.   6. Buckley, Jerome Hamilton.
I. Buckley, Jerome Hamilton.   II. Lockridge, Laurence S., 1942–
III. Maynard, John, 1941– .   IV. Stone, Donald D.
V. Staines, David, 1946–
PR463.N56   1989
820'.9'008–dc19   88-18673   CIP

ISBN 0 521 34181 7

CE

Contents

CONTENTS

Contributors

RICHARD D. ALTICK is Regents' Professor of English, Emeritus, at the Ohio State University. His essay in this volume is a result of the conjunction of interests represented in two of his numerous books, *Lives and Letters: A History of Literary Biography in England and America* (1965) and *Paintings from Books: Art and Literature in Britain 1760–1900* (1985).

MARGARET ATWOOD is a Canadian novelist, poet, editor, and critic. Among her most recent works are *The Handmaid's Tale* (1986), *Bluebeard's Egg and Other Stories* (1986), and *Selected Poems II* (1987).

MORTON N. COHEN is Professor of English, Emeritus, at the City College and the Graduate Center of the City University of New York. The editor of *Rudyard Kipling to Rider Haggard: The Record of a Friendship* (1965) and of *The Letters of Lewis Carroll* (1979), he is currently writing a biography of Lewis Carroll.

NORMAN KELVIN is Professor of English at the City College and Graduate Center of the City University of New York. He is the author of *A Troubled Eden: Nature and Society in the Work of George Meredith* (1961) and *E. M. Forster* (1967) and the editor of *The Collected Letters of William Morris* (1984–).

ROBERT KIELY is Professor and Chair of the Department of English at Harvard University. His publications include *Robert Louis Stevenson and the Fiction of Adventure* (1964), *The Romantic Novel in England* (1972), and *Beyond Egotism: The Fiction of James Joyce, Virginia Woolf, and D. H. Lawrence* (1980).

J. Hillis Miller is UCI Distinguished Professor at the
University of California at Irvine. The author of many works of
literary criticism, his most recent books are *Fiction and Repetition*
(1982), *The Linguistic Moment* (1985), and *The Ethics of Reading*
(1987).

Phyllis Rose is Professor of English at Wesleyan University.
Her writings include *Woman of Letters: A Life of Virginia Woolf*
(1978), *Parallel Lives: Five Victorian Marriages* (1983), and *Writing of
Women: Essays in a Renaissance* (1985).

John D. Rosenberg is Professor of English at Columbia
University. He is the author of *The Darkening Glass: A Portrait of
Ruskin's Genius* (1961), *The Fall of Camelot: A Study of Tennyson's
'Idylls of the King'* (1973), and *Carlyle and the Burden of History*
(1985).

Margaret Diane Stetz, founding editor of the journal *Turn-
of-the-Century Women*, has written widely on Victorian and
modern literature. Co-author, with Mark Samuels Lasner, of
England in the 1880s: Old Guard and Avant-Garde (1988), she
teaches English and Women's Studies at Georgetown University.

Carl Woodring is G. E. Woodberry Professor of Literature at
Columbia University. Among his books are *Victorian Samplers*
(1952), *Wordsworth* (corrected edition 1968), and *Politics in English
Romantic Poetry* (1970).

The Editors: Laurence S. Lockridge is Professor of English
and Co-Director of the Poetics Institute at New York University.
He is the author of *Coleridge the Moralist* (1977) and *The Ethics of
Romanticism* (1989).

John Maynard is Professor and Chair of English at New York
University. He is the author of *Browning's Youth* (1977) and
Charlotte Brontë and Sexuality (1984).

Donald D. Stone is Professor of English at Queens College.
His publications include *Novelists in a Changing World: Meredith,
James, and the Transformation of English Fiction in the 1880s* (1972)
and *The Romantic Impulse in Victorian Fiction* (1980).

THE BIBLIOGRAPHER: David M. Staines is Professor of English at the University of Ottawa. Among the books he has written or edited are *The Canadian Imagination: Dimensions of a Literary Culture* (1977) and *Tennyson's Camelot: The 'Idylls of the King' and its Medieval Sources* (1982).

Jerome Hamilton Buckley

To read Tennyson or Dickens seriously in the late 1930s and early 40s was, Jerome Hamilton Buckley recalls, "a matter of perversity." He began to focus his attention on the Victorians while a graduate student, at a time when nineteenth-century literature was under a cloud. "Few ... can fully appreciate," one of the contributors to this volume, Richard D. Altick, has noted, "how recently, and from how low a starting point, this particular branch of English literary study rose." That Victorian studies have risen so vigorously is owing, in good measure, to the dedication, scholarship, and inspiring influence of Jerome Buckley.

Canadian by birth, he took his undergraduate degree at the University of Toronto, studying Elizabethan literature with Northrop Frye and Shakespeare with Edward John Pratt. As a young critic and poet, Buckley reviewed new works by Virginia Woolf and Robinson Jeffers, and won a prize for an essay entitled "New Techniques in Contemporary Fiction." He had chosen, by happy coincidence, to study at Victoria College, the most literary of the Toronto colleges; and things Victorian would increasingly matter to him when, like many Canadian literary students of this century, he chose Harvard Graduate School. His essay on the Ruskin–Whistler trial won the Ruskin Prize. A seminar with Howard Mumford Jones on Victorian critics stimulated Buckley's interest in William Ernest Henley. In his second year at Harvard, he studied with Robert Frost, whose publisher David Nutt had also been Henley's publisher, and who encouraged his students' interest in the late nineteenth- and early twentieth-century poets. Buckley's dissertation on Henley eventually became his first book, *William Ernest Henley: A Study in the Counter-Decadence of the 'Nineties* (1945), which received strong critical attention.

With the publication in 1951 of *The Victorian Temper*, Buckley's reputation as a leading Victorianist was firmly established. The book has remained, for four decades, the most incisive introduction to the study of Victorian culture. His next work of Victorianist revaluation, *Tennyson: The Growth of a Poet* (1960), reestablished Tennyson's reputation for modern literary studies. Buckley's books have tended to follow a pattern wherein the study of a particular figure leads to a work of cultural synthesis. Upon completing the study of Tennyson, he turned to the challenging topic of time in the nineteenth century. Always a philosophical reader of literature, Buckley, in *The Triumph of Time* (1966), investigated the conflict of personal with public time. Thereafter, he focused on the temporal growth of the individual in time, as reflected in the genre of the *Bildungsroman* (*Season of Youth: The Bildungsroman from Dickens to Golding*, 1974). This standard work led, in turn, to the comprehensive study of literary autobiography. *The Turning Key: Autobiography and the Subjective Impulse since 1800* (1984). In addition to authoring so many of the seminal books in Victorian studies, Buckley has found time to oversee anthologies, editions, and secondary source books in the field.

His teaching career has taken him from the University of Wisconsin (1942–54) to Columbia (1952–53, 1954–61), and finally to Harvard (1961–), where he was named Gurney Professor of English Literature in 1975. (Douglas Bush, his predecessor as Gurney Professor, welcomed Buckley to Harvard "with open arms . . . filled with theses.") He has guest-lectured from Hawaii to Norway, and has won honours that include the Christian Gauss Award of Phi Beta Kappa and two John Simon Guggenheim Fellowships.

Jerome Buckley is known to his literally hundreds of former students now in the profession as Jerry. It is a nickname never used without affection. We were not surprised to find that everyone shared our own sense of love and gratitude to such a caring mentor and friend. All spoke of the same generous person through the differing perspectives of their own relationships with him. One would speak of his good nature – how he approved and encouraged, even to the point of a supportive kind of intellectual indulgence. Another marveled at his freedom from possessiveness, his ability to allow growth, even to revel in others' growth. He has a humility, only too rare in our profession, that allows him to focus on students' needs and to tease out strengths in them. Another noted how Jerry took him into account and responded to him personally and to the interests he had. He would actually listen, talk, and then listen *again*. Another noted how he never stints in any personal favor or professional obligation. His grace, speed, and efficiency are remarkable, his readings of others' work responsible, incisive, helpful. For his students, his magisterial scholarship became a permanent possession through his personal presence. Victorian England continues to be, one person said for us all, the one Jerry taught us. Another told us he always starts a major new project by drawing once again on Jerry's reserve of indulgence and discussing it thoroughly with him.

In all our discussions, Jerry's comic spirit, his sense of fun kept coming up. He is damned funny, one said; like some Victorians he loves he has a genuine eccentricity in his humor. Many recalled his wonderful performances in taking on the personalities of writers he discussed. Who can forget how Jerry *became* Dickens, or how he sang or danced to make his points or did that outrageous Trabb's boy: "Don't know ya."

The hospitality of Jerry and his wife, Elizabeth Adams Buckley, who is also an educator, was much on our minds. Former students from other countries recalled Jerry and Elizabeth's very welcome Thanksgiving spreads. They regularly invited students to their home, one recalled, and didn't seem to make social distinctions between students, young professors, and senior colleagues. Wisconsin when Jerry was there, Columbia with Jerry, the days of the Harvard Victorians, MLA dinners, or more exotic international conferences, all came alive once again to former students and colleagues as they remembered the friendship and warmth of Jerry and Elizabeth. We know students and friends everywhere join our distinguished contributors who delight, as we do, in celebrating Jerry Buckley as a remarkable man and scholar. We dedicate this volume to him with great intellectual respect and deep affection.

Preface

A principal question raised in these essays is what it means to narrate a life. Drawing largely on nineteenth-century texts, the ten contributors explore boundaries of fact and fiction. They tend to see a merging of biography, autobiography, and the novel within the broader genre of narrative – a merging which can be understood from a purely theoretical perspective but which has also been increasingly witnessed in modern literary history. Margaret Atwood, J. Hillis Miller, and Phyllis Rose frame the discussion most generally. Atwood writes: "The biographer, like the novelist, is a constructor of narratives; it's just that the ground rules are a little different." Determining what these ground rules are in their difference is a recurring interest in these original essays, which otherwise range from the trope of prosopopoeia to grandmother's diary to the life of Darwin.

Several contributors consider the fictional, figurative, and mythic components of biographical form. Carl Woodring calls *The Prelude* a *Bildungsroman* in verse, a form in which the poet can ironically achieve a greater "sincerity" because he is not tied to a standard of literal fact. Within this form Wordsworth cannot strictly lie about the facts of his own life. As a graduate student, Atwood was taught *The Prelude* as an autobiographical text and felt "squirmy" about how gossipy minutiae of a life might subvert our sense of literary value. She then recognized that biographies are only stories of lives, with no privileged authority to fix a life forever or exhaust the truth about it.

Nineteenth-century writers often merge categories of fact and fiction through indirection, or even in violation of their expressed intent, as scrutiny of rhetorical figures can reveal. Miller is most extreme in his claims for the inevitably figurative nature of autobiography. He takes the morbid trope of prosopopoeia – the summoning of the mask of the dead – to be its mastertrope. In *Praeterita* Ruskin attempts to dissever himself from tropes, in keeping with his attack on the "pathetic fallacy." In his Preface he presents himself as a harmless drudge, an archivist who eschews any attempt to give a shaped life under the illusion of a coherent "I" laid out in purposeful narrative. If Wordsworth disavows the generic expectations of autobiography by swerving toward the novelist, Ruskin disavows them by swerving toward the mere chronicler. Miller presents some textual evidence that Ruskin himself employs prosopopoeia.

Like Ruskin, Darwin sets himself up as a dispassionate, objective narrator, who, as John Rosenberg observes, does not attempt a novelistic unity of narration. He gives us mere "recollections" instead of autobiography. In a discontinuous narrative he collects moments of his earlier life as specimens for disinterested analysis. Rosenberg finds the "grand organizing metaphor of autobiography" to be the journey, which Darwin enacted in his own literal voyage on the *Beagle*. Other "ancient archetypes" inform Darwin's ostensibly detached and objective writings: the Book of Genesis is naturalized in *The Origin of Species*; the primal Edenic transgression is repeated in his account of stealing apples from his father's orchard as a young boy.

Norman Kelvin thinks Morris's life, like Darwin's, enacts a metaphor, derived in his case from the structures of his own art. Just as the often violent narrative content of Morris's painting finds containment and "rest" in a decorative frame, so his career as a political activist makes up the violent narrative content to which his career as a designer provides a frame – a ratio reversed when Morris becomes so passionately committed to his art and "Morris & Co." that politics is displaced to the frame. This instrumental metaphor for reading the patterns of Morris's life is, in one sense, Kelvin's, but he thinks it is also Morris's – a metaphor consubstantial with the life because embedded in Morris's own artistic constructions.

That biography *ought* to be enhanced by the tropes of fiction is argued by Richard Altick and by Rose, who suggest the grounds on which literary value judgments can be made. Altick finds that in many nineteenth-century art biographies there is a fear of fictionalizing – combined with an "indiscriminate inclusiveness" of fact – which makes the majority of these deservedly neglected. Only in a biography such as Gilchrist's of William Blake, where the more discriminating and artful conventions of literary biography come into play, does one find a production that answers to our sense of literary value. Rose, in turn, believes we are now at a period when biographers are effecting a "mimetic shift" in aspiring without apology to the condition of the novel. Biographers should break away from their naive worship, she argues, of "fact." Nor should they necessarily write biographies on the artistic model of fictions from the past. She notes that biographer Justin Kaplan narrates a basic discontinuity in Walt Whitman's life; he declines to structure this biography on the convention of strict temporal sequence; and he employs more than a single narrative point of view. Rose implies that the novelistic paradigm for biographers might more appropriately be the experimental than the conventional novel.

The novel has of course already found a renewed vitality in turning, contrariwise, toward journalistic fact, as in the novels of Capote and Mailer. This development has its precedents. Margaret Stetz describes the aggressive violation of boundaries of fact and fiction in the guilt-ridden novels of the 1890s, in which novelists portray the contemporary reader-as-avenger transported into their own fictions. Altick notes the irony that Thackeray's novel *The Newcomes* tells us more about the world of contemporary art than the art biographies themselves. Interestingly, Rose thinks contemporary novelists may be seeking "to regain the amplitude and solidity of the Victorian novel."

Whether one considers the novel or the biography, these observations relate to the nature and professed power of the narrator. Miller argues the presumption of the biographical narrator; he links Ruskin's seeming self-effacement to his tacit recognition that only God can grant himself the power of summoning the dead. Ruskin necessarily goes on being God in spite of his professed humility. Atwood agrees: although biographers are telling only stories of lives, they imitate God in attempting to subsume all "possible incarnations" of a person "in one form"; the biographer's "peculiar art is to raise the dead." Woodring remarks that Wordsworth "looking into a poet's mind is an Adam observing beings that need names." But he also remarks on poetic indeterminacy, seen in Wordsworth's sense that there are limits to "the utmost that we can know." The Blind Beggar chastens divine emulation in *The Prelude*. Wordsworth invites the reader to join him in constructing a self out of his poem. Down the scale of professed power, we find Darwin, who amiably situates himself counter to the dramatic situation of prosopopoeia. Hardly a god summoning the dead back to life, he calls himself "a dead man in another world looking back at my life."

As in the novel, the role played by the biographer-as-narrator may be determined less by the given rules of the genre than by how particular biographers choose to present themselves. Whether they are living gods who summon back the dead, or dead persons who summon back the living, may be a matter of compositional choice. Some might present themselves as "nobodies" in Robert Kiely's third sense of the term: persons "of no importance or authority," self-effacing whether writing of themselves or, more likely, of some other person. Or they might present themselves as nobodies in Kiely's second sense – disembodied spooks or spirits, rather like Darwin. Rousseau, of course, chooses a different voice in *The Confessions*: "I have bared my secret soul as Thou thyself hast seen it, Eternal Being!" He declares his enterprise to be without precedent, and his own life to be "different" from all others.

Most of the contributors raise questions about the formal qualities of biography. Yet the more traditional search for fact and discovery necessarily preoccupies many of the contributors. Morton Cohen confronts a textual lacuna in the evidence of Lewis Carroll's life, and is confident that, with some sleuthing and a bit of good luck, he can ascertain what the facts are. The sleuthing motive is seen in Miller, who discovers a contradiction that betrays Ruskin's own pathetic fallacy. Though well aware of the mythic resonance of Darwin's writings, Rosenberg sets out to ascertain what the case was – for instance in Darwin's relationship with his father, who has been thought by earlier biographers to have been a largely negative force in his son's career. Some aspects of a life are, as he says, "rooted in fact." And Altick can tell us confidently when a biography such as Walter Thornbury's *Life of J. M. W. Turner* resembles a bad novel in its hyperbole and distortions of fact and character.

If a biographer were convinced, before all investigation began, of the wholesale fictionality of biography, one wonders what the compelling motive for "investigation" would continue to be. Though they do not agree on the nature of biography, perhaps all our contributors would agree that it retains some connection with finding out things about a person, in addition to "doing things with words."

Acknowledgments

The editors wish to express their gratitude to the many persons who have offered such generous help in preparing this volume: Margaret Atwood, Henry Auster, Andrew Brown, Morton Cohen, Brook Hopkins, Norman Kelvin, James Kincaid, Harriet Ritvo, John Rosenberg, David Staines, Carl Woodring.

1

Biographobia: some personal reflections on the act of biography

MARGARET ATWOOD

My grandmother died at the impressive age of ninety-four. I knew her as an austere old lady, a Nova Scotia rural matron with stringent views on washing your hands before meals, a person you had to tiptoe around verbally; there were certain things – quite a few things – that could not be discussed in her presence. She did not smoke, drink, or swear, and she handled difficult social situations by talking about the weather. She was said, by her daughters – my mother and my aunts – to have had a sense of humour.

After she was dead, one of my aunts discovered a short diary my grandmother had kept in the summer of 1899, when she was sixteen. It was written in pencil, on cheap scribbler paper, with many abbreviations, dashes and exclamation marks. My aunt transcribed this diary and sent copies to interested relatives, myself among them.

My reaction to this act was twofold. First, horror. This was a private diary! What would my straightbacked grandmother have thought about such a violation of her privacy? But then, the question that must have occurred to every biographer who has ever set pen to paper intruded: why did my grandmother keep her diary? Why did Pepys keep his? Why do people write diaries, if they don't want people to read them, ever? Is it only to remind themselves of what they were like when they were younger? If you were the last person alive on the earth, if you were marooned on the moon with no chance of rescue, would you keep a diary?

What is it that impels people – even people like my grandmother, the last sort you would expect – to so novelize their lives, to attempt to impose some sort of selection, form and meaning upon them, and then to save the results? If people do these things, don't they intend – like every other writer – to be read? Perhaps my aunt's transcription was not a violation after all, but a discovery, of a message to the future, half-mischievously hidden away by my grandmother eighty-seven years ago. Perhaps she had not been writing only to herself at all. Perhaps she had also been writing to me.

My second reaction was amazement, for when I began to read the diary – in a contest between horror and curiosity, curiosity usually wins – I discovered a person I did not realize had ever existed. On July 15, 1899, she writes – and I notice myself using the present tense, as if she is still alive, as if she is, in fact, sixteen and it is still July 15, 1899 – she writes, "I made a strawberry shortcake for tea on Monday night and it was fairly good – I put in the soda this time. Tuesday morning I started reviewing the Latin; then Abbie and I went out and walked the fence in the lane for awhile; and then we went down to the washing pool and waded – I got my underclothes soaking. *You must never tell or let on to anybody* that you know about the last two, for *it's both scandalous and ridiculous* for a great girl like me to walk fences and go wading."

Later she says, "I wish to goodness I knew when to keep my tongue still but alas, alack I do not."

And later still: "Now, mind you it's Tuesday & I haven't written oh, what a girl am I? I'm ambitious too, have never studied my Latin a bit! Oh, you lazy, lazy, lazy good-for-nothing thing!"

No one would have suspected, meeting my grandmother in her later years, that a fence-walker and pond-wader, who considered herself too talkative and lazy, was hidden somewhere within her. Yet this was the case, for do authentic manuscripts lie?

Another mystery: why did my grandmother's confession of what she considered to be her faults make me think better of her? Was it simply a little of the unattractive glee we experience at the sight of human fallibility when it doesn't happen to be our own? Or was it because I knew more of the story than the writer of the scribbler pages could possibly have known? I knew she was to get married, to have six children, one of whom would not survive, to outlive her husband, to become a ferocious bridge-player, and to die, finally, confused and unsure of where she was. It was my knowledge, not the writer's, that made her high-spirited jottings so poignant for me. I knew also that her sister Abbie, her fellow fence-walker and pond-wader, was to die almost blind, almost deaf, almost paralyzed, but with her mind clear and active. I knew that she would say, to my visiting aunt, "I am lying here telling myself the story of my life. When I get to the end, I will close the book." I knew that she did.

My position *vis-à-vis* my grandmother's manuscript is that of the biographer, who feels compelled to make, of other people's lives, a story. You can make a story when you know the end, and when you get to the end, you close the book. Our stories of our own lives are always incomplete; it is left to others to complete them.

My grandmother's diary ends: "Well, half the holidays are gone, never to come back, so goodbye, goodbye, goodbye books." As far as I know, these were the last words of deliberate self-revelation she was ever to write.

When I was in university, I hated biography. I hated it so much that I refused to study Wordsworth for my English Romantics examination, because the approach to Wordsworth taken by the professor had been largely biographical. I did not want to know about Dove Cottage. Dove Cottage embarassed me. If the famous daffodils had been actual daffodils, actually glimpsed by Wordsworth in the course of an actual walk and duly recorded in Dorothy's journal, I wished to remain in ignorance of it. The only piece of Wordsworth's biography that I welcomed was the news that Lucy had never existed.

But in fact the only biographies I hated were those of writers. I read, avidly, the biographies of other people, people who, I felt, had the right to have biographies written about them; for, not being writers themselves, they had no access to the word, to the "story" part of the story of their lives, and they needed help. Also they had done real things, in the external world, whereas writers, usually, had not; all they had done was scribble,

scribble, scribble, like Mr. Gibbon. So what was there to say about the lives of writers? I read biographies of military men such as General Rommel and Napoleon, and of politicians such as Disraeli. I read biographies of scientists and explorers, even of painters, actors, musicians and dancers. None of them gave me any qualms. But when it came to the biographies of writers – which I had to read, in the course of my studies, whether I liked it or not – I felt squirmy.

I wonder, now, what accounted for this squirminess of mine. Possibly it was that I intended to be a writer myself, and reading the biographies of writers made me self-conscious. Despite myself, I would start thinking of myself in the third person. "It is April the second, nineteen sixty one. She walks along the street, contemplating the distance between herself and the next street-car stop. She is thinking about Kafka. Her feet hurt. She is thinking she should have worn a different pair of shoes." This sort of thing, if it went on long enough, drove me mad, partly because, in the third person, I sounded much less dramatic than I would have liked. Perhaps my uneasiness in the face of writers' biographies was caused by the thought that my own would come out dull.

But also I didn't want to be spied on. I knew, from reading biographies, what ragbags of conjecture could accumulate around a cryptic letter, a chance remark made by a third person, a shred of malice. Did Keats have syphilis? Did Shelley drown on purpose? Why didn't Jane Austen ever get married? Could *Paradise Lost* be explained by blind Milton's shoddy treatment of his stenographic daughters? Did it matter that Poe was a drunk and Pope a hunchback? If the smell of cabbage cooking was supposed to enter into the poem, which particular cabbage, cooked when, had merged itself with *The Waste Land*? What light did Tennyson's aside about his suspenders, at the garden party, cast on *Idylls of the King*? Did Byron's remark about the poetry of Keats – that it was "Johnny Keats's *p-ss a bed* poetry" – illuminate the "Ode to a Nightingale"? It seemed to me that a lot got into critical biographies that, if it had been exchanged over the back fence instead of typeset and hardbound, would have been called bubbleheaded gossip. Biography seemed to me subversive, a danger to art.

4

And what about me? I was, after all, a budding female writer, and such people were, at that time, rarer and therefore more subject to mythology than they are now. I had already heard some interesting rumours about myself which would have been more interesting, to me, if they had been true. What would be made of me, by the misguided, when I wasn't around to set them straight? Would someone, sometime, ever chronicle my wardrobe (scanty and, at that time, mostly black), make caustic remarks about my hairdos (dubious), try to unearth my boyfriends? I hoped not.

Every attempt I made to keep a journal was blighted by the venomous fogs of biography. "Went to Eaton's. It rained. Dinner with D." That was about all I could bring myself to squeeze out. Occasionally I tried to be more literate, and to write about what I was trying to write; but my profound literary thoughts, once I had got them down on the page, looked either too pompous or too stupid for words. My embryonic journals, which lurched between staccato and bloat, seldom survived three days. What person's life, I mused, looked at through a microscope, comes out admirable? Mankind cannot bear too much biography.

There was yet another problem. I was a budding *female* writer, and, whether I liked it or not – and I didn't – what the biographers had to say about female writers was not encouraging. This was the early sixties, when the dread hand of Togetherness lay heavy upon the land and couples prayed to Our Freud, and most biographies of woman writers were veiled warnings. Emily Dickinson was weird, skipped about in white dresses, hid in cupboards, and she never got married. Christina Rossetti looked at life through the wormholes in a shroud, and also she never got married. Charlotte Brontë died of pregnancy, they said, Emily of TB, and also *she* never got married. George Eliot looked like a horse, and although she did get married, it was awfully late in life and she never had children. Then there were Virginia Woolf and Sylvia Plath, who had one-upped everyone else in the self-destructive department. Could it be that I wasn't gloomy or crazy enough to be an authentic female writer? There wasn't a lot of uplift in these biographies; all and all, these woman writers had not fulfilled their femininity, the way you were supposed to. Safer by far for the aspiring woman writer just to read their books, and to leave the stories of their warped, doomed or discouraging lives alone. And so, for a while, I did.

But not forever. I suppose I began to like the biographies of writers when I began to recognize them for what they are: the stories of lives, the *stories* of lives. They were not the truth, the whole truth, nothing but the truth, the bare-naked truth; they were composed of selected truths, and therefore subjective; they were not the only possible version of a given life. I didn't have to take the biographer's word for it; I could have second opinions. Maybe the women writers weren't as miserable as their biographers said they were. Maybe they liked their lives, at least some of the time, even if they never got married.

The biographer, like the novelist, is a constructor of narratives; it's just that the ground rules are a little different. Novels have to convince the reader that the imagined is true, and therefore they have to be plausible; whereas biographies, having some grounding in factuality, can cross the boundary between credibility and the totally bizarre with more impunity. All novelists know that the truth, if not stranger than fiction, is at least more unbelievable. If you were to read, in a novel, that a man had presented his son, on his twenty-first birthday, with an account for all the expenses incurred in his upbringing, including the doctor's bill for his delivery at birth, you'd think the novelist was exaggerating; but the bill really existed, and the son was Ernest Thompson Seton. (Seton paid it.)

I suppose I began to think about biographies, in their Platonic form, when I was travelling in Wales and someone told me the history of the man who had fought a successful battle to institute cremation. The Christians opposed him: what would happen to the resurrection of the body if, when the time came, there was nothing around but a pile of ashes? I'd never thought about the resurrection of the body in such concrete terms before. I began to wonder *which* body God would see fit to resurrect. If you'd died at ninety, was that the body you'd be stuck with, arthritis and all? Or would you be sixteen? If your mother had died when you were sixteen, what a shock it would be to her, and how cruel really, if you came back ninety.

I do not wish to suggest the biographers confuse themselves

with God, but they do have a problem in common: in a nutshell, which body? Which point in time marks the real person? Which act, which detail, which comment is the most revealing, the most typical? And the biographer's solution must be to try to imitate God, and to subsume all possible incarnations in one form. The biographer stands in the place of Set, the God of the Underworld, before whom the souls of the dead must stand to have their lives weighed and judged, and who, incidentally, is shown with the head of a jackal. For – it must be admitted – there is a slight odour of scavenger about the biographer, a slight air of sniffing about among rags and shreds, a discreet crunching of bones.

No one seems to write biographies of biographers. If they did, and if they did it well, we would speculate a good deal more than we do about the motives of the biographers themselves. The lives of great men used to be presented to the reader as examples worthy of emulation, but that pretense appears to have fallen by the wayside. What now drives the biographers on? What draws them to their subjects? Is it affinity and admiration, or a desire to villify and debunk, to slay the sacred cow, to play David to the overinflated reputation of some paper Goliath, as is frequently the case? Are they riddle addicts, determined to follow the maze of a famous personality to the core of a hidden mystery which they assume is there? Do they believe in an ordered universe, are they determined to make sense of apparent contradictions? Are they novelists *manqué*? They are certainly, as a breed, more sombre than novelists, because, though a novelist may choose to end her story with a marriage, a child, a bend in the road, all biographers, unless they take the risk of embalming a living subject, must end theirs with a death. But surely their peculiar art is to raise the dead and cause them to live again among us; a good biography makes the dead feel less dead. What do they really think they're up to?

For a time I preferred the biographical style of, say, Lytton Strachey: a little caustic, a little wry, a little mean, like a strict, sarcastic nanny who sees through every subterfuge, discounts all excuses, distrusts all motives. No hiding the dirty fingernails, the smashed window. But perhaps the best biographies are written out of a more generous impulse, out of the desire to do justice to a life, to weigh its acts and choices, to see it whole and in its best light. I think of Margaret Drabble's biography of Arnold Bennett. Here's how she ends it, after she has described the inevitable death:

So I, too, feel depressed, unreasonably enough, by his death. He was a great writer from a stony land, and he was also one of the kindest and most unselfish of men. Many a time, re-reading a novel, reading a letter or a piece of his journal, I have wanted to shake his hand, or to thank him, to say well done. I have written this instead.

"To shake his hand." I suppose this may be what we really want, when we read biographies and when we write them: some contact, some communication, some way to know and to pay tribute. Time flows only one way, it seems: from past to future, from them to us. I can't go back to 1899, shake the hand of my dead grandmother as she existed before she had ever imagined me. Half the holidays are gone, never to return; all I have of that "great girl" with the soaking underclothes is the one small paper trace she left behind her, fragile as an eggshell. If she had re-read her own diary, much later, when she was ninety-four, would she ever have recognized it?

Such multiple versions of our multiple selves populate our lives; we play Mr. Hyde, constantly, to our various Dr. Jekylls; we supersede ourselves. We are our own broken puzzles, incomplete, scattered through time. It is up to the biographers, finally, painstakingly, imperfectly, to put us together again.

2

Shaping life in The Prelude

CARL WOODRING

In the study of English autobiographies, *The Prelude* has been awarded a place near the center. As an explorer of the heart less suspect than Rousseau, Wordsworth had a demonstrable effect on Victorian literature of childhood and growth even before *The Prelude* became known in 1850. With the availability of Wordsworth's manuscripts, the version of 1805 in thirteen books on "my earlier life or the growth of my own mind" has become a seminal document of search into origins.[1]

For much of the late nineteenth and early twentieth centuries, *The Prelude* was drawn upon so heavily for autobiographical fact that George W. Meyer felt it necessary to write a book on Wordsworth's childhood utilizing sources clearly distinguishable from the account in the poem.[2] Somewhat autobiographical in the form of its search, and containing passages of inquiry into memories and events, the poem is nonetheless not an autobiography. In all the ways of distinguishing autobiographical poetry from autobiography, *The Prelude* is a poem. Like Byron's extension of Fielding's *Tom Jones* as an "epic poem in prose" in ways that make *Don Juan* an epic poem in prose in verse, *The Prelude* can be called a *Bildungsroman* in blank verse.[3] Of its relation to the facts of Wordsworth's life, one could paraphrase what he said to Isabella Fenwick concerning his "Ode: Intimations of Immortality": "I took hold of the notion of preexistence as having sufficient foundation in humanity for authorizing me to make for my purpose the best use of it I could as a Poet."[4] Henry Nelson Coleridge, nephew and son-in-law of S.T.C., recorded in October 1829 a statement of Wordsworth's that "it is impossible to reconcile the exact truth with poetry," and paraphrased further remarks from the same conversation: "He thought himself entitled to avail himself as a verseman of many notions which he was not prepared to defend literally as a proseman, and he complained of the way in which he had been made answerable for mere plays of the Imagination."[5]

Poetry called for a higher truth than fact could provide. Coleridge, to whom the poem is addressed, would know that the "high argument" concerning an individual mind required a universalizing of personal experience. He would know that a poem needs enough originality in metaphor and the metaphorical to afford the pleasure of surprise. A poet's contract with the reader always contains a clause authorizing "mere plays of the Imagination." Is there in *The Prelude*, then, no reliable relation to what those who knew the poet well could regard as datable facts? Truth in the Wordsworthian sense of embodying emotion with thought in fidelity to the best moral judgment he can bring to the study of his own mind is important to his purposes and to his accomplishment. In receiving such truth, the reader is not to expect scrupulosity toward actual, accidental fact. In autobiography, Rousseau, Mill, and Newman ask their readers to believe that actual physical and mental events in the particular life at issue can bear the interpretation offered. Mill and Newman plead with the reader to get pleasure and instruction not only from asking whether the words before them persuasively interpret ascertainable facts, but also from answering Yes, this author is attempting a faithful interpretation of actual events. *The Prelude* asks the reader for no equivalent response.

The author of *The Prelude*, like the authors of *Jane Eyre* and *David Copperfield*, asks the reader to believe that the words chosen offer truth of value to the reader concerning *a* life, a representative life; if the reader asks whether this life was Charlotte Brontë's, or that life Charles Dickens's, evaluation of their words is unchanged whether the answer is Yes, No, or Arguably. Neither assignment to genre nor literary evaluation depends in any way on knowing how far a work of fiction under consideration is autobiographical. Newman does not wish to be called a liar, and a reader of his *Apologia* assigns a demerit for each degree of disbelief. Dickens, as the author of *Copperfield*, can be false or inadequate to Victorian consciousness, but he cannot in a novel lie about his own life. Wordsworth goes from fiction toward Mill and Newman in encouraging the reader to accept his life-story as representative *because* the author has struggled to find words true to the life he has undergone, the one mental life he can know. His words of the author's yesterday are to convey usable truth for the reader's tomorrow: a probable life, not one possible merely because it happened. It is not entirely fiction that the poem is addressed to a friend who is asked to remember memorable days, and the poet in the poem does share with Wordsworth at line 61 of Book Sixth in 1804 "Four years and thirty, told this very week," but the "I" in *The Prelude* is not an actual person you can sue in a court. Wordsworth cannot lie in *The Prelude*. Even "told this very week," untrue thereafter, remains to make it vivid for readers other than Coleridge. How far the "Vaudracour and Julia" story involves Annette Vallon is a question for Wordsworth's biography, but not one raised by *The Prelude* for readers of poetry.

Wordsworth challenges the meanings of "truth" common in his time. Where fidelity had been to truth that is externally and ideally *right*, Wordsworth, with an influence on Mill and Newman, sought fidelity that is *sincere* to a corresponding breeze of inspiration within.[6] The dream near the beginning of Book Fifth, of the Arab fleeing across a sea of sand to rescue the stone of geometry and the sounding shell of poetry from imminent Deluge, was attributed to a friend in 1805 but to the poet's "I" in 1850. Whether the "friend" derives from the actual Michel Beaupuy who may have told the actual Wordsworth of a similar dream, with or without saying that it had been attributed by others to Descartes, is less significant than the affirmation of the poetic "I," in 1850 as in 1805, that he shared the willingness of the Quixote–Arab to leave wife and children in the cause of saving Shakespeare and Milton (and geometry) from the Deluge that threatens the fragile physical containers of the highest accomplishments of human mind.[7]

Contemplating life, Wordsworth is sincerely faithful to the Romantic mode of the particular. The mode does not require fidelity to fact. Henry James, in declaring that a novelist seeks to convey the appearance of morality, rather than morality itself, makes a distinction similar to the one attributed to Wordsworth between a "verseman" and a "proseman." The task of a poet tracing the growth of an individual mind is, like Conrad's, to make you *see*. To enjoy seeing plainly the appearance of morality will not make you less moral. James's language concerning *appearance* is anticipated in Wordsworth's supplementary essay of 1815: "the appropriate business of poetry (which, neverthe-less, if genuine, is as permanent as pure science) . . . is to treat of things not as they *are*, but as they *appear*; not as they exist in themselves, but as they *seem* to exist to the *senses*, and to the *passions*."[8]

The courtesan Harriette Wilson's *Memoirs of Herself and Others* (1825) begins with an attempt to establish credibility: "I shall not say why and how I became, at the age of fifteen, the mistress of the Earl of Craven." Her power over the "others" in the title of her book is the threat to tell all. The sting of her book lies in its claim to reveal facts. Augustine and Rousseau call their accounts of transgression in adolescence "confessions," but like Words-worth they sharpen points about universal human nature by personal revelation. Wordsworth writes in the spirit of August-ine's insistence that he must have been a selfish baby because all babies are selfish. Readers in a later era may treasure the poem for its evidences of alienation, but the alienation is specific, though double: the author describes himself as lost now in the effort to recover and communicate his feelings, and as alien in the period when his environment became one alienated from him, alien to his human need.

Coleridge at every stage urged Wordsworth to write the great philosophical poem, doctrinal to a nation, that he thought Wordsworth alone could write, in order to eradicate the general disillusionment that had followed the French Revolution. In the poem in process from 1798 through 1805, Wordsworth asks how far circumstances working on his inherent abilities have made him capable of restoring joy in the way Coleridge solicits – in something like the way Coleridge very much needs. An epic task, partly faced with trepidation and partly evaded.

As a major difficulty, the usual problem of a writer – where to begin – was exacerbated because the poem as we have it had beginnings before Wordsworth set about to begin it. Before he could commence a philosophical poem he felt that he must assess his experience and abilities. But before he began the assessment he had already worked a number of memories and epiphanies – "beauteous colours of my early years"[9] – into passages of blank verse related subterraneously to each other but with the surface relationship not initially determined. Not initially determined, and never fixed. Since Ernest de Selincourt's parallel texts of 1926 we have had several editions that juxtapose the 1805 and 1850 versions of particular passages. As helpful as these editions are in revealing origins and changes, the poem that undulated fluidly in Wordsworth's consciousness would be more faithfully represented, not in two editorially fixed versions staring at each other, but in a postmodernist form that allowed multiple juxtapositions of narrated memories and their more discursive explanations. Wordsworth was never quite certain which discursive explanation belonged with which vivid memory. As reconstructed in language, several specific memories were too precious to abandon, but he kept asking in various ways what it meant to remember them. Variations from one version to the next show him asking which were the most communicable meanings that would not be palpably untrue.

Language was as important to him as memory; he was building and altering with memories and words. But uncertainty about the meaning of his life did not leave him attached only to his words. It would have taken a fool indeed to compose 8,000 words as a phrase-maker. Attention to sound and suggestion in language, whether regarded from the poet's viewpoint or the reader's, only partly explains the memorable phrases. The poem consists chiefly, more or less as an autobiography might, of re-created episodes, sometimes offered to illustrate an assessment or a belief, sometimes intruded as if spontaneously and then interpreted. Wordsworth looking into a poet's mind is an Adam observing beings that need names, but interpretation of the undefined required new combinations of familiar words, often in the form of metaphor, discovering likeness where only unlikeness had been seen before. He was building with memories, words, and metaphors. The metaphors interweave. The statue of Isaac Newton as the marble index of a voyaging mind

13

has a less vivid but equally subtle counterpart in a couplet on such minds as Newton's, "powers" ever on the watch

> Like angels stopped upon the wing by sound
> Of harmony from heaven's remotest spheres . . .   (14.98–99)

Angels and the music of the spheres are as commonplace as gravity because higher minds voyaging ever at watch on strange seas discovered their reality.

He designs phrases to show that he has something to say, and more to ask, about language. The distinctively Wordsworthian phrases, as the poem itself declares, make "Breathings for incommunicable powers" (3.190). They give names to states of semi-consciousness in a stretch toward realities always out of reach: "unknown modes of being"; "the sentiment of Being"; the soul with "obscure sense" of "possible sublimity" – "Remembering how she felt, but what she felt / Remembering not"; "Strength came where weakness was not known to be, / At least not felt"; a "renovating virtue" in recollected "spots of time."[10] Often the memorable phrases gain strength from unexpected but telling imprecision, as when he tells how he and a friend, in late adolescence, recited aloud inferior "glittering verse":

> Lifted above the ground by airy fancies
> More bright than madness or the dreams of wine . . .
>
>   (5.569–70)

The "dreams" that might have been expected from madness come as a surprise on their delayed arrival with wine. Rarely but effectively the imaginative imprecision includes synesthesia: the infant "Drinks in the feelings of his Mother's eye" (2.238). It is not complexity of sensation that the poet points to, but the fusion of pleasure and frustration in ineffability.

The phrases quoted most frequently by exegetes are (to steal from Matthew Arnold on the language of the Bible) words thrown toward the idea of interchange with external nature, "unconscious intercourse with beauty" (1.562):

> An auxiliar light
> Came from my mind which on the setting sun
> Bestowed new splendour . . .   (2.369–71)

14

Wordsworth "Saw blessings spread around [him] like a sea" (3.396). The active mind feeds on the active universe, disintegrating it, penetrating it, imagining it, and imagining a common source, a noumenal Royal Exchange, for mind and external nature. The spousal imagery often includes also an anti-Cartesian, unifying interchange of the physical and mental: a "giddy bliss" that "works along the blood"; "my blood appear'd to flow" for "its own pleasure"; "The calm and dead still water lay upon my mind"; "It seemed the very garments that I wore / Preyed on my strength."[11] The human body with a mind perceives the intervenient imagery of nature as a physicality inspired: black drizzling crags spoke as if "a voice were in them" (6.631–33). These interfusions of the physical and spiritual carry through the poem the "correspondent breeze" of inspiration that quickened to a tempest in the glad preamble (1.35–38). Related to the breathings of the poem "for incommunicable powers," the poet as boy felt the presence of "rocks and streams" (now addressed) when he and his companions "breathed" along "the sides of the steep hills" (3.190, 2.131–35). The word "intercourse" had not contracted in Wordsworth's day to mean a merely sexual copulation, but it incorporates at all times in *The Prelude* physical conjunction as metaphor. Intercourse with Nature is for the poet intercourse with the mother's breast, except that physical touch is not felt in isolation from affection:

> a Babe, by intercourse of touch,
> I held mute dialogues with my Mother's heart . . .
>
> (2.268–69)

As the poem grew, it had to be shaped, and reshaped, and counter-shaped. Although Abbie Potts was dependent upon the faulty reconstructions attempted by Arthur Beatty in the absence of aid from the custodians (before 1950) of Wordsworth's manuscripts, there is still value in her attempts to describe how the alternative structures developed as the poet proceeded: wanderings, journey, pilgrimage, cycle of seasons, places of residence, a changing life marked by conversion.[12] Organization of content raised Augustine's double question: What is time, and how is memory related to time? In studying the "growth" of a mind Wordsworth often questioned the assumption of growth: is the movement of a life linear, dialectic, stairstep, cyclic, spiral, discontinuous, fated, random, or several of these in turn or at once? The figurations of time underlying *The River Duddon* (1820) and *Ecclesiastical Sketches* (1822) make clearer why pilgrimage and journey were inadequate concepts for progress in (and on) *The Prelude*. Even if the poet's sole task in this work were a survey of mental change, a life like a river has its intriguingly obscure source; it has an ever-changing flow directed by the slowly changing *other* of banks not unaltered as the river, affected by gravity, deposits sediment; like a river, a life searches for an outlet unpredictable from its origin (14.194–202). Moreover, as the mind leaps selectively in the effort to get from consciousness to source and downstream to poem, the observing, recollecting, and creating poet is carried toward an indeterminate end in whatever discontinuous way the mind of a poet who would be representative moves.[13] This figure is given in microcosm as an observer hanging over the side of "a slow-moving boat," discovering much at "the bottom of the deep," but fancying more, and pleasantly perplexed in vision by intermixed reflections of sky, mountains, sunbeams, "his own image," and "wavering motions" of indeterminate source (4.256–76). Our poet continues to lean from that boat.

With a consciousness not unified in the years of writing, the poet seeking unity grappled with a variety of memories of self-division. Reconstructed memories had found their phrasing, but how could the sequence of passages be settled? Despite the problems, some of them never conclusively solved, the poem found a structure, a Gaudian architecture, not greatly unlike the structure that Coleridge proposed, predicted, or found in the completed work:

He was to treat man as man ... then the pastoral and other states – assuming a satiric or Juvenalian spirit as he approached the high civilization of cities and towns, and then opening a melancholy picture of the present state of degeneracy and vice – thence revealing the necessity for and proof of the whole state of man and society being subject to and illustrative of a redemptive process in operation – showing how this Idea reconciled all the anomalies, and how it promised future glory and restoration.[14]

What Coleridge leaves out is the subjective poet; one thing his account helps to explain, however, is why the completed work, with the subjective, self-assessing poet at its center, is a "prelude" to what was projected and a preemption of the philosophic end.

Book First, beginning with a "glad preamble," continues as a prelude to the chronology, with enough of boyhood to make Book Second, on growth from infancy to age seventeen, partly reprise. Book First asks not only, Have I been conditioned to write the poem Coleridge asks for, but also, Am I fortunate, am I special, and if so, how? In "Was it for this" (*Hoc erat*), Vergil's Æneas, looking back from escape, asks his mother Venus if it was only to see his father, wife, and son all bloody that she snatched him from the fires and weapons of his enemies. In Book First Wordsworth asks if he was raised by the river Derwent and released from the city only to have writer's block: could vagrant imagination be recovered? Books Third – Tenth, on Odyssean wanderings in the quest, give wider scope to the question, "Was it for this?" Alternate books, Third, Fifth, and Seventh, are scherzos, with Book Ninth, revolution as promise, preparing for Book Tenth (including Eleventh in the 1850 version), the prodigal son's disillusioned descent – "and then opening a melancholy picture of the present state of degeneracy and vice." It is in the core, Books Third – Tenth, that Wordsworth encounters the mayhem and slaughter that Æneas recollected from Troy. The antepenultimate book, with the spots of time accumulated, explains how the individual mind recovered imagination; the penultimate book democratizes the "Same Subject" (imagination) – "thence revealing the necessity for and proof of the whole state of man and society being subject to and illustrative of a redemptive process in operation." The concluding book universalizes the human mind from a single experience on Mount Snowdon, what Potts after Coleridge called "Redemption," with Mary the beloved, Dorothy the beloved sister, and Coleridge the loved inspirer as preparatory Redeemers.

In Coleridge's account of the poem as he would have it, the words "assuming a satiric or Juvenalian spirit as he approached the high civilization of cities and towns" deserve special attention. Shelley's critics are divided over the question of his competency as a satirist. Wordsworth's admirers have generally regarded satire as lower than any ground he trod. Wordsworth is not supposed to be able to laugh, in one sense of "supposed," and in another he is not supposed to try. The urn of the Intimations Ode, well-wrought when "Shades of the prison-house begin to close" upon the growing boy who will be led into blindness by blind adults, is said to sink in stanza 6 with the homely nurse of prose romances (the physically bountiful Earth) and to crack in stanza 7 with the pigmy actor fretted by adults into playing store.[15] An elevated ode is said to have no business stooping to a satiric tone.

Sympathy with Wordsworth's general purposes could foster such a view. In a period when the two most popular forms of literature were sermons and virulent satires in couplets, he determined "to steer clear of personal satire . . . as far as concerns the *private* vices of individuals."[16] In his third essay upon epitaphs (1810), he explained why the "obtuse moral sensibility" of Dryden and Pope was consonant with their attention to "division," "perpetual obliquities," and "evil passions thwarting each other in various ways."[17] In the Preface of 1815, however, with a bearing upon his practice in *The Prelude*, he observed that out of "The Idyllium," the "Didactic," and "philosophical Satire like that of Horace and Juvenal ... has been constructed a composite order, of which Young's Night Thoughts, and Cowper's Task, are excellent examples."[18]

Satire is one of the elements of "worthy purpose" in *The Prelude*. Because the satiric strain is sometimes neglected and sometimes noticed but denigrated, it deserves more than a glance as a motivating force distinct from the autobiographical in the poem. The satire darkens the *Bildungsroman* sometimes by underscoring negative forces that checked the poet's education; less often but in a darker shade, by defining cultural evils common to the era but escaped by the poet. His own nurture by the River Derwent made the miseducation of child prodigies more evident. Both the presence of satire and the way it alternates with affirmation are important elements in the shaping of a life into a major poem. Following Raymond Williams, James Turner says that "rural poetry is always partly satirical."[19] That is, pastoral poetry by its very existence comments adversely on the conditions of urban life. Pope and Dryden, says Wordsworth, reflected in their poetry the internal divisions, obliquities, and mutual thwarting of the urban persons they wrote about. Books Third, Fifth, and Seventh of *The Prelude* satirically employ devices of multiplicity to represent the dreary fragmentation encountered by the poet in Cambridge, in forced prodigies of learning, and in London. "Questions, directions, warnings, and advice" (3.23) came fast in this "recreant age" of "Folly and False-seeming' (3.403–04), with ears accustomed to tranquility vexed by unresting bells and "chattering Popinjays" (3.415–21, 447). When Osbert Sitwell chose to have it said in his biography in *Who's Who* in the 1930s that he was educated "during the holidays from Eton," he was indebted to *The Prelude*.

The satiric negative always implies its polar opposite. Unity and communion are rural experiences, absent from college and concealed from the prodigy. Deprived both of the sense of unity in sound and scene that came unexpectedly to the Boy of Winander and of the variety in the "race of *real* children" ("Fierce, moody, patient, venturous, modest, shy"), the little "miracle of scientific lore," stuffed by utilitarian adults,

> can read
> The inside of the earth, and spell the stars;
> He knows the policies of foreign Lands;
> Can string you names of districts, cities, towns,
> The whole world over, tight as beads of dew
> Upon a gossamer thread; he sifts, he weighs;
> All things are put to question; he must live
> Knowing that he grows wiser every day
> Or else not live at all, and seeing, too,
> Each little drop of wisdom as it falls
> Into the dimpling Cistern of his heart. (5.319–29)

"All things are put to question"; readings for the "noosed," stringed, and stalled prodigy, prepared with questions, warnings, and advice, are shorn of imagination and feeling in the way of an owner who keeps his ox stalled until a mower can fell the growing grass and flowers (5.240–47).

In Book Seventh the poet who had first thought the Cambridge spectacle a museum of "Doctors, Students, Streets, Courts,

Cloisters" and further confusion so comic he must be dreaming it, and then found it a nightmare of misdirection, including "Feuds, factions, flatteries, enmity, and guile" (3.604), found mountebanks everywhere in the "too busy" show of London. Minstrels, clowns, ballad-singers, monkeys, cripples, "the begging Scavenger," gilded ladies, blaspheming women, Malays, Lascars, the dwarfs and conjurers of Sadler's Wells, a vomiting jumble of "out-o'the-way, far-fetched, perverted things" (7.714) – none of these prepared the youth "Fostered alike by beauty and by fear" for the encounter with still further artifice in the pulpit, on the "great Stage" of Parliament, and in ermine on the bench.

Wordsworth is not "Peter Pindar" or William Gifford; in a work of "a composite order" satire is a servant subordinate to higher purpose. By 1820 Book Seventh itself apologizes to Burke for "the pen seduced" by "specious wonders," although the apology includes praise of Edmund Burke's "Keen ridicule" of "upstart Theory" (7.512–29). The fate of the artless Maid of Buttermere and her lovely child needs poignant telling to show how ruthless the city slicker, "the Spoiler," can be (7.297–381). Book Seventh begins with the "monstrous Ant-hill" and, except for a final declaration of the poet's openness to the Spirit of Nature and the Soul of Beauty, returns to end on the "blank confusion." It begins in awe that denizens of the city are all strangers to each other, and in scorn that urban buildings must wear lettered names to be identified,[20] but just before the end Book Seventh's catalogue pauses over a prospective emblem of unseeing fragmentation. A blind beggar propped against a wall wears a paper written by another, unreadable by him, to explain "whence he came, and who he was" (7.642). It is unimportant whether William Wordsworth had this experience in London, but it is invaluable that the "I" of the poem, now reconstructing experience in a search for source and origin, at some *then*, not now, turned mentally around as if from the might of waters, "As if admonished from another world." The reader is lifted out of London when the poet declares the blind beggar's label emblematic of "the utmost we can know" both "of ourselves and of the universe." And this is the great indeterminacy of *The Prelude*: the search morally braces-and-scrubs and poetically excites the reader of our time, but the end of the search is unreachable.

The value and strength of satire in an affirmative poem is evident in the language of descent: first, Pitt's Ministry, by declaring war on France and liberty, tearing "at one decisive rent" from those Wordsworth knew to be "the best Youth" their "joy in England" (10.300–03), soured and corrupted the poet's own sentiments (11.175–78) – those shepherds who soon at home made "the guardian crook of Law / A tool of murder" (11.63–65). As a consequence of Britain's open war on liberty (as distinct from the ministers' devious corruption of law), tyrants among the revolutionaries in France began "vengeful retribution"; with the poet as anxious witness, the "goaded land waxed mad" (10.331–50). The next stage of descent, into personal nightmare of innocent victims forced into solitary confinement and of forced pleading before unjust tribunals (10.399–415), is presented without satire, rather as theater of *Sturm und Drang*. These accumulative nightmares make it clearer, however, that in the Quixote–Arab dream the Deluge in the desert is in one aspect the Revolution in France validated by dessicated rationality. In the final descent into hell, the nethermost *bolgia* of sterile ratiocination – an anatomizing, questioning attempt to apply dry logic to moral complexities – the language ends in the sublimity of deprivation, "the crisis of that strong disease" in which "blessed Reason" is totally drained of imagination, "Sick, wearied out with contrarieties," "the soul's last and lowest ebb." The initially satirical entry into these lines on the region "Where passions had the privilege to work, / And never hear the sound of their own names" (11.230–31), gives a satiric edge to the rest of the passage:

> So I fared,
> Dragging all precepts, judgments, maxims, creeds,
> Like culprits to the bar . . .   (11.293–95)

Comedy exposes its characters as intellectually deficient, foolish; satire accuses its culprits of immorality affecting others. Comedy laughs at a character for trying to cheat; satire charges that an immoral act has been perpetrated. Satire injects morality into a descriptive poem. So it is in *The Prelude*.

The lines on the Boy of Winander can serve to illustrate both the positive cohesion utilized to resolve the fragmentation satirized and the unreachability of final conclusions. The first known, jotted version begins, "There was a boy ye knew him well, ye rocks," but then identifies that earlier boy with the now-speaking poet by continuing in the first person – "Responsive to my call."[21] That the boy had been killed and the speaker had stood "Mute – looking at the grave," in a version given to the public in 1800, was enough to keep him more than symbolically dead in 1805. Even without this prod, the boy who was answered by owls appears in Book Fifth as the ideal opposite to the child prodigy. This objectivity of presentation, tempered by the poet's memory of his own *memory* of an earlier boy's experience, makes more persuasive the ensuing self-congratulation: the poet who had had the good fortune of a "Parent Hen" who could recognize nutriment had as one result the further good fortune to read of Robin Hood and Jack the Giant-killer. With poetic aptness the dream of shell and stone is transferred to the "I"; with a corollary aptness, the boy surprised by a sense of oneness with the universe provides, instead of autobiography, outer (externalized) confirmation of the poet's own experience. In his final version of *The Prelude* Wordsworth forced the episode of the drowned man of Esthwaite into Book Fifth, "Books," with an *ad hoc* argument that it illustrated the value of reading fairy tales as preparation for encountering actual ghastly shapes, a process so successful it turned a corpse retrieved by grappling hooks into the ideal grace of "Grecian Art, and purest Poesy" (5.428–61). These indeterminacies in different versions of *The Prelude* invite the reader, not to make her or his own poem from it, but to make a self.

Satire fades as the final books declare in affirmation exactly what harmony with external nature and within one's own nature could achieve. Juxtaposition even of the final books with passages of discursive assertion in *The Excursion* (1814) ought to show how seldom and how little *The Prelude* is discursive, but the poet's message becomes declaratively lucid near the close. Wordsworth revised the concluding book, particularly, into greater and greater summarizing clarity. The subject has been the stream of imagination, rising from obscurity at birth into "clearest insight," dimmed in an awful time (14.189–205). In Book Third, it would be vanity to look ahead because "we see but darkly" when we look behind to judge our choices in an imperfect world (3.482–86). In the summary, imagination is lost sight of, not because of any epistemological uncertainty or any ambiguity concerning its powers, but biographically because the protagonist coincides with the poet who was for a time "bewildered and engulphed" by ratiocination. In a poem written and revised for nearly half a century, the conclusion in 1850 retains, with reference to the life surveyed, a movement upward to the recovery of imagination and hope culminating in 1799; the revisions after 1805 leave 1804–05 as the date of assessing that life. In an insertion much later than 1805, "we have reached / The Time," in chronicle not later than 1799,

> When we may, not presumptuously, I hope,
> Suppose my powers so far confirmed, and such
> My knowledge, as to make me capable
> Of building up a Work that shall endure . . .   (14.306–11)

With reference to 1799, the work at issue is the great philosophical poem, *The Recluse*; referring to 1804–05 and 1827–50, the work can be the autobiographically philosophic poem in steady process of accomplishment, *The Prelude*. *The Excursion* is not significantly at issue in the confirmation of powers, although it shares the heuristic optimism of the concluding book of *The Prelude* in its final form.

Division of consciousness had intrigued the poet sufficiently to give him confidence that his exploration of division would interest the reader. The voice that concludes the work has learned from "timely exercise to keep / In wholesome separation the two natures, / The one that feels, the other that observes" (14.345–47). Paradoxically, the poet who observes the younger protagonist declines to make that distinction for either the observer or the observed, and the entire poem, in its later, fuller versions, declares to the student, whatever scholars and teachers may say, that there should be no separation between the reader who feels and the reader left free by reason to multiply distinctions.

NOTES

1 The alternative phrasing appears in a letter to Sir George Beaumont, December 25, 1804, *The Letters of William and Dorothy Wordsworth: The Early Years*, ed. Ernest de Selincourt, rev. Chester L. Shaver (Oxford: Clarendon Press, 1967), p. 518. From early 1804 through 1806, Wordsworth usually referred to the work in progress as "the Poem on my own life" or "on my own earlier life" (*Letters*, pp. 436, 451, 454, 470, 513, 586, 605); Dorothy similarly said "his own life" (pp. 440, 617, 650). The title page of the manuscript declares it a yet-untitled poem "addressed to Coleridge."

2 *Wordsworth's Formative Years* (Ann Arbor: University of Michigan Press, 1943).

3 On its place in the development of the *Bildungsroman* in English, see Jerome H. Buckley, "Autobiography in the English *Bildungsroman*," in Morton W. Bloomfield (ed.), *The Interpretation of Narrative: Theory and Practice* (Cambridge, MA: Harvard University Press, 1970; *Harvard English Studies*, no. 1), pp. 93–96, expanded in Buckley, *The Turning Key: Autobiography and the Subjective Impulse since 1800* (Cambridge, MA and London: Harvard University Press, 1984), pp. 54–61 and *passim*.

4 *The Poetical Works of William Wordsworth*, ed. Ernest de Selincourt, rev. Helen Darbishire (5 vols., Oxford: Clarendon Press, 1940–49), v, 464.

5 MS at the Harry Ransom Humanities Research Center, University of Texas, Austin; published in *Table Talk*, vol. I, p. 550 in *The Collected Works of Samuel Taylor Coleridge*, general editors Kathleen Coburn and Bart Winer (Princeton: Princeton University Press).

6 For a noble gateway to this subject, see David Perkins, *Wordsworth and the Poetry of Sincerity* (Cambridge, MA: Harvard University Press, 1964).

7 William Wordsworth, *The Fourteen-Book "Prelude"*, ed. W. J. B. Owen (Ithaca, NY: Cornell University Press, 1985), p. 97. Unless otherwise indicated, references to *The Prelude* will be to this edition, parenthetically cited by book and line (here 5.155–67).

8 *The Prose Works of William Wordsworth*, ed. W. J. B. Owen and Jane Worthington Smyser (3 vols., Oxford: Clarendon Press, 1974), III, 63.

9 *The Prelude, 1798–1799*, ed. Stephen Parrish (Ithaca, NY: Cornell University Press, 1977), p. 81.

10 1.393, 2.402, 2.316–23, 4.155–56, 12.208–18.

11 1.583–84, 2.187–88, 2.171, 4.295–96.

12 Abbie Findlay Potts, *Wordsworth's Prelude: A Study of Its Literary Form* (Ithaca, NY: Cornell University Press, 1953).

13 Of several studies of indeterminacy in *The Prelude,* the most usefully suggestive are Kenneth R. Johnston, *Wordsworth and the Recluse* (New Haven: Yale University Press, 1984), and Susan J. Wolfson, "The Illusion of Mastery: Wordsworth's Revisions of 'The Drowned Man of Esthwaite,' " *PMLA,* 99 (October 1984), 917–35.

14 21 July 1832, in Vol. I of *Table Talk,* ed. Carl Woodring, pp. 307–8.

15 These satiric terms are intensified in *The Prelude* in the account of the child prodigy, culminating in the grief of "old Beldame Earth" at the distortion and contraction of the child's natural bent (5.300–42).

16 Letter to Francis Wrangham, 7 November 1806, *The Letters of William and Dorothy Wordsworth: The Middle Years,* Part 1, ed. Ernest de Selincourt, rev. Mary Moorman (Oxford: Clarendon Press, 1969), p. 89.

17 *Prose Works,* II, 80.

18 *Prose Works,* III, 28.

19 *The Politics of Landscape* (Cambridge, MA: Harvard University Press, 1979), p. 117.

20 Home on vacation he could re-read "the face of every neighbour," for "each was known to all" (4.67, 199).

21 From MS JJ, in *The Prelude, 1798–1799,* ed. Parrish, p. 87.

3
Writing the life of J. J. Ridley
RICHARD D. ALTICK

I

Thackeray was the first English novelist to describe the contemporary world of artists. In *The Newcomes* (1853–55) he told his readers what they could learn from no other source, whether fiction, biography, or history. Nowhere else did it all come together: the pleasures of being an artist, including the hopeful years of developing one's talents at Gandish's school, and the financial precariousness of the profession; the deep-seated prejudice against art as an occupation unworthy of a gentleman, expressed in half-regretful but nonetheless forceful terms by Colonel Newcome, who humours but hardly supports his son's eccentric choice, and, more bluntly, by a chorus consisting of Charles Honeyman, Hobson and Ethel Newcome, Major Pendennis, and Lady Kew; and the crucial role of popular taste in determining whether, talent apart, an aspiring painter would fail (Clive) or succeed (J. J. Ridley).[1]

The Newcomes is nominally set in the late 1830s and early 1840s, but in most ways the distanced setting is scarcely distinguishable from the immediate moment of the mid-1850s. Ridley's success as a painter of genre subjects, the more sentimental the better, is as typical of the latter period as of the former, when pictures from that inexhaustible source of anecdotal artists' inspiration, *The Vicar of Wakefield*, were so numerous as to require, said Thackeray in one of his reviews of the year's crop at the Academy exhibition, a separate room for their display. Indeed, the devotion to outmoded historical painting which Thackeray used to exemplify

Clive's lack of realism in respect to his own very modest gifts (like Thackeray's, they extended no further than a facility in sketching) and his indifference to the decisive power of popular taste, had even greater point in the fifties than in the early forties. The series of competitions, beginning in 1843, that were the instrument of the government's proposal to subsidize "high art" in the form of colossal frescoes on national themes to be painted on the walls of the new Houses of Parliament had brought history painting, traditionally the most ambitious category in the hierarchy of art, to public attention and momentarily restored something of the repute it had enjoyed toward the end of the previous century. But thanks to bureaucratic shilly-shallying and other complications, the enterprise largely failed, and history painting, now more than ever regarded as unsuited to the native genius of the country, fell into still lower esteem. Readers of *The Newcomes* would have recognized that Clive had backed a losing horse.

The audience for Thackeray's novels greatly outnumbered the readership that had so far constituted the market for biographies of artists and books on other art-related subjects. Probably this was because the fine arts were an aspect of contemporary culture that was of less popular interest than, say, literature. The very nature of the product involved restricted its appeal. While books were easily available to the entire middle- and upper-class population, original works of art – paintings and statuary – figured in the experience of relatively few. Most people knew them, if at all, only at second hand, through inadequate reproductions. There were hosts of readers; there were not all that many gallery-goers.

Although literary reviews proliferated and a few general periodicals like *Fraser's Magazine* printed art criticism, in this period there was but one periodical dedicated to the visual and plastic arts, the *Art-Union*, founded in 1839 and given the name by which it is better known, the *Art Journal*, ten years later. It had no serious rival in the field until *The Portfolio* appeared in 1869. No book about an artist ever came near to being a bestseller, and none had stirred as much public controversy as, for example, Thomas Moore's *Letters and Journals of Lord Byron, with Notices of His Life* had ignited in 1830. No painter – though Henry Fuseli, with all his ineradicable "foreignness" and manifold peculiarities, would have been an ideal subject for such treatment – was memorialized by a book like John Thomas Smith's *Nollekens and His Times* (1828), a quirky, malicious portrait of a quirky, dirty, uncouth, and gigantically miserly sculptor. Nobody in the ensuing decades collected a living painter's reminiscences and his wide-ranging opinions on art and life as had William Hazlitt, who published the results of his interviews as *Conversations of James Northcote, Esq., R. A.*, which appeared piecemeal in various periodicals in 1826–30 and in book form in the latter year. Nor was any living artist as famous as Dickens had been for almost twenty years, and as Thackeray had become after the success of *Vanity Fair*.

And so *The Newcomes* revealed an enclave in their very midst about which most readers knew little but now wanted to learn more. The Westminster cartoon competition had been well publicized – and ridiculed – in places like *Punch*, and when, at length, it disappeared from the news, another, livelier, art topic turned up in the form of Pre-Raphaelitism. In 1851 Ruskin's pamphlet defending the new dissident movement touched off a sustained wave of reviews, polemics, and satire that engaged a public most of whose members had hitherto been so indifferent to British art that they could not tell a Fuseli from a Wilkie. Art was in the air, and *The Newcomes* could not have been published at a more opportune moment.

In that novel, written by a man who had turned to fiction after failing to become an artist and then succeeding as an art critic, the art world overlapped the literary, as it had repeatedly done since Pope's time. J. J. Ridley's circle included Frederick Bayham, the busy miscellaneous journalist and fine arts critic for the *Pall Mall Gazette*, and Arthur Pendennis, also a member of the *Gazette*'s staff. As a close friend of Clive Newcome, Pendennis, the narrator of the novel, wrote of himself as Clive's "present biographer." To that extent, *The Newcomes* can be looked upon as the biography of an artist, though of course Clive's chosen occupation is incidental to several other, more important considerations. At the very end of the novel, Thackeray, writing now in his own person, raises this question: "why did Pendennis introduce J. J. with such a flourish, giving us, as it were, an overture, and no piece to follow it? J. J.'s history, let me confidentially state, has been revealed to me too, and may be told some of these fine summer months, or Christmas evenings, when the kind reader has leisure to hear."

What Thackeray had in mind, he revealed to his friend Whitwell Elwin in 1856, was "to show J. J. married, and exhibit him with the trials of a wife and children. I mean to make him in love with another man's wife, and recover him through his attachment for the little ones." This story, Elwin noted in a memorandum, "I begged him not to write."[2] But he did reintroduce J. J. in his last completed novel, *The Adventures of Philip* (1861–62). Still a bachelor, J. J., a prosperous academician with prematurely silver hair, dined out in the best company and played favorite uncle to his friends' young children, who drew omnibuses on the landscape sketches he dashed off for them.

What if Thackeray, still clinging to his intention to write a full-length life of J. J. but heeding Elwin's advice to avoid a domestic story of the kind he proposed, had concentrated not on J. J.'s temptation – a version of Thackeray's frustrated love for Mrs. Brookfield – but on J. J. as an exemplary artist of the day? Would he again have used Arthur Pendennis as the fictive author, or would he have enlisted instead the more experienced and knowledgeable Frederick Bayham? There was ample precedent for professional writers to compose biographies of artists. Allan Cunningham, like Bayham a miscellaneous author, who had earlier earned some reputation as "the English Vasari" with his six-volume *Lives of the Most Eminent British Painters, Sculptors, and Architects* (1829–33), lived just long enough to finish his *Life of Sir David Wilkie* (1843). Wilkie Collins's first book (1848) was his *Memoirs of the Life of William Collins*, his father, a well-known genre painter. Anna Elizabeth Bray, author of a long string of historical romances, published her *Life of Thomas Stothard*, her first husband's father, in 1851. Tom Taylor, a popular playwright and *The Times*'s art critic, "edited and compiled," as the title page put it, the *Life of Benjamin Robert Haydon, Historical Painter, from His Autobiography and Journals* (3 vols., 1853), and edited Charles Robert Leslie's *Autobiographical Recollections* (1860). He would go on to continue and conclude, greatly enlarging in the process, Leslie's *Life and Times of Sir Joshua Reynolds: With Notices of Some of his Cotemporaries* (2 vols., 1865). Gainsborough's first biographer, excluding the notorious adventurer Philip Thicknesse, who published a brief catchpenny "sketch" of the artist immediately after his death, was removed from the main stream of literature but flourished on its rural banks. George Williams Fulcher was a printer and bookseller at Sudbury, Suffolk, a leading citizen of the town and editor of the annual *Sudbury Pocket Book* in which he published the poems of William and Mary Howitt, James Montgomery, Bernard Barton, and other minor celebrities of the time. His modest monograph, *Life of Thomas Gainsborough, R. A.* (1856), conceived as a tribute to Sudbury's most famous son, was based on a fair amount of research Fulcher accomplished locally.

On the other hand, if Clive Newcome, lacking literary credentials but possessing at least as impressive artistic ones as Thackeray, had written J. J.'s biography, he would have found himself in good company. Northcote, Reynolds's assistant for some five years and his lifelong admirer, prefaced his *Life of Sir Joshua Reynolds* (2 vols., 1813; 2nd ed., enlarged, 1819) by saying:

It is my fixed opinion, that if ever there should appear in the world a Memoir of an Artist well given, it will be the production of an Artist: but as those rarely possess an eminent facility in literary composition, they have avoided the task; and the labour of writing the lives of Painters has been left to depend solely on the skill and ingenuity of men who knew but little concerning the subject they had undertaken, in consequence of which their works have been rendered useless and insipid.

On this premise, Edmund Burke, Edmond Malone, and Boswell, the three potential biographers Northcote mentioned, would have been ill-qualified to write the book that he did in fact write, in default, he said, of their more capable pens. The ample quantity of anecdotal material he had at his disposal, involving not only Sir Joshua but his friends Dr. Johnson, Goldsmith, and Garrick among others, virtually ensured that his biography would be more interesting than most. The painter Leslie, who would later write his own, expanded life of Reynolds, probably used it as a model also for his well-informed *Memoirs of the Life of John Constable* (1843; enlarged ed. 1845). It is less certain that William Bell Scott, an artist as well as a poet, had it in mind when he memorialized his late brother in his *Memoir of David Scott, R. S. A.* (1850).

What form would the life of the estimable Ridley have taken? (For the purpose of the present exercise we must assume, regretfully but not without grounds – in *The Adventures of Philip* he was said to be "weakly and almost infirm of body" – that J. J.'s prosperous career was cut short by death. Like authors, artists were not then eligible for formal biographical treatment until they were safely in the grave.) To speculate on the kind of book Bayham or Clive might have written in the early or middle sixties, given the nature and quality of other art biographies written before it, offers a useful perspective on both the biographical form as it was practiced in Victorian times and the place the artist occupied in the public mind.

In 1762, Horace Walpole remarked in his *Anecdotes of Painters in England*, "This country, which does not always err in vaunting its own productions, has not a single volume to show on the works of its painters." Compared with the increasing dignity literature enjoyed as evidence of the nation's long cultural heritage, British painting was of small concern to any but a handful of connoisseurs and collectors and, as yet, none at all to biographers. Painters at large, including landscapists and the contrivers of huge, unsalable historical canvases, had little social standing; only a few portraitists, headed by Reynolds, enjoyed the emoluments of fashion. Authors of established reputation were more likely to be the subjects of biographies. Even before Boswell laid the massive foundation on which modern literary biography rests, there had been scores of lives of poets from Chaucer to Pope. Such biographies would continue to outnumber lives of artists if only because the nation's pantheon and its annexes contained several centuries' worth of literary men, and, by the time *The Newcomes* appeared, less than a century's worth of painters, Lely and Kneller apart, who claimed any remembrance whatsoever.

Literary biography, art biography's stronger and more prolific sibling, had prospered despite the view, current as early as 1688 when Thomas Sprat mentioned it in his life of Cowley, that authors were, as a class, unpromising material for life-writing. In

31

1778 Walpole observed, with a characteristic measure of ironic wit, that

> The deep and extensive learning of a man of letters is but a barren field for biography . . . The date of his publications and their editions form the outlines of his story; and frequently the plans or projects of works he meditated are taken to aid the account; the day of his death is scrupulously ascertained; – and thus, to compose the life of a man who did very little, his biographer acquaints us with what he did not do, and when he ceased to do anything.[3]

By substituting a portrait painter's sitters' book and the record of the pictures he showed at the annual exhibitions for the publication dates of an author's books, Walpole might well have enlarged his observation to cover painters as well. And, in fact, a quarter-century later a very minor artist, Edward Dayes, did just that. Prefacing a collection of brief "Professional Sketches of Modern Artists" which was included in a volume of his works published in 1805 to benefit his widow – he had taken his own life in the preceding year – he had remarked, "Unchequered with events, as the lives of artists generally are, it may to many appear superfluous to mention them." He added, however, that "to preserve the names of those who have labored to elevate the character of humanity, is but justice" (p. 315).

In his own practice, Walpole's description of the lives of authors as "a barren field for biography" did not extend to artists. His *Anecdotes of Painting in England; with Some Account of the Principal Artists; and Incidental Notes on the Other Arts* (2 vols., 1762, and further volumes to 1782), derived from the collectanea of the engraver and antiquary George Vertue (1684–1756), was the spring from which the whole tradition of English art biography flowed.[4] Walpole was supplemented by Edward Edwards's *Anecdotes of Painters Who Have Resided or Been Born in England* (1808). On the eve of the Victorian period, the biographical history of the nation's art contained in these compilations was further extended, and rewritten for a popular audience, in Cunningham's *Lives*.

Down to the end of the eighteenth century, the only British artist to receive a degree of biographical notice that exceeded the entries in Walpole was Hogarth, whose celebrity, uniquely for the time, reached far beyond the select circle of connoisseurs. His engraved pictorial moralities and no-nonsense personality appealed to a middle-class audience that was otherwise uninterested in, and uninformed about, art and the lives of artists. He was, as Thackeray was to describe him in one of his lectures on the English humorists, "a jovial, honest London citizen, stout and sturdy; a hearty, plain-spoken man, loving his laugh, his friend, his glass, his roast beef of old England." It was this congenial character, shared by no other artist of his time with the possible exception of Gainsborough, that explains why John Nichols had envisioned a market for his *Biographical Sketches of William Hogarth; with a Catalogue of His Works Chronologically Arranged* (1782, "enlarged and corrected" 1785), and why John Ireland had prefaced his *Hogarth Illustrated*, a two-volume album of reproductions and running commentary (1791, supplement 1798) with "Anecdotes of an Artist."

In that hesitant dawn of English art biography there was a brief eruption of scandalmongering, reminiscent of the vicious *ad hominem* Grub Street pamphleteering of Pope's day and Samuel Johnson's candid (and mythmaking) life of Richard Savage (1744). Even while the talented but extravagantly dissolute George Morland was still painting away in his squalid garret, Edward Dayes wrote of him:

It is a great misfortune for the arts, when the world entertain an opinion, that a man cannot be a genius without being mad; or, in other words, be a brute or scoundrel. This makes many a weak head run into excess to acquire a reputation. The many stories of excess related to this artist, would fill a volume of some magnitude; yet, I most fervently hope that no one will be at the pains to transmit them to posterity, as the surest way of disappointing all who may set out in life with such views. Whatever his professional talents may be, he is a disgrace to the name of man, and a blot on the credit of the art . . . No gentleman can deal with him; he has often taken half the money for a picture before it was begun, and sold it to a stranger for the other half. (*Works*, pp. 338–40)

Notwithstanding Dayes's hope, within three years of Morland's alcoholic death in 1804 no fewer than four small volumes transmitted the stories of his various excesses. The earliest and most restrained of these was by his friend the picture dealer William Collins, who arranged for Morland to teach his son, Wilkie

Collins's father. In a curious piece of bookmaking, the biography of Morland was sandwiched between the two volumes of a fictional concoction by Collins entitled *The Memoirs of a Picture* (1805).

There is no evidence that any subsequent writers of artists' lives read the Morland volumes. Although other painters after him lived more or less irregular lives (to borrow a favorite Victorian euphemism), the moral climate of the years to come inhibited any repetition of the sensation-streaked biography. But by the middle of the century, prospective biographers of English painters had a number of other models to select from, their choice depending on the nature and quantity of the available materials, the special character and career of the subject himself (Northcote's and Leslie's elaborate treatment of Sir Joshua Reynolds, a public figure, would not have worked with the retiring Thomas Stothard), and the literary bent of the biographer.

Most art biographers were either close relatives or, like Pendennis, Bayham, and Clive Newcome in J. J.'s case, friends of the painters concerned. Whatever advantage their intimate personal knowledge of their subject may have given them was more than outweighed by their lack of objectivity and expertise in life-writing. Two early biographies by artists' friends illustrate the depths to which the form could sink when the only equipment the writers had for their chosen task was good intentions. William Hayley, an uninspired poet, patron of Blake, and friend and biographer of Cowper, was closely associated with George Romney from 1776 to 1799, when, broken in body and mind, the painter returned to Kendal to be nursed by the wife he had deserted at the outset of his career. Hayley's *Life of George Romney, Esq.* (1809) is little more than a recital, in an intolerably discursive, huffing-puffing style, of that acquaintance; Romney is seldom seen except in the presence of the complacent Hayley, the most intrusive of all art biographers. In fact, the book might have been more accurately titled *Romney's Life with Me*. In the midst of all the verbiage, there was little residue of prosaic fact. Its place was taken by generous swatches of Hayley's execrable verse, culminating at the end of the book in the heavily annotated texts of his "Epistles to Romney, First Printed in the Year 1788".[5]

Although it lacked Hayley's ornate style as well as poetry of any kind, John Knowles's biography of Fuseli, in the first of the three volumes of his *Life and Writings of Henry Fuseli* (1831), shared Hayley's other faults. Little is recorded of Knowles, who was a civil servant in the Navy Office (1806–32) and, as his title page proclaimed, "Corresponding Member of the Philosophical Society at Rotterdam." (The *Dictionary of National Biography* identifies him solely as the "biographer of Fuseli," adding, somewhat bleakly, that "as a biography the work has some merit.") But Knowles announced his unique qualification to write Fuseli's life:

The daily intercourse and sincere friendship which subsisted for many years between this great artist and myself, afforded me the opportunity of witnessing his domestic habits, hearing many of the incidents of his life, and watching his career as an artist; and, being executor to his will, his professional as well as private papers came into my possession.

("Advertisement")

Knowles's readers must have been at a loss to discover what he had done with all that intimate knowledge, because the bland, vaguely outlined figure called Fuseli had nothing in common with the profane, eccentric artist and teacher later glimpsed in the memoirs of some of his pupils. This person was as absent from Knowles's drab pages as the living Romney was from Hayley's florid ones.

Hayley made no effort to enlarge his portrait of Romney from the testimony of others, and Knowles said only that he had corresponded with Fuseli's family at Zurich to obtain particulars of his early life. The more energetic biographers who succeeded them cast a wider net, and some had access to considerable quantities of their subject's letters, the result being what became in the course of the Victorian era the standard form of biography where suitable materials were available. Following the lead of literary biographers ever since the "memoirs" William Mason prefixed to his collection of the poems of Thomas Gray (1775), and reacting against the self-indulgence represented by Boswell's prominence in his life of Johnson, post-Hayleyan writers of artists' lives relied heavily on the familiar but porous argument that the best biography was one told by the subject himself in his letters and, in some instances, diaries and other personal documents. Such a premise was, in essence, an evasion. Once the unavoidable necessity of describing his subject's childhood was somehow dealt with and the young man's earliest letters took up the story, it was much easier for a biographer to transcribe his letters, with whatever deletions and alterations he deemed prudent, than to distil their contents into prose of the biographer's own composition. The author lapsed into the passive role of editor, at a heavy price so far as the resulting book was concerned. The fatal flaw in a letters-based biography was that it severely distorted the contours of the life it purported to tell, concentrating as it did upon those events that happened to figure in the artist's surviving correspondence at the expense of other events of equal if not greater importance.

In a typical letters-based biography, the early letters were given some cohesiveness by narrative bridges written by the author/editor, but as the chapters wore on and, one suspects, the biographer tired of his task, the supplied transitions became fewer and fewer and the uninterrupted sequences of quoted material longer and longer. The degree of authorial intervention, either by way of occasional comment on the content of the letters or by the supplying of connective tissues to tighten and smooth the narrative, varied from biographer to biographer. Allan Cunningham earned comparatively high marks in this respect; until he grew weary, and probably ill, in the third volume of his life of Wilkie, he kept the letters in their place, subservient to the narrative rather than the other way round. Compared with the easy-going practice of his peers, Alexander Gilchrist, writing his *Life of William Etty, R. A.* (2 vols., 1855), was actually heroic. He printed few of Etty's letters as they stood, but absorbed thousands of tiny phrases from them into his own running text, a procedure that signally increases the modern reader's comfort and pleasure despite the inevitable profusion of quotation marks.

Leslie, too, was comparatively judicious in his use of Constable's letters as the basis of his biography, and this is one reason for the book's lasting appeal. (It has had two twentieth-century editions, by the Hon. Andrew Shirley in 1937 and Jonathan Mayne in 1951.) Probably a more compelling reason is

Constable's gift as a correspondent: he wrote more engaging, self-revealing letters than any other nineteenth-century painter before Rossetti and that all too obscure master of informal English prose, Rossetti's sometime protégé James Smetham.

It would seem that, like Reynolds and Turner, J. J. Ridley was no letter-writer.[6] The biography to be written of him would not, therefore, have belonged to the conventional life-and-letters genre. Nor, because he had died so recently, was he qualified to be the subject of a life-and-times biography such as Leslie had undertaken of Reynolds but not finished before he died in 1859. But this last, most ambitious type of biography must be briefly glanced at in order to complete the gamut of options available to the mid-Victorian narrator of an artist's life.

Leslie's principal model and source was Northcote's earlier life of Reynolds, which supplied many of the anecdotes and personal details that allowed the painter to be seen more fully – in the round, as it were – than any other artist of his day. But Northcote did not attempt to correlate Reynolds's career with external (public) events or with happenings in fashionable society, the world of his sitters. When Leslie was collecting his materials, a widely, and for the most part favorably, discussed literary biography was John Forster's *Life and Times of Oliver Goldsmith* (1854), a major two-volume enlargement of his successful *Life and Adventures of Goldsmith* which had appeared six years earlier. Seeing Reynolds's friend portrayed against a lavish background of contemporary events, with ample coverage of his relations with the Johnson circle, doubtless encouraged Leslie in his ambition to write a similarly comprehensive biography of Reynolds himself. Completed by Tom Taylor and published in two heavy volumes (1,178 pages) in 1865, the book was the first major effort to place an eminent British artist in his historical context.

It was also a source biography, heavy with quoted documents and, like Northcote's, arranged in the form of annals, Reynolds's year-by-year activities as recorded in his pocket books being accompanied by a chronology of public events. Taylor, in addition to picking up the narrative where it had fallen from Leslie's failing hands, supplied extensive annotations to the text. The huge index (in Volume I) of proper names is sufficient indication of the book's density. But apart from laying on a thick impasto of Reynolds's personal and professional milieu, Leslie, and after him Taylor, made no real attempt to establish a significant connection between the artist and his times.

Nor were such vital linkages more frequent in art biography in general. Only a few widely scattered and in any case fleeting efforts were made to discover causal relationships between aspects of an artist's life and the society and culture of his age. Influenced by the associationist philosophy of the time, which sought to reveal developmental connections between "genius" and the social, intellectual, and physical environment, John Galt attempted something of the sort in his *Life and Studies of Benjamin West, Esq.* (2 vols., 1816–20). West was a special instance, growing into precocious artist-hood in what was then regarded as the primitive culture of the distant American colonies. The marvelous Pennsylvanian child's good fortune, Galt argued, was due in part to the accident of his being commissioned to paint portraits in

the town of Lancaster, a place at that time remarkable for its wealth, and which had the reputation of possessing the best and most intelligent society to be then found in America . . . It was exactly in such a place that such a youth as Benjamin West was likely to meet with that flattering attention which is the best stimulus of juvenile talent.　　(I, 34)

Galt's version of West's early life was, in fact, an incongruous and no doubt anachronistic mixture of Parson Weems, Horatio Alger, and Hippolyte Taine, with even a trace of Rousseau thrown in.

Once in a while, a biographer mentioned in passing that "public events" disturbed the artist's concentration and diverted his mind, as well as affecting his patronage. Wilkie Collins wrote in his memoir of his father:

Those momentous public occurrences, the outbreak of the cholera, and the Reform Bill agitation, of which England was the scene during this year [1831], produced that long and serious depression in the patronage and appreciation of Art which social and political convulsions must necessarily exercise on the intellectual luxuries of the age. The noble and the wealthy . . . had little time, while engrossed in watching the perilous events of the day, to attend to the remoter importance of the progress of national Art . . . At such a time, to attempt any new experiments or superior achievements in painting would have appeared to those of this opinion as hopeless a waste of labour and anxiety as could well be undertaken. (I, 344–45)

Leslie noted that in the same year he called on Constable and "found him in a state of mind which magnified every anticipation of evil. The Reform fever was then at its crisis, and he talked much of all that was to be feared from the measure." The impact of contemporary affairs on a certain artist's consciousness was more fully illustrated when Tom Taylor published, in his life of Haydon (1853), that tempestuous painter's uncompleted autobiography and selections from its source, the journals he kept for thirty-four years. Although Taylor explained that he omitted "Haydon's political disquisitions [and] letters, which at this time [1834] are both numerous and long," he printed from the journals enough evidence to show that the artist was "an ardent reformer, in spite of his old high Tory predilections" and that in all likelihood "his political speculations sorely interfered with his painting" (II, 358).

II

Of the score or so of English painters who were the subjects of book-length biographies down to the middle of the century, none conformed to the developing stereotype of the Romantic artist, singlemindedly committed to a quasi-sacred calling, entertaining visions of what he might create under such inspiration, a man of violently shifting moods, a sufferer for a noble cause in an uncaring Philistine society. As far as the public was concerned, such a person existed only in the idealistic formulations of Romantic poets and critics, not, certainly, in the pages of any art biography.

In 1850, however, just as the first Pre-Raphaelites were beginning to personate the (toned-down) Romantic artist in some if not all of his aspects, William Bell Scott, a trained and practicing artist with ties to the group, published his memoir of his brother David, who had died the previous year at the age of forty-three. David Scott, as revealed in his letters and journals, was virtually the model of the Romantic art-figure. In some ways, his temperament and fortunes were reminiscent of Keats's: his inherently abnormal sensibility was exacerbated by ill health, and his poems, some of which his brother touched up before printing, referred to "some profound affection of long standing, deep as life in his heart" – one thinks inescapably of Fanny Brawne. "Perhaps," William remarked, "there never was a man with passions more violent, absorbed though they were in the ideal of art and intellectual ambition" (pp. 302, 310). It was no accident that his eerily prophetic picture, *The Hopes of Early Genius Dispelled by Death*, bore Milton's lines, "Fame is the spur that the clear spirit doth raise, / (That last infirmity of noble minds) / To scorn delights and live laborious days." His life was a series of calamities dominated by the utter failure of his grandiose painting of *Vasco da Gama Passing the Cape of Good Hope and Meeting the Spirit of the Storm* when it was exhibited at Edinburgh.

In recounting his brother's tortured life, William Bell Scott was torn between deep sympathy and (we can read between the lines) a persistent measure of embarrassment. He was enough of a proper middle-aged Victorian – he was seventeen years older than Rossetti, for example – to be discomfited by the hyperbole of an incorrigibly Romantic temperament. He was as candid as he could be about David's solipsistic "mental state" "which assists and participates in the pains, pleasures, and struggles of none other about it – it scarcely acknowledges any identity but its own – the insatiable *me* sees nothing but obstacles in the *not me*" (p. 227).[7] Only three years later Tom Taylor might have used those very words to describe the Haydon who bared his soul to his journal. David Scott and Haydon had much in common: vaulting ambition, an apparent will toward self-destruction if not martyrdom, paranoia, a fatal attraction toward outsize canvases and grand themes. Scott's biography would have fallen into the hands of few readers, if only because neither its subject nor its author was well known. The Haydon book, by contrast, was about a figure who had long been in the public eye because of his insatiable bent for controversy and confrontation in behalf of his obsessive cause – governmental support for the fine arts – and his relish for establishment-baiting, with the Royal Academy as his perennial *bête noire*. People still remembered his histrionic suicide in 1846, following the failure of his last exhibition when his fellow occupant of rooms at the Egyptian Hall, Barnum's General Tom Thumb, siphoned off all the crowds.

Tom Taylor extracted only a small portion of Haydon's voluminous journals, but he printed enough to provide a vivid, if incomplete, self-portrait. Like David Scott, Haydon lived at a high pitch. His aim as an artist, to storm the heights of history painting, comported with an irrepressible urge for self-dramatization. In an early page of his autobiography he wrote, typically:

> I got home before Wilkie, ordered the canvas for my first picture (six feet by four) of "Joseph and Mary resting on the road to Egypt;" and on October 1st, 1806, setting my palette, and taking brush in hand, I knelt down and prayed God to bless my career, to grant me energy to create a new era in art, and to rouse the people and patrons to a just estimate of the moral value of historical painting. I poured forth my gratitude for His kind protection during my preparatory studies, and for early directing me in the right way, and implored Him in his mercy to continue that protection which has hitherto been granted me. I arose with that peculiar calm which in me always accompanies such expressions of deep gratitude, and looking fearlessly at my unblemished canvas, in a species of spasmodic fury, I dashed down the first touch.
>
> (I, 49–50)

The final "touch" in this description is particularly characteristic. Haydon repeatedly portrayed himself attacking his canvas with ferocious confidence, momentarily forgetting his troubles as he wielded his (to him) God-inspired brush. He conveyed a Browningesque sense of the artist's unique joy in creation – a total absorption in work, an escape, in his case, from the monotonously revolving door of the debtors' prison and his frustration as he sought, futilely, to reform the Academy and establish the grand style as the norm of British painting.

Except for their wholehearted dedication to palette and brush, Haydon and J. J. Ridley had little in common. Haydon painted large and epic, Ridley painted small and sentimental. In terms of worldly success, Haydon was a failure, his big canvases going unsold, his personal effects periodically seized by his creditors, his ambitions necessarily sacrificed to turning out pictures of Napoleon at Elba and Wellington at Waterloo in the same quantities in which Browning's Pictor Ignotus mass-produced endless series of Virgin, Babe, and Saint. J. J.'s career, on the other hand, was one of quiet, steadily growing success.

J. J. therefore was an artist with whom readers of his biography would feel comfortable. He was not a mercurial, self-assertive Haydon but an equable, modest Leslie, a sober-suited Victorian rather than a Promethean Romantic. No division of mind, no torture over impossible ideals unrealized, set him apart from his fellow artists. As an exemplary character in two mid-Victorian novels, J. J. was an ideal subject for a mid-Victorian biographer. His uneventful rise in his profession emblematized the current state of English art: a talented though scarcely inspired painter instinctively perceiving what a middle-class public, replacing the old aristocratic patronage, wanted to buy, and willingly producing it.

As J. J.'s creator, Thackeray firmly set his moral dimensions and boundaries, and even the best-informed of his potential biographers, Pendennis, Bayham, or Clive, would have had nothing to hide from their readers.[8] In this they were luckier than some of their real-life counterparts, who shared the mealy-mouthedness for which Victorian biographers in general are deservedly notorious. Restive though they may subconsciously have been under the constraints of the prevailing moral climate, as Thackeray memorably proclaimed himself to be in the preface to *The History of Pendennis*, none went on record to that effect. The obligation to tell no tales out of school applied to all biographers and editors, irrespective of their personal ties, and most stringently of all when there was any danger of giving offense to surviving relatives. Even personal relationships to which no breath of scandal was attached came under this informal censorship. Readers of D. E. Williams's *Life of Sir Thomas Lawrence, Kgt.* (2 vols., 1831) – a superior example, in its more than a thousand pages devoted to a relatively uneventful life, of the indiscriminate inclusiveness that was a bane of the genre – would not have learned how close Lawrence's ties had been to the Kemble family, especially Mrs. Siddons, her daughters, and her niece Fanny. The fact that several Kembles were very much alive in 1831 was enough to trigger the ultra-cautious discretion that was an indispensable part of the biographer's equipment.

J. J. Ridley played an eminently moral role in *The Newcomes*, as the industrious apprentice opposite Clive as the idle one. (Clive's weakness however was not totally invincible laziness – he could apply himself to his work quite seriously if he had nothing better to do.) From the outset, art biography had been infused with an element of didacticism. Edward Dayes's apology for memorializing the lives of artists echoed the familiar eighteenth-century tenet that the "praise of excellence" is valuable to

the youth pursuing a similar course of study. All the great arts require reflection, and a perpetual inquiry into the sublime parts of Nature: to which end, it is necessary that the young mind be roused into action; and this cannot be done so effectually, as exhibiting as bright examples, those who have excelled in the profession. (*Works*, p. 315)

The first volume of Galt's life of West was punctuated with edifying scenes and sentiments. Even Haydon sought to instruct and inspire.

I write this life for the student [he said in his autobiography]. I wish to show him how to bear affliction and disappointment, by exhibiting the fatal consequences in myself who did not bear them. I wish to give him spirits by showing how rashness is to be remedied, vice resisted, and a great wish persevered in, when the last resource is a prayer to the Almighty. Is there a reader, in or out of the art, who will presume to ridicule such a resource, – the resource since the world began of all the greatest minds in their greatest sorrows? (II, 183)

Like Haydon, J. J. was a workaholic, a studio-dwelling exemplification of Carlyle's cardinal moral principle. Arthur Pendennis wrote that day after day he began painting at first light and worked happily away until nightfall. Had he been the sort of artist who kept a journal, he might have written in it, as Haydon did in his as late in his much-harried life as April 1845, "Worked with such intense abstraction and delight for eight hours, with five minutes only for lunch, that though living in the noisiest quarter of all London, I never remember hearing all day a single cart, carriage, knock, cry, bark, of man, woman, dog, or child" (III, 274).

J. J.'s story was additionally worth recounting to a mid-Victorian audience because he was of humble birth, the son of a couple who kept a lodging house – his mother, former housekeeper to Squire Bayham of Bayham; his father, major-domo to the Right Hon. John James Baron Todmorden, after whom J. J. was named. Although Anna Maria Bray exaggerated somewhat when she wrote in 1851 that "Young artists of the present day are, for the greater part, young men of poor circumstances and station" (p. 197) – most of the new arrivals actually came from the mercantile and professional classes – it was pleasant to believe that low-born artists with determination proportionate to their gifts had an equal chance at the prizes their profession now offered. This was part of the self-help ethos of the day, a belief given definitive utterance in 1859 in the chapter on "Workers in Art" in Samuel Smiles's celebrated book:

Gainsborough and Bacon were the sons of cloth-workers; Barry was an Irish sailor boy, and Maclise a banker's apprentice at Cork; Opie and Romney, like Inigo Jones, were carpenters; West was the son of a small Quaker farmer in Pennsylvania; Northcote was a watchmaker, Jackson a tailor, and Etty a printer; Reynolds, Wilson, and Wilkie were the sons of clergymen; Lawrence was the son of a publican, and Turner of a barber ... It was not by luck or accident that these men achieved distinction, but by sheer industry and hard work. Though some achieved wealth, yet this was rarely, if ever, the ruling motive. Indeed, no mere love of money could sustain the efforts of the artist in his early career of self-denial and application.[9]

Smiles singled out Turner, Wilkie, and Etty, among self-made painters, for special attention.

Smiles added currency to the stories of precocity that figured in the biographies of so many English artists. He began with a familiar anecdote of West:

When only seven years old, struck with the beauty of the sleeping infant of his elder sister whilst watching by its cradle, he ran to seek some paper and forthwith drew its portrait in red and black ink. The little incident revealed the artist in him, and it was found impossible to draw him from his bent.

So with Richard Wilson, who, "when a mere child, indulged himself with tracing figures of men and animals on the walls of his father's house, with a burnt stick"; and Reynolds, who "forgot his lessons, and took pleasure only in drawing, for which his father was accustomed to rebuke him"; and Blake, a hosier's son, who "employed himself in drawing designs on the backs of his father's shop-bills, and making sketches on the counter"; and Hogarth, who, "though a very dull boy at his lessons, took pleasure in making drawings of the letters of the alphabet, and his school exercises were more remarkable for the ornaments with which he embellished them than for the matter of the exercises themselves"; and Wilkie, who, "though he was a negligent and inapt scholar . . . was a sedulous drawer of faces and figures" (pp. 171–72). Like Wilson, Wilkie was addicted to defacing with the end of a burnt stick any household walls within reach: graffitism in the service of future Art.

Smiles, had he chosen to do so, could have multiplied examples. Knowles reported that when Fuseli was a child in Switzerland, his parents wanted him to become a clergyman, but "he bought with his small allowance of pocket-money, candles, pencils, paper, etc., in order to make drawings while his parents believed him to be in bed" (I, 7), and Williams, who devoted several pages to other examples of precocity, said that young Lawrence could not only recite any speech in the Pandemonium passage in *Paradise Lost* upon request, but could make instant pencil portraits of guests at his father's inn: "A high chair was placed at the table, pencils and paper were brought, and the infant artist soon produced an astonishingly striking likeness" (I, 41).

It is noticeable that most of these precocious artists were said to have indulged their compulsion to draw at a time when, according to the common wisdom, their energies should have been channeled into book learning. Fulcher wrote of the child Gainsborough:

Presuming, perhaps, on the forbearance of his relative [an uncle who ran the grammar school he attended], most of the hours which should have been devoted to study, were employed in making rude sketches on the covers of his books, and when they were filled, those of his schoolfellows were put into requisition, who were delighted with his ready pencil, and proud to have them thus adorned. Whilst he was engaged in sketching some well-remembered landscape or laughter-loving face, they busied themselves in preparing his arithmetical exercises, and extracted the cube roots of the vulgar fractions with an accuracy which completely imposed upon his worthy relative, leaving young Gainsborough to pursue his ruling passion.   (pp. 23–24)

J. J. followed the pattern, though lacking the pleasing detail of the cooperative deskmates. "At school," wrote Pendennis, "he made but little progress," with the result that his father "thought him little better than an idiot."

The similarities between these stories are reason enough to believe that they represented periodic outcroppings of a myth that reached far back in the biographical department of art history, to Vasari's time at least. Cimabue, Vasari recorded, "played truant often from school" in order to watch artists at work, and Giotto, herding sheep, "was for ever drawing, on stones, on the ground, or on sand, something from nature, or in truth anything that came into his fancy." Fittingly enough, it was Cimabue, by then an established master, who happened upon Giotto drawing a sheep on a "flat and polished slab, with a stone slightly pointed, without having learnt any method of doing this from others," and so took him on as a pupil.[10] Only Alexander Gilchrist, writing the life of Etty in which the usual stories of precocity and self-training figured, implied some skepticism. "The reader of artists' biographies," he said at the outset of a chapter entitled "Obstacles 1787–1805," "is familiar with prodigies achieved by Genius in short coats ... Gossip of the stereotype sort does not fail, as to Etty's childhood. A famous artist's infantile cartoons are the *only* notabilia, reminiscents [*sic*] of his early years can call to mind. An infant Apelles he (fifty years later) turns out to have been" (I, 15–16). The "fifty years later" was a sly allusion to the autobiographical fragment Etty published in 1848 in the *Art-Union*, one of a number of autobiographical and biographical sketches the magazine and its renamed continuation, the *Art Journal*, ran in those years. Quite plainly, Gilchrist believed that Etty had decorated the facts of his childhood to bring it into line with the almost obligatory mythical pattern.

Biographers who were closely related to their subjects sometimes crossed the boundary between respect and adulation, none more egregiously than Mrs. Bray in her short life of Stothard. His imagination, she declared, was "so wonderful in itself, so comprehensive in its exercise, that, as no other country has ever yet produced a painter who excelled him in this, the highest attribute of genius, so an age may pass away before we again, if ever, shall number among our most illustrious men his equal, as a second Stothard in the annals of our English Schools of Art" (p. 226). Such familial piety, which as often as not turned the memoir of an artist into a solemn memorial, would not have been a consideration of J. J.'s case, because he had no relatives besides his parents, who obviously did not qualify as life-writers. Despite Thackeray's intention which Whitwell Elwin so promptly shot down, J. J. never married. Had he done so, his biographer would have been free to describe his domestic life, though this was by no means an essential part of biography. Galt said nothing about West's, Knowles nothing about Fuseli's, Wilkie Collins next to nothing about his father's (and when he did venture upon innocuous personal matters, he apologized for having "dwelt somewhat too much at length upon matters generally held by the world to be of too delicate and private a nature for the public eye" [1, 118]).

The reluctance to penetrate beneath the public surface applied even more emphatically to the inner lives of artists. It was one thing to allow diarists and letter-writers to reveal themselves in their own words, with due editorial circumspection, of course. It was quite another thing for biographers to go beyond their subjects' recorded statements and indulge in psychological speculation or downright interpretation. Most of what biographers chose to say about the character and temperament of their subject was relegated to that lamentable convention of nineteenth-century life-writing, the concluding chapter or chapters that bore the same relation to the preceding narrative that lees bear to an indifferent bottle of wine. Here the biographers swept together the miscellaneous data supposedly reflecting the subject's essential qualities as man and artist that modern biographers, more sophisticated in their craft, are at pains to distribute at appropriate places along the way. One rare, perhaps unique, exception to the general reticence was William Bell Scott's memoir of his brother. He called his chapters "Letters" and wrote as if to a friend:

The materials will be used as if addressed to you alone, with no public in the background. I can propose to myself no treatment to meet any supposed improprieties, but merely note down whatever may assist in working out the narrative of his career, rather psychologically than circumstantially. This is the point of view which alone can be taken with profit, and, fortunately, his long and lonely evenings would appear to have been devoted frequently to expressing his experiences . . . All these diaries and notes that he guarded from alien eyes, secretive and sensitive as he was, living so much apart, now lie before me. (pp. 6–7)

But though he quoted only the less fragmentary and chaotic documents and admitted that some of his brother's "sacred things" could not be used at all, Scott pursued his psychological inquiry throughout the book, not loath to confess that he was disturbed by David's "morbid and solitary nature" (p. 227). Tom Taylor suffered a similar unease, though it had different origins and he did not express it so openly, as he worked through the masses of Haydon's starkly revealing journals and chose those passages which he felt would not too deeply offend the anti-Romantic bias of his readers in 1853.[11]

One possible reason for Victorian biographers' aversion to psychologizing was their fear of contaminating their product with stray ingredients of fiction, that lesser form of literary art, where motives and moods were staples of the writer's craft. If it was Arthur Pendennis, author of the well-received semi-autobiographical novel *Walter Lorraine*, who wrote J. J.'s life, he might have been tempted to go beyond the data of his personal observation and, if only to keep his gifts limber, invent scenes and dialogue, but this would have been a gratuitous embellishment. There was unfortunate precedent for art biography lapsing into the condition of fiction. Although at the time John Galt wrote his life of West (1816–20) he had produced no fiction except for one story that a reviewer bluntly said was "scarcely a novel," it was apparent in the West biography that his natural bent was in that direction. Only a month after the second volume appeared (May 1820), his *Ayrshire Legatees* began to be serialized in *Blackwood's Magazine*, and its success confirmed that supposition. The book was "compiled," as the title page of the first volume said (the second volume had "composed"), "from materials furnished by [West] himself," but much of the narrative, at least in the form he gave it, could only have come from inside Galt's imagination: an implausibly tinted account of the young American's first impressions of Rome, reported conversations, confident renderings of West's "reflections" and the workings of his sensibility. Whatever the raw materials may have consisted of, Galt, writing in the heyday of his friend Byron, attributed a recognizably Romantic temperament to a painter who was anything but Romantic in personality.

One would hope that, following Thackeray's example in *The Newcomes*, J. J.'s biographer would have provided a warm picture of gregarious young English artists' way of life in the thirties and forties, a way of life that was more *gemütlich* than Bohemian in the French fashion (Murger's *Scènes de la vie de Bohème* was serialized in 1848). Precedent existed, after all, in painters' autobiographies – in Haydon's faintly Thackerayan portrayal of the high spirits and hopes of the talented youths who attended the Royal Academy schools with Fuseli as their friendly mentor, and in Leslie's *Autobiographical Recollections*, which recalled, at least, the amiable relations that prevailed among the artists of his time, even if many of Leslie's anecdotes, like so many others in Victorian volumes of reminiscence, had little point. J. J.'s biographer might also have provided, as Thackeray did in several places in *The Newcomes*, evidence of the social status of the profession and of the whole cocoon of circumstance in which artistic talent was nurtured, tested, and, in fortunate cases, brought to fruition.

If so, he gave his readers more than they were accustomed to expect to find in formal biographies of artists. Before Leslie studied Reynolds's career, life-writers were not much interested in either the social context or the implications of their subjects' professional lives; they had no desire to borrow the historian's mantle. Such few references as they made to the place of the art profession in society were remarkable more for their brevity and offhand nature than for any acute perceptiveness. The general drift was that things were better than they had been. As early as 1820, Galt asserted that "so great and eminent a taste for the fine arts as that which had been diffused throughout the nation, during the reign of George the Third [who had died a few months earlier], was never before produced in the life-time of one monarch, in any age or country" (II, 26).

Not all biographers were sanguine, however. William Bell Scott took a cheerless view of the situation at mid-century, declaring that in the present age, and in this country, especially in the limited sphere of Edinburgh, high art of an original kind, and on an adequate scale, is not required by any desire in the public mind – that pictures take their value nearly exactly in proportion to their workmanship, and scarcely ever by their intellectual expression – that the high art we now have is of the revival kind, and aims at foreign standards, or merely academic excellences ...   (p. 54)

The older Leslie agreed: "I think it cannot be denied that painting is in a much lower state in this country now than in the year 1822 ... Those who have since come forward, however they may hereafter rank, cannot, I think, at present be considered as forming anything like such an assemblage of excellence, as the English school could boast of thirty years ago." But if the quality of English art had declined, patronage had dramatically increased, and Taylor made a special point of this shift in the economic basis of art, from which Leslie had much benefited:

The nobleman is no longer the chief purchaser of contemporary pictures. It is mainly to our great manufacturing and trading towns that the painter has to look for the sale of his works. The class enriched by manufactures and commerce is now doing for art in England what the same class did in earlier times in Florence, Genoa, and Venice, for the art of Italy; in Bruges, Antwerp, and Amsterdam for that of the Low Countries and Holland. The change may have its evil as well as its good. There may be some risk that it will multiply the manufacture and increase the homeliness of pictures, to say nothing of less direct and obvious ill-consequences.

But against such risks is to be set the likelihood that purchasers of this class will, in the main, insist upon something like fidelity of nature, and truthfulness of expression and sentiment. They are rarely beset by prejudice in favour of old schools of time-honoured conventions; *ceteris paribus*, they are likely to prefer pictures which are the growth of the time, and appeal to the time, to those which belong to the past, and speak to the past – or, in other words – living to dead art.

(Leslie's *Autobiographical Recollections*, pp. xviii–xix)

The words are Taylor's but they might also have been those of J. J.'s biographer, explaining, as tactfully as possible, why J. J. sold, for steadily increasing prices, his "pretty" and "sweet" pictures (Pendennis meant this to be praise) of ladies and their children. His "A Cradle," a painting of Charlotte and Philip Firmin's firstborn, featuring the baby's "two rosy little feet," "brought," said Pendennis, "I don't know how many hundred guineas apiece to Mr. Ridley" (chapter 33). Meanwhile, Clive, whose pretentious *The Battle of Assaye* failed to make the cut at the Royal Academy exhibition, had to be content with selling sporting and mail-coach sketches to printsellers, beginning at seven and sixpence each and eventually reaching a top price of fourteen shillings.

Only seldom did biographers refer to art-world topics that were current at the moment they wrote. In his memoir of Constable, Leslie quoted the artist's opinion that "should there be a National Gallery (which is talked of) there will be an end of the art in poor old England," because "the manufacturers of pictures are then made the criterions of perfection, instead of nature." "Constable's inference seems hasty," commented Leslie in 1843, six years after the National Gallery had actually opened in Trafalgar Square:

Neither connoisseurs nor legislators can promote the rise or hasten the decline of the arts in any material degree. A multitude of concurring circumstances, varying in every age and nation, contribute to these; meantime, it is something that a collection of fine pictures should be accessible to the public; and if the National Gallery should help, only in a small degree, to keep our young artists from the dissipation of their time, and the injury their unformed minds receive while running all over Europe, in quest of the art, which can only be acquired by years of patient and settled industry, it may effect some good.   (p. 97)

The chronic loser David Scott was among the victims, in his brother's opinion, of the much-vexed series of Westminster cartoon competitions; he had submitted suitably large entries that, like Haydon's, won no prizes. Gilchrist, writing the life of Etty five years later, recalled the first contest in 1843, and wrote an epitaph of sorts for that protracted governmental misadventure in the field of fine art:

The revival of Fresco, – already a stale marvel in Germany, – was the artistic wonder of the hour in England: over which deluded persons were raising their prolonged cackle, as of a new Epoch for the British School, and rehabilitation of Art itself. Under the impetus of alien influences, and of a petty, pedantic taste, the novelty was engrossing far more attention than it could ever repay: in a School whereof the chief triumphs had been attained in precisely opposite directions.

(II, 149)

But biographers in general felt that their volumes were no place to debate the issues of the 1840s and 1850s, to which the *Art-Union* and *Art Journal* gave adequate coverage. They were, after all, writing the lives of individual artists, not leading articles for the press.

No matter how skillfully J. J. Ridley's biographer told the story of his life, the book was bound to have imperfections. But these would have been overlooked, and the writer showered with praise, if the biography appeared, as we may postulate, in the early 1860s. Any such study would have shone like pure gold when set beside a leaden two-volume work that appeared in November 1861, Walter Thornbury's *Life of J. M. W. Turner*.[12]

What little is known of Thornbury suggests that he was an opportunistic journalist who might have worked for the *Pall Mall Gazette* in an inferior capacity (although Fred Bayham, Pendennis, *et al.* were unimpeachably honest practitioners of their trade, as Thornbury certainly was not). When Turner died in 1851, there had been some expectation that Ruskin, his first and now magisterial champion, would write his life, but, as Ruskin wrote to his father, biography was not his forte; he looked upon it as one of the lower branches of literature. When Thornbury's book was published ten years later, Ruskin wrote, again to his father: "That is a dreadful book of Thornbury's – in every sense – utterly bad in taste and writing; but the facts are sorrowful things. Hamlet is light comedy to it."

Ruskin was not given to understatement, but here he failed to do justice to the book's unenviable distinction. It was a witches' brew of everything that was worst in the art biographies of the past half-century, with a number of new aberrations thrown in for good measure. It began with a sentimentalized narrative of the artist's childhood against a background of period color laid on with a giant palette knife. There were imputed states of mind and invented scenes galore, and in the chapter entitled "Love and Ambition" Thornbury attributed to Turner a blighted love affair, an episode recalling the "Jessamy bride" confection that had wrung the hearts of readers of Goldsmith biographies – comparable, in fact, both to Clive's "sentimental disappointment" that drove him to Italy to seek forgetfulness in work, and to poor, misshapen J. J.'s hopeless romantic attachment to Charlotte Firmin, the surviving remnant of Thackeray's plan, in *The Adventures of Philip*.

Once he had ushered Turner into manhood, Thornbury tired of writing this very bad novel and turned to other literary and scholarly malfeasances instead. He finished off Turner's career toward the end of the first volume, and then, relieved of any chronological obligation, he filled the remainder of his pages with a chaotic farrago of unreliable information on Turner's contemporaries, a capsule history of watercolor painting, another of engraving, an extended account of Turner at Petworth, and much else. No sooner had the book appeared than the pages of *The Athenaeum* bristled, week after week, with indignant letters from people cited in Thornbury's record-setting list of credits, who disclaimed the statements he had attributed to them and called attention to hundreds of errors.

The book received the worst press notices any art biography had elicited down to that time. The long, devastating article in the *Quarterly Review* for April 1862 typified the general tenor of the criticism. Thornbury, wrote the critic James Craigie Robertson,

has no idea of method or order, of digesting his materials, or of constructing a narrative ... Things are repeated over and over and over, – sometimes with variations which leave us in uncertainty as to the truth, or which show that the compiler has not understood the information supplied to him ... Blunders are heaped on blunders; contradictions are perpetually clashing ... The ordinary style is that with which the readers of country newspapers are familiar in the jaunty letters of "our London correspondent" ... frequently relieved by passages of bombastical rant, caricatured from the worst manners of Mr. Carlyle and Mr. Ruskin, with a mixture of Mr. Charles Reade, and of the grandiloquence which is supposed to belong to the dramatists of the Victoria Theatre. (pp. 457–8)

After this catastrophe, the fortunes of English art biography had nowhere to go but up. And, in the manner of a decided action being followed by an equally powerful counteraction, not much more than a year later appeared the best book yet written about an English artist, Alexander Gilchrist's *Life of William Blake* (2 vols., 1863). Since the publication of his biography of Etty in 1855, Gilchrist had devoted more research to his new subject than any previous biographer except Leslie (on Reynolds) had expended on a similar project. He died, however, before the book was finished, and the task was completed by his wife, assisted by Dante Gabriel Rossetti and his brother William, who were responsible for the accompanying *catalogue raisonné* of Blake's works.

It may be that the superior quality of Gilchrist's *Blake* was due to the fact that it was written more as a literary biography than as a life of an artist.[13] The best of the many literary biographies so far published had furnished Gilchrist with a higher standard of accomplishment to aim at than did their counterparts in the field of art biography. Gilchrist was, in any case, a superior life-writer. He sought out all the surviving persons who had known Blake and obtained their reminiscences; he even did some field work, reporting on the present state of sites associated with Blake's life, the cottage at Felpham near his patron Hayley's home and various London localities, including one that was mistakenly identified (it was on the other side of the street). He enriched his straightforward narrative with historical perspective and paid satisfactory attention, though more subdued than in Thornbury's extravaganza, to period setting and contemporary figures Blake had known. He also made a serious attempt, rare for the time, to get inside Blake's mind, as in the chapter on his "mentally physiognomic" annotations in a copy of Lavater's *Aphorisms*.

The book enjoyed the kind of reception it deserved. It was enthusiastically reviewed, sometimes at great length, in all the leading journals, and today it commands the respect of the many Blake specialists who depend on Gilchrist for basic information about the painter–poet that is obtainable nowhere else. No biographer of the time, in contrast to Thornbury, had a keener sense of scholarly responsibility. And the book is readable as well.

No doubt the life of J. J. Ridley would have been readable too; and critics would have written in appreciation of J. J.'s character.

But the limitations of its subject – an unassuming, uncomplicated man leading an uneventful and prematurely terminated life, making no waves and, as far as that is concerned, no memorable pictures either – would have prevented it from entering the same class as the *Blake*. The best that could confidently be said of our hypothetical biography is that it would not have been as bad as Thornbury's or as good as Gilchrist's. J. J.'s memoirist, whoever he might have been, would have been burdened by the sclerotic practices of the past, a set of conventions and taboos that militated against a biographer's availing himself of the opportunities for narrative writing and character portrayal that give his art the appeal it possesses today. The books so far produced in what was to remain a small backwater of English life-writing for almost another century represented, with the possible exception of Leslie's *Constable* and certainly of Gilchrist's two biographies, a standard of mediocrity so oppressive as to discourage any effort to do better. They were, at best, journeymen's work, and by amateur journeymen at that. Their ambition reached only as far as putting a body of selected facts on the art-history record and, in most cases, erecting a memorial tablet if not a mausoleum over the remains of a painter of some gifts or contemporary repute. Such books doubtless served their modest purpose in their time, but their deficiencies, especially in the case of artists about whom relatively little else is known, place modern biographers under a more severe handicap than is suffered by most of their colleagues in literary biography, whose subjects' lives ordinarily are considerably more fully documented. As a class, they now sleep on the shelves, deservedly undisturbed except by the occasional student bent on extracting from their too often ponderous and inconsequential pages such facts (and fancies) about the careers and characters of long-dead English artists as their authors were able, or disposed, to set down.

1 There have been recent suggestions that J. J. was modeled to some extent after Richard Doyle, Thackeray's friend from *Punch* days and the illustrator of *The Newcomes*, and/or William Henry Hunt. See Viola Hopkins Winner, "Thackeray and Richard Doyle, the 'Wayward Artist' of *The Newcomes*," *Harvard Library Bulletin*, 26 (April

1978), 193–211 (especially pp. 197–98), and Margaret Diane Stetz, "Thackeray's *The Newcomes* and the Artist's World," *Journal of Pre-Raphaelite Studies*, 3, no. 2 (May 1983), 80–95 (especially pp. 83–85). Another valuable treatment of the art theme of the novel as represented by J.J. is Stephen Canham, "Art and the Illustrations of *Vanity Fair* and *The Newcomes*," *Modern Language Quarterly*, 43 (March 1982), 43–66.

2 "Memoir of Whitwell Elwin," in Elwin's *Some XVIII Century Men of Letters*, ed. Warwick Elwin (London: John Murray, 1902), I, 157.

3 *Life of the Reverend Mr. Thomas Baker*, quoted in Richard D. Altick, *Lives and Letters: A History of Literary Biography in England and America* (New York: Alfred A. Knopf, 1965), p. 39.

4 Instead of the modern meaning, the word "anecdotes" in such titles means "secret, private, or hitherto unpublished narratives or details of history" (*OED*) – a decidedly more enticing title-page description of the life-writer's product than the neutral *life* or *biography*.

5 The Rev. John Romney's *Memoirs of the Life and Works of George Romney, Including Various Letters, and Testimonies to His Genius, etc.* (1830) was, in part, a reply to Hayley, whom he regarded as his father's evil genius. With a venom ill befitting a clergyman, he wrote of Hayley's having

> with very imperfect knowledge of what he has presumed to relate
> . . . invaded the sanctuary of domestic life, and with unholy hand
> rent that sacred veil which screens every private family; confounding fiction with reality, and exaggerating or misrepresenting
> circumstances, which might have been omitted altogether as not
> being essentially connected with Mr. Romney's professional life
> . . . If Mr. Hayley had had any gratitude in his heart, or delicacy in
> his nature, he would have shewn more tenderness for the memory
> of his deceased friend, and more respect for the feelings of the
> surviving relatives of that friend; but how could delicacy, or
> feeling, be expected from a man, who has blazoned his own
> dishonour! (p.36)

More specifically: Romney, flattered by Hayley's "Epistles," allowed himself to come under the poet's "in many respects injurious" influence:

> Mr. Hayley's friendship was grounded on selfishness, and the
> means, by which he maintained it was flattery . . . By this art he
> acquired a great ascendancy over the mind of Mr. Romney, and
> knew well how to avail himself of it for selfish purposes . . . By
> having intimated an intention of writing Mr. Romney's life, he
> made him extremely afraid of doing anything that might give
> offence. (pp. 138–39)

Despite its polemic tone and pompous style, which easily matched Hayley's, the book was at least more factual and it did provide a chronological narrative of Romney's career, understandably scanting rather than concentrating on the Hayleyan years.

6 Turner's recently collected correspondence occupies only a slim volume. Again like Turner, J. J. was not much of a reader. "The painter," said Arthur Pendennis in *The Adventures of Philip*, "had been too busy in life over his easel to read many books. His ignorance of literature smote him with a frequent shame" (chapter 6). All he had in an old cabinet in his studio was a "simple little stock of novels and poems," which he read and re-read, "with much artless wonder and respect" (chapter 11).

7 Abnormal states of mind presented recurrent problems to art biographers. Hayley made much of Romney's "mental instability" or "mental affliction," especially his "deep depression of spirit." John Romney, as was to be expected, played down this misfortune, calling it "nervous irritability, and quick susceptibility, [which] only became an infirmity when his health was injured by application and age" (p. 140). Or, in a succinct phrase wholly untypical of this writer and all his fellow biographers, "his mind was thrown off its pivot" (p. 250). It would have been interesting to see how Leslie, in the biography he planned but never executed, would have dealt with the insanity of the promising painter Gilbert Stuart Newton, who died in a Chelsea madhouse. Alexander Gilchrist in his life of Blake forthrightly headed one of its chapters "Mad or Not Mad?" but this was not a true sign of increased candor among biographers. Blake was long dead and had left no relatives to be distressed by any speculation about his sanity.

8 Numerous skeletons in Victorian painters' closets were the subject of contemporary gossip but were referred to in print, if at all, only in guarded, evasive language, leaving to modern biographers the task of discovering the facts behind the innuendo. In 1830 the thirty-seven-old artist Francis Danby suddenly left for the Continent and did not return until 1839. Considerable mystery surrounded the episode, but it is now known that he had deserted his wife for a younger woman. The Royal Academy council, always sensitive to behaviour that might bring disgrace on art, seems to have pressured him to go into exile. (It is not on record that the council took similar action against another fairly well-known artist, Paul Falconer Poole, when he left London with Mrs. Danby.) William Mulready's entire career was dogged by an old scandal, his disastrous marriage at the age of seventeen to a girl from a prominent family of artists (the Varleys) from whom he separated soon after she had borne four sons

in quick succession. Recently discovered documents show that Mrs. Mulready later accused him of homosexuality, but of course there is no hint of this in contemporary memoirs. In his last years Edwin Landseer was a heavy drinker and his mind gave way; Lord Frederick Hamilton went so far as to describe him as "hopelessly insane, and during his periods of violence, a dangerous homicidal maniac." Learning of Landseer's death in 1873, Queen Victoria noted in her diary, "A Merciful release, as for the last three years he had been in a most distressing state, half out of his mind yet not entirely so." (See, respectively, Eric Adams, *Francis Danby: Varieties of Poetic Landscape* [New Haven: Yale University Press, 1973], chapter 4; Kathryn Moore Heleniak, *William Mulready* [New Haven: Yale University Press, 1980], pp. 8–16; and Campbell Lennie, *Landseer: The Victorian Paragon* [London: Hamish Hamilton, 1976], pp. 233–39.

9 *Self-Help*, Centenary edition, intro. Asa Briggs (London: John Murray, 1958), p. 169.

10 Giorgio Vasari, *Lives of the Most Eminent Painters, Sculptors and Architects*, translated by Gaston Du C. DeVere (10 vols., London: Macmillan and Medici Society, 1912–15), I, 3, 71–72.

11 Only a few days before he took his life, Haydon sent the twenty-six folio volumes of his journals to Elizabeth Barrett, asking that she arrange for their publication. They were, she wrote Robert Browning (5 July 1846), "as unfit as possible for the general reader – fervid & coarse at once, with personal references blood-dyed at every page . . . I only know that without great modification, the memoirs should not appear at all . . . that the scandal would be great if they did" (*The Letters of Robert Browning and Elizabeth Barrett*, ed. Elvan Kintner [Cambridge, MA: Harvard University Press, 1969], II, 847). In the event, Tom Taylor managed to avoid much of the offense that worried her by severely cutting and rewriting the journals.

12 See A. J. Finberg, *The Life of J. M. W. Turner, R.A.* (2nd ed., Oxford: Clarendon Press, 1961), pp. 1–5.

13 Ruthven Todd's Everyman edition of Gilchrist (London: Dent, 1942) is the most scholarly edition of any Victorian art biography – a tribute to Gilchrist's lasting value. See the appreciation of Gilchrist in G. E. Bentley, Jr. and Martin K. Nurmi (eds.), *A Blake Bibliography* (Minneapolis: University of Minnesota Press, 1964), pp. 12–14.

4

Charles Dickens: the lives of some important nobodies

ROBERT KIELY

When speaking of "nobodies" in Dickens, one may as well begin with Sairey Gamp's Mrs. Harris from *Martin Chuzzlewit* since sooner or later she is bound to force her way into the conversation. She is clearly nobody and, less than that, a nobody's nobody, the invention of a marginal character as negligible in the main outlines of the plot as she is in the socio-economic system depicted. It may seem that Mrs. Harris can be disposed of quickly so that we can move on to more important nobodies. But it is hard to suppress the fact that Sairey is never "dispoged" to drop the subject of Mrs. Harris. The non-existent woman repeatedly asserts herself at moments when there seems to be no reason that she should.

But Mrs. Harris is not simply a nuisance. Of the four classes of "nobodies" that commonly appear in fiction, she is a type of that which is most disturbing because it embraces all the others. The first meaning of the term "nobody" is "not any person." This can, of course, indicate a pure lack, but it just as often suggests a person who does not exist, and, therefore, designates all fictional characters, including Sairey Gamp and the entire clans of Chuzzlewits and Pecksniffs. Whatever humor one may find in Sairey's imaginary friendship must have a disturbing or at least reflexive quality since it would be hard to say with conviction why Sairey's suspension of disbelief is any more foolish than that proposed by the text as a whole.

The grounds on which the characters in the novel are asked to "believe in" Mrs. Harris do not seem phenomenologically different from those on which the reader is asked to "believe in" the rest of the characters. When a text calls attention to non-existent persons and goes so far as to introduce them into the fictional discourse, it points to the emptiness behind its own enterprise and to the presumption of language that claims to be about somebodies. The gesture is always ironical, often paradoxical, part apology and part boast, a reminder to the reader to be on guard against characterizations weighted down with false substantialities and, at the same time, to recognize the sheer inventive playfulness in the art of making something out of nothing.

The second most common definition of the term "nobody" is "a person without a body," literally "no body." This may be a spirit, a ghost, a spook, or more generally, the memory of an absent person, one who is far away or dead. This is the felt presence of a person physically not there. In literature, these "nobodies" are introduced through the dialogues of those who re-call them by naming, describing, and quoting them. They may also be recalled through a token that was once in their possession, by a portrait, or by a relative or other person who resembles them. This kind of "nobody" is known through some form of substitution, a replacement that fills in a part of the gap left by his or her absence. Rhetorically, this version of the "nobody" is revealed through metaphor or a metaphorical personification that calls attention to difference while establishing itself on grounds of similitude.

The third definition of "nobody" is social, political, and psychological rather than ontological. This is the kind of nobody that takes the indefinite article. "*A* nobody" is a person of no importance or authority, particularly from the point of view of those who consider themselves "somebody." Yet the term is not so much dismissive as it is reductive. Whether thought of in literary or social terms, those persons of no great significance are necessary to the exercise of power and even to the contours of the existence of those in privileged positions. Jane Austen's *Emma* needs Miss Bates, both in fictional and in social terms. Of course, textual and social hierarchies are not always parallel, especially in Dickens. Lizzie Hexam and Georgiana Podsnap are "nobodies" of a different order in *Our Mutual Friend*, but whether the hierarchy is of the book or of the society, the positions within it derive their status from those above and below. Hence, rhetorically, these "nobodies" are typically represented through terms of contingency, of that which is a subsidiary of a larger structure, an auxiliary or synecdoche. In *Bleak House*, the paralyzed limbs of Sir Leicester Dedlock and the strong arm of George Rouncewell derive their significance from one another and from a text that creates a society that marginalizes both.

The fourth kind of nobody is "an unknown person," missing or forgotten or only vaguely identified by associative indirection. This is the nobody who is anonymous, heard about but not heard from, a nameless, faceless creature. This is the no one who is everyone, the man in the street, the man from nowhere, alternatively a person lost in the crowd and the crowd itself, society with a capital "S" or the mob. Like Nemo in *Bleak House* or the authors of literary works, it leaves traces and signatures, but is impossible to find. This is "nobody" as a diffuse presence, everywhere and nowhere, a voice without a mouth, a hieroglyph without a complete system through which it can be decoded. Its language is that of hints and clues that do not lead by means of substitution or linear progress to a single solution, but rather play against one another in shifting juxtapositions that continually enlarge the circumference of possibilities. Rhetorically, this nobody makes itself known through metonymy, loose associations of figures that insist on nothing, neither beg for interpretation nor force equations. The effect is cumulative, often unremarkable in detail yet powerful in its totality.

Dickens's cast of "nobodies" is not entirely restricted to these four categories and few belong exclusively within the limits of a single definition of the term. There is a good deal of mixing and overlapping. But whatever the variations and combinations, Dickens's "nobodies" raise questions in which linguistic play and social concern are interlocked in ways that demand attention. There are moments in Dickens when a sensitivity to the collective welfare gives way to brilliant linguistic improvisation that appears to have no point of reference outside of itself. And there are others when the narrative discourse becomes such a transparent ideological rhetoric as to resemble propaganda. I am interested in what seems a more typical pattern in which the writing both teases and points, a discourse that defines for itself a space between the ingenious but ultimately empty display of arbitrary and opaque signs, and an equally ignenious but ideologically packed array of signifiers directing attention away from themselves.

This tension or balance is present throughout Dickens's fiction and can be traced in nearly all of its structural and thematic elements. Its peculiar concentration in the character of the "nobody" is a curiously Dickensian variant of what Wolfgang Iser calls the "blanks" that exist in all narratives.[1] Iser refers to structural segmentation, a mosaic patterning that leaves spaces for the reader to fill in with an interpretation. According to Iser's argument, the text does not force a particular interpretation. Readers will differ according to cultural, historical, and individual distinctions, yet the arrangement of the segments does not allow for random or arbitrary reading either. The patterning does not insist but it does suggest.

Iser's approach is helpful in considering "nobodies" since they too represent odd breaks in structural and thematic continuity. These are the fictional characters or non-characters who belong to the narrative without quite having earned the right to do so. Their self-assertions are oddly intrusive digressions, interruptions of plot not with subplot but with an "other's" plot, like "The History of a Self-Tormentor" (Miss Wade's confession in *Little Dorrit*) or the various inset tales in *Pickwick Papers*. The "nobody" may also represent the opposite of a digression if he or she has no other story to tell, but rather exists as a kind of negation of the main plot, a drain on its vitality, a hole in its center (like that created by the "man from nowhere" in *Our Mutual Friend*) or a perforation in the margins like that made by Oliver Twist's orphan friend Little Dick or Brooks of Sheffield in *David Copperfield*.

As the reader rushes to fill in these personified "blanks" with interpretive possibilities, he is bound to consider not only the relationship of the empty character to those whose contours and internal traits are amply sketched, but also the relationship between the language of narrative discourse and the source and nature of its authority. One of the first gestures involved in literary interpretation is naming. The reader, through paraphrase, selective quotation, analytical translation or literary allusion, renames the situation or characterization encountered in a text. Frequently this naming is a form of intertextual categorization by analogy. To call a character in a novel "Job-like" or "another Wife of Bath" is a conventional shorthand way to indicate a complex group of traits. "Nobodies" create a special problem in this regard as well as in others, but perhaps even more than in others, they beg for inclusion in a literary nomenclature. Among the most suggestively paradigmatic names for Dickens's "nobodies" are Ariel and Cordelia, not because of direct literary ancestry, but because their situations raise similar questions about the nature of language and authority, both within the text and within a socio-political world to which the text sometimes refers.

Ariel, as Prospero's slave, invisible to all but Prospero and the audience, seems a pure instrument of authority. He is a projection of an authoritative figure and inseparable from the will of that figure. Since Prospero calls him "*my* spirit," he can be taken as an intangible element of Prospero's being and as a creation of Prospero's mind. Yet Ariel is no "idle" invention; he is nothing if not active and effective. If Prospero's word is his command or if he is the very breath of Prospero's speech, he is the word as a missile of direct consequence. By moving winds and ships and people, he literally keeps the story going. Though bound to Prospero, Ariel is also, in a sense, a free spirit. His true freedom lies in the future when Prospero will release him from captivity, but his playful and musical nature suggests liberties already taken not so much in direct rebellion against the authority as unnecessary to it. There are moments in *The Tempest* when Ariel is a personification of what Bakhtin calls the "carnivalesque," in his sheer delight in reversing and thwarting the "official" order of things.[2] Yet it can never be forgotten that Ariel's rascality and disruptiveness are in the service of the higher, nobler, legitimate order which Prospero is in the process of restoring. Ariel is slave and free, empty and full, frivolous and functional, a perfect blend of language as nothing but air and language as a powerful instrument of social order.

Dickens's novels have a surprising number of paired characters whose relationships bear a resemblance to the Prospero/Ariel paradigm. Some examples might include Mr. Pickwick and Sam Weller, Fagin and the Artful Dodger, Nicholas Nickleby and

Smike, and Aunt Betsy Trotwood and Mr. Dick. In each case, the primary character is in a position of some authority that is expressed through, reinforced by, and to some extent derived from the secondary character. And while these secondary characters are not invisible spirits, their connection to the primary character is of a kind not fully explained by their social status as servant or companion. Functionally they are inseparable from the primary character; as autonomous creatures they have no existence.

The airiest of these Ariel-figures in Dickens is Sairey Gamp's Mrs. Harris and it is to her that we now return. Like Ariel, Mrs. Harris can be seen by none but her creator. She is a derivative of Sairey Gamp; she is at her beck and call; she will do and say what Sairey tells her to do and say. As the bond-servant and closest, dearest companion of her mistress, she is a sign of her isolation and limitation, yet in the ever-expanding variety of her sayings and activities, she is also a sign of her free-wheeling inventiveness. Like Ariel, Mrs. Harris is the language of her maker (or teller) set into narrative motion. She is the author's word activated into story.

Yet, of course, it is obvious that unlike Prospero, Sairey Gamp is not in control of the main plot or even of any of its secondary parts. She is a woman, childless and widowed, a servant, and a drunk: the anti-type it would seem of the sober, noble, fatherly figure personified by Prospero who, though exiled, appears from the very beginning with his authority intact. Whatever credibility Sairey Gamp has with the other characters and the reader and whatever her minor function in the story she must talk herself into and earn again with each appearance. If she is one of the many images of the author in Dickens, she is an author who cannot take the reader's respect for granted. She must hustle (verbally) just to be heard and hope that she might receive some modest compensation for her services. One of Mrs. Harris's main functions is to serve as a public relations agent for Sairey. " 'If ever there was a sober creetur to be got at eighteen pence a day for working people, and three and six for gentlefolks – ... you are that inwallable person,' " Sairey quotes Mrs. Harris as frequently remarking.[3]

In addition to using Mrs. Harris as a promoter of her career and reputation, always ready with words of praise, Sairey employs her cooperative friend as a source of stories told to entertain, amaze, and impress her listeners. When the subject is beauty, Sairey is reminded of Mrs. Harris's "husband's brother bein' six foot three, and marked with a mad bull in Wellington boots upon his left arm, on account of his precious mother havin' been worrited by one into a shoemaker's shop" (II, 208). When the subject is children, she recalls Mrs. Harris's sister's baby born dead and preserved "in spirits in a bottle" and exhibited for a price at Greenwich Fair "in company with the pink-eyed lady, Prooshan dwarf, and livin' skelinton, which judge her feelins wen the barrel-organ played, and she was showed her own dear sister's child" (II, 322).

These absurd and grotesque narrative fragments can be read as parodies of the main plots that deal with the perverse and tangled relationships within bourgeois families controlled by rich fathers. By means of Mrs. Harris, Sairey Gamp introduces (or tries to introduce) the working class and mothers into the story. She, of course, fails to link her digressive anecdotes effectively to the main plot. They are not sustained and do not cause change. Instead, like Mrs. Harris, they leave a "blank" between themselves and the major characters and actions of the text. The reader can pass quickly over these "blanks," but it is difficult to ignore them. They call into question in the same rhetorical gesture of paradox the socio-economic breadth of this story about money and families and the sources of validation for narrative discourse.

On one side of the paradox Sairey and therefore Mrs. Harris have no standing in the formal or social framework of the novel. Sairey makes her last effort to wheedle her way into a position of advantage in the third to last chapter of the book in which old Martin Chuzzlewit finally emerges from inaction, denounces Pecksniff as a fraud, and, like Prospero, sets things in motion for happy pairings and a just conclusion. As events advance swiftly toward their destiny, Sairey becomes restless and creative for one last time: "Mrs. Gamp had observed, not without jealousy and scorn, that a favorable impression appeared to exist in behalf of Mr. Sweedlepipe and his young friend; and that she had fallen rather into the background in consequence. She now struggled to the front, therefore, and stated her business" (II, 322).

Sairey's last narrative, of course, involves Mrs. Harris and is also a self-recommendation for a position in the Chuzzlewit household. Old Martin, however, reads her out of the house and out of the story ("Here we will close our acquaintance, Mrs Gamp"). He sees to it that she is paid off and tells her landlord to advise her to have "a little less liquor, and a little more humanity, and a little less regard for herself, and a little more regard for her patients, and perhaps a trifle of additional honesty" (II, 323). Sairey, exposed to the stern judgment of the family patriarch, exits swooning and muttering faintly to herself. Struggle as she may, she has had no power to break permanently into the main plot and certainly has nothing to say about how the story ends.

Or does she? Can Old Martin really rule her out of order and effectively eliminate her from the fictional and social network?

The other side of the paradox says No. Sairey and Mrs. Harris are permanent and disturbing fixtures in the linguistic and socio-economic scheme. Judged and dismissed by Old Martin, their presence also has a judgmental and dismissive effect on him. In the first and ontological sense of the term, he is as much of a "nobody" as Sairey. And his eccentric schemes and pretenses are no less fraudulent or fictional than hers. If her relationship to reality is ambiguous, so is his; if her honesty is questionable, so is his; if the grounds on which she attempts to establish her authority are shaky, so are his. He finds his voice and she loses hers with equal and illogical suddenness.

If Sairey is a mock-Prospero with nothing to offer but nerve, words, and a non-existent friend, Old Martin can hardly be seen in simple and sharp contrast to that image. It is laughably plain that Sairey has a way with words but almost no effect on events. But Martin, despite his age, gender, wealth, and designs has remarkably little influence on the complex twists and turns of the plot until almost the very end. If he is not a mock-Prospero, he is a withered, worn, weakened one who shares stage center with Pecksniff, a personification of patriarchal authority as a hollow fiction. Sairey is not a minor foil to old Chuzzlewit, an insignificant speck that can be dusted off, but a curiously stubborn counterpart. They sink or swim together. If she is a mere fiction, a cluster of words with no substance, capable of generating nothing and nobody, he is, considered by empirical standards, exactly the same.

Furthermore, their symbiosis extends beyond the verbal to the social. If she, as a woman and a member of the working class, "fallen into the background ... struggling to the front," must compete with a huge and discordant chorus of other voices in order to "state her business," he, as an aged grandfather of an ageing and increasingly embattled bourgeoisie, must do the same. There is no single central authority either in the text or in the world it represents. Old Martin's belated assumption of authority is a fictional convention with a mixed message. And so is the humbling of Sairey and her comic exit. Martin may have the last word and in his way tie up the loose ends of the plot. But Sairey, a diachronic failure, is an irrepressible synchronic success. Beginnings and endings are all the same to her: "She went to a lying-in or a laying-out with equal zest and relish" (I, 331).

There is a strong sense in which Sairey and Mrs. Harris, by virtue of their being "nobodies," are beyond Old Martin's power of exclusion. Bakhtin refers in his study of Rabelais to a Latin "History of Nemo" in which *Nemo* or "nobody" is interpreted as a proper noun: "Thus, everything impossible, inadmissible, is, on the contrary, permitted to *Nemo*. Thanks to this transposition, *Nemo* acquires the majestic aspect of a being almost equal to God, endowed with unique, exceptional powers, knowledge (he knows that which no one else knows) and extraordinary freedom (he is allowed that which nobody is permitted)."[4] Sairey may not be equal to God, but she, like *Nemo*, possesses paradoxical power and freedom that the main plot cannot fully suppress.

Sairey's absurd parody of patriarchal power suggests another more serious literary type of the "nobody" who challenges authority. In Shakespeare, Cordelia's refusal to employ words excessively is an exercise of power by means of negation. Her "Nothing, my lord," may be modest and true, but it is also a denial of a linguistic and courtly convention. She creates and points to a hole in the fabric. Lear's "Nothing will come of nothing" (Act I, scene i) appears to make mathematical and proverbial sense, but it is in fact almost immediately contradicted by his own angry response. The main action of the play follows directly upon Cordelia's "Nothing, my lord." And though these actions are specifically set into motion by the authority of the King's commands, it is really Cordelia's negative authority, her articulated silence, that is the force behind much of what occurs, including her own banishment. Lear spares his daughter's life, but he disowns her, and marries her off without a dowry. For him, she is to be "a stranger to my heart," "my sometime daughter," a non-person. Until the end of the play, she is off-stage even if not quite outside the text. Her absence, like her verbal negation, assumes a power and a voice not anticipated by the old King. A hint of this is given when Lear banishes Kent for coming to Cordelia's defense. Kent pleads with the King: "Let me still remain / The true blank of thine eye" (I, i). The play of the word "blank" as "bull's eye of a target" and "empty space" suggests that what is not filled by a presence is not necessarily de-centered.

Cordelia's replacement in closeness to Lear and bluntness of language is the Fool, yet like metaphor, he is an imperfect substitute, a rough equivalent who reminds us as much of difference as of similarity. He is not a transformation of Cordelia but a personification of her absence, a figure for one who is not there. Since Cordelia's exit and the Fool's entrance coincide with the loss of Lear's authority and sanity, they may also be thought of as occupying the "bull's eye," the empty space at the center of the King's being. "Thou has pared thy wit 'o' both sides, and left nothing i' the middle," says the Fool to Lear. "Now thou art an O without a figure ... I am a fool, thou art nothing" (I, iv). "Nobodies" proliferate in this play. Edgar, Edmund, Gloucester, and Kent are all characters whose legitimacy, authority, and identity are called into question. At the center of it all is the collapsed King who in a few gestures has disempowered himself, disinherited his daughter, and created a gap that only a fool would try to fill.

In the form of abandoned, neglected or disinherited daughters and their childlike and sometimes comic counterparts, the Cordelia/Fool doubling appears frequently in Dickens. Esther Summerson and Charley Neckett, Florence Dombey and Little Paul, Lizzie Hexam and Jenny Wren, Little Nell and Kit Nubbles suggest some variations on the pattern. One of the earliest and most memorable Lear figures in Dickens is the grandfather in *The Old Curiosity Shop*.[5] But the mature novel in which "nobodies" and their foolish substitutes seem to multiply with every chapter and in which their non-being is related to the collapse of language and of paternal authority is *Little Dorrit*. In many ways the novel appears to be an oddly splintered, mirrored and attenuated version of the Lear story as if the whole family had survived the King's downfall and madness and had to settle down in Victorian London. Old Dorrit, the Father of the Marshalsea, is a Lear who has adjusted to his own madness and turned his prison into a court. Tip and Fanny are the greedy and disrespectful Goneril and Regan; Little Dorrit is the good daughter whom the father needs but discounts; and the simple-minded Maggy is the Fool who "counted as nobody."[6]

As always in Dickens's hall of mirrors, there are multiple reflections of the devalued or absent daughter: Tattycoram, Miss Wade, Pet's dead sister. But the most prominent of the "nobodies" in the novel, the counterpart of Little Dorrit and the character most frequently referred to as "nobody" is Arthur Clennam. He is not merely a Cordelia, but a combination of Lear, Cordelia, and the Fool. As a middle-aged male named Arthur, heir to a family business, he bears the Victorian traces of patriarchal authority. Yet we also know that he and his father were banished to China by his iron-willed "mother." Like Cordelia, he is honest, sparing of words, innocent and inexperienced despite his age. Like the Fool, he is a person with no status. He gives up his claim to the family business and to falling in love. He sees himself as an outsider, an observer, an interpreter, one who has no place in the society to which he has so recently and belatedly returned or in the novel which has by some cruel accident drawn him into the large open space ordinarily reserved for a hero.

The sketching of Arthur's character as it is gradually introduced into the text is filled with "erasure marks" and therefore forms a peculiar contrast with the many characters whose outlines and outstanding features are inscribed with Dickensian sharpness. First encountered (hardly seen) in conversation with Mr. Meagles, Arthur is referred to as "the other," "the second speaker," "a grave dark man of forty" in a series of verbal evasions of naming and detailed description. When Arthur is finally named and begins talking about himself, he says that he is a "waif" and a "stray," that he has "no will" and that he is "the child of parents who weighed, measured, and priced everything; for whom what could not be weighed, measured, and priced, had no existence" (I, 22). The third-person narration cannot get a fix on this character any more than he can seem to get one on himself. We see him as he sees himself in terms of what he is not. Even his forty years do not add up to a mature sum. In his own eyes he is still a discounted child, and when he is greeted at the door of his house after a twenty-year absence, the old servant observes him: "Your figure is filled out, and set . . . but you don't come up to your father in my opinion. Nor yet your mother" (I, 34).

That Arthur is a "figure" of some kind and that this "figure" is already "set" discourages the reader, as it does Arthur, from trying to fit his narrative into the trajectory of a young person of potential still trying to discover a true self in some future resolution or recombination of promising parts. Arthur is a "set figure," an inadequate substitute for a missing self. Again, he is both Cordelia and the Fool: an absence and a slightly absurd replacement. This doubleness, not so much a moral or psychological duality as an ontological split, is expressed in a variety of ways, including, most persistently, in Arthur's relation to language.

Arthur's spoken dialogue is courteous and conventional, but like Cordelia's, it is notably sparing and uninflated in comparison with most of the talk that surrounds him. Some of his most extended "speeches" are never uttered; yet it would not be entirely accurate to say that they remain within his mind or even in literary terms that they are a version of narrated interior monologue. They are speeches not spoken and thoughts he does not dare to have about a self that does not exist. When he first visits the Meagleses at home, he is attracted to their daughter Pet, but thinks that he is too old for her and probably should not let his feelings lead to disappointment. The situation is a familiar one and not in itself particularly difficult to grasp. What complicates it is not the subtle nuances of awkwardness, pleasure or obsession in Arthur's unfulfillable relationship with the young woman (as one might expect in Henry James or Thomas Mann) but his ambivalent relationship with his non-existent self.

The text cooperates with this ambivalence in a relentless dialectic of narrative forms and tones. When Arthur muses to himself at the end of the chapter, which is entitled "Nobody's Weakness," quotation marks and the phrase "so his thoughts ran" signal the reader or seem to signal the reader that these are direct quotes of direct thoughts. But indirection belies the punctuation from the outset: " 'Suppose that a man,' so his thoughts ran, 'who had been of age some twenty years . . . ' " (I, 213). The separation of Arthur's older from his younger self, that is, the separation in time, is complicated by a separation in grammatical mood between the conditional and the implied indicative, and the syntactical interruption that divides the "man" from "his thoughts." The language performs a set of separations more disturbing and puzzling than the somewhat conventional one that it describes. Arthur goes on to picture a self that is easily recognized by the reader: "diffident," "deficient," "a stranger in the land," with "nothing in his favor" (I, 213–14). And then he supposes that such a man might hope to win the love of a young girl and concludes, "What a weakness it would be!" (I, 214).

If Arthur's self-portrait did not correspond so accurately to what the reader has already seen, it would be difficult to keep from taking these self-effacing lines as Pamela-like (or Uriah Heep-like) false protestations of unworthiness. Even as it is, the associations and therefore the response are impossible to eliminate altogether. The literary reputation of elaborately articulated self-effacement is not good for the obvious reason that genuine self-effacement is silent. It is true that Arthur does not speak his thoughts. He does not even directly address them to himself but rather narrates them as part of an imaginary story about an unnamed and nondescript person. Yet we know who and what he is thinking about; moreover, we know that he knows who and what he is talking about. The indirection of the language thus presents itself as an intrusion, as a kind of pure rhetoric that cannot be easily translated into moral terms (like hypocrisy or false modesty) but also cannot be ignored. This is Arthur's form of circumlocution, not puffed-up language concealing indolence and greed, but language that does not derive its momentum, direction or meaning from a single identifiable source, but rather moves in circles around an empty space that divides the self from itself.

That space is further widened when the third-person narration takes up Arthur's musings and extends them outside of the boundary of quotation marks: "Why should he be vexed or sore at heart? It was not his weakness that he had imagined. It was nobody's, nobody's within his knowledge" (I, 214). The language of this passage, like the "knowledge" to which it refers, belongs to and does not belong to Arthur. It is suspended between the full awareness and control of an omniscient narrator and the repressed consciousness and passivity of an observant but only partially informed character. Within the third-person narration, the word "nobody" is an archly ironic label for Arthur, equivalent to the narrator's winking at the reader and saying, "You know who!" As a verbal approximation of Arthur's mental state, the repetition of "nobody" suggests a denial that reaches beyond Arthur's immediate attraction to Pet to life in general. "He thought . . . that it might be better to flow away monotonously, like the river, and to compound for its insensibility to happiness with its insensibility to pain" (I, 214). The ill-equipped stand-in for nobody sees one solution for his split voice and personality in the "monotone" of the river, an image of oblivion.

But even Arthur's inclination toward death is shadowed by doubt, and only "*might* be better" than his present state. He does not attain univocity or unity of purpose. And the text does not allow its "nobody" to die. The chapter following "Nobody's Weakness" introduces Henry Gowan, Pet's lover, and is entitled "Nobody's Rival." Arthur dislikes Gowan and sees that he will make an irresponsible husband, but determines not to speak of these matters or dwell on them in his own mind. In a chapter entitled "Nobody's State of Mind," the third-person narration depicts Arthur's attitude toward Gowan as self-sacrificing and generous and then follows this with the observation that "such a state of mind was nobody's – nobody's" (I, 330). At the end of the chapter, after a visit to Gowan's mother, Arthur is troubled by the old woman's snobbery and greed. He falls into a disturbed silence, a "state of mind" which the text declares "rendered nobody uneasy" (I, 340). It goes on to say that if he had allowed himself to ponder these matters, "he would have thought. . . ," and then proceeds to say what he would have thought. Once again, Arthur's unarticulated musings are given utterance by a text that does not locate itself squarely in his mind. His problems – psychological, social, epistemological – are split and given pseudo-articulation and personification in a brooding "nobody" who is a pathetic cousin of the comically garrulous Mrs. Harris.

What is striking and highly characteristic of Dickens is that Arthur's "problem," his repression and self-alienation, neither dominates the novel nor stands alone as a unique personal dilemma. On the contrary, the further one reads, the more Arthur's difficulty in finding an identity and a language appears to be a variation on a complex and much-repeated theme. Rather than isolating individual psychology or the ontological riddles of metafiction, Dickens does everything possible to associate them with a social condition, a collective malaise. Class, wealth, or gender are no guarantee of invulnerability. Each experiences Arthur's problem in its own fashion. In the last of the "nobody" chapters, "Nobody's Disappearance," the nonentity who has disappeared is not Arthur but the servant Tattycoram. She has run away with Miss Wade, who sees one major similarity between the girl and herself: "She has no name. I have no name" (I, 353). Arthur also learns that Pet and Gowan have become engaged so that the "hope that had flickered in nobody's heart" at last died (I, 357). But even in the matter of the engagement, Arthur is not alone in his sense of loss and the emptiness within himself. Mr. Meagles compares Arthur's loss of Pet with the death of Pet's twin sister many years ago, a death he and his wife have denied by imagining the child as if she were growing up beside Pet. Little by little, the book adds to its long list of erasures and cancellations – whether through death, neglect, denial, or repression – and the odd, imperfect substitutes that try to fill their place.

As has been suggested in Arthur's case, one of the indicators of the self aware of itself as an absence is a kind of fractured utterance, an articulation of the sayable and unsayable, the voice of the impersonator and the would-be voice of the missing person. The malady of the Circumlocution Office spreads well beyond the walls of a single bureau. Nearly all of the characters in the novel engage in some form of "speaking around," not that they are all hypocritical scoundrels or are aware of a subject that they wish to avoid. There are other forms and causes of circumlocution. When, for example, in a conversation with Arthur, Pet refers to Gowan as "one I need not name," her indirection betrays more than delicacy of feeling toward a would-be suitor. The text has already hinted that the suave Gowan who has been courting Pet is a polished front for a less certain, indeed a hidden character. Pet herself has been so pampered that her own character is not clearly formed. Her little evasion is not simple reticence but a signal of a gap in her self-certainty. Her servant Tattycoram's counting to five-and-twenty when she is out of temper is a parodic variant on the substitution of neutralizing meaningless signs for an unexpressed or inexpressible self.

The pattern is one in which inheritance and disinheritance begin to resemble one another. The children of this novel seem to be similarly disabled by parents, especially fathers, who are absent and therefore silent or who are present and have much too much to say for themselves. Derrida has observed that " 'the speaking subject' is the father of his speech," and that "*logos* is a son ... a son that would be destroyed in his very *presence* without the present *attendance* of the father. His father who answers. His father who speaks for him and answers for him. Without his father, he would be nothing but, in fact, writing."[7] According to this view, speech has an authority, a force, a self-verification that writing, as an "orphan," lacks. In fact, "the instant it reaches inscription [writing] scarcely remains a son at all and no longer recognizes its origins."[8]

In *Little Dorrit*, fathers as well as sons and daughters are like orphaned writing cut off from the authority of the spoken word. The three most talkative fathers in the book are Meagles, Old Dorrit, and Christopher Casby, the Last of the Patriarchs. Meagles cannot stop Pet's marriage, improve Tattycoram's temper, or bring his dead daughter back to life with his words. Old Dorrit, the Father of the Marshalsea, is much given to speech-making. He is a victim of the Circumlocution Office but he is also one of the great practitioners of empty talk. He is honored and catered to in prison out of pity and force of habit more than because his words carry any weight.

But if Dorrit is a benevolent windbag, Christopher Casby is a malicious patriarch, the landlord of Bleeding Heart Lane, who gives oily speeches while wringing money out of his poorest tenants by means of an agent. When Mr. Pancks unmasks Casby, he does so in a manner that calls attention to another form of circumlocution, language as dislocated brutality, violence by metaphor: "You're a driver in disguise, a screwer by deputy, a wringer and squeezer and shaver by substitute!" (II, 399). As though words do not have sufficient force to perform the complete task of exposing Casby, the metaphor disfigures its origin. Pancks cuts off Casby's locks and wrecks his hat (two signs of the Patriarch's would-be dignity): "A bare-polled, goggle-eyed, big-headed lumbering personage stood staring at him, not in the least impressive, not in the least venerable, who seemed to have started out of the earth to ask what was become of Casby" (II, 402). Stripped of fine speech and long hair, Casby is shown to be a kind of mannequin, a nobody, a fake father whose word is not a living son or daughter but a dead letter. Pancks, the rebellious agent ("son") does not reveal an evil authority but an absent one, an emptiness.

Of all the patriarchal figures in the novel, the one with the most power in economic and social terms is also the least loquacious. Mr. Merdle has little to say for himself even at the dinner parties held in his own magnificent townhouse. He is not given to speech-making and, in fact, his wife complains that he does not cut a sufficiently impressive figure in "Society." His defense, that she supplies the "manner" and he the "money," suggests with unexpected candor that they both are in service to a phenomenon that has its origin outside of their powers of definition and control. Guests flock to the Merdle household and line up to request favors from their rich host, but quickly leave his company once they have stated their business. He appears to have no self apart from the trappings of material success. He is a sign of power, not its source. When left alone in his own house he wanders around like a lost waif or a phantom without a body: "Let Mrs. Merdle announce, with all her might, that she was at Home ever so many nights in a season, she could not announce more widely and unmistakably than Mr. Merdle did that he was never at home" (I, 425).

Mr. Merdle's financial collapse and subsequent suicide in the Baths expose, as in the case of Casby, not malice, or lust, or even a clearly defined case of ambition, but fraudulence, the pretense of being that which he is not. "He had sprung from nothing, by no natural growth or process that anyone could account for" (II, 301). Merdle is not so much a self-made man as a self-invented one. His own last word about himself is left in writing, in a letter to his physician (not to his wife or offspring) and, though the letter is not quoted directly, it makes known that "Mr. Merdle's complaint had been simply Forgery and Robbery" (II, 302). In writing, the powerful patriarch at last names himself and makes his signature known. His self-betrayal goes a step further than the separation of the written from the spoken word, as described by Derrida; he separates the written word from itself, compounds the break between the authority of speech and the parentless, unauthorized inscription.

His hallmark is a species of writing, not as a distortion of truth or as a partial representation of it, but as a counterfeit, that is, a doubly dislocated figure, an image of an image, a sign in imitation of a sign behind which there is nothing, no money or person "that anyone could account for." But as is the case with Arthur Clennam's absent self, his continually having to contend with the "nobody" who accompanies and speaks for him wherever he goes, Mr. Merdle's forgery is duplicated in numerous forms throughout the text. It is an instance of an economy "sprung from nothing, by no natural growth or process," based on speculation, chance, and sources of labor and production that are invisible in that they are not recognized or rewarded by the system of which they are an essential part.

But if Mr. Merdle's forgery is a sign of an economy without solid grounding or generative consequences, it is also a disturbing example of a kind of writing that calls into question the possibilities of the written word ever overcoming its alienation from the authoritative. Recalling the origins of the word "forge" and Joyce's ambiguous use of it at the end of A Portrait of the Artist as a Young Man,[9] one is faced with the double notion of writing as shaping something substantial, new and perhaps even useful, or as a kind of counterfeiting that does not always result from bad intentions but from the nature of the medium in which the artisan is condemned to work.

The question is whether Mr. Merdle's forgery is an aberration, both in reference to language and social ethics, or a repulsive variant of a common pattern reflected in all the characters and in the language of the narrative itself. As figures of authority (and authorship) the patriarchs in the novel differ from one another most widely not in degree of pretension, but in the credulity of those who interpret their words and thereby lend power to them. The Father of Marshalsea is not limited by self-restraint, but by his audience, the impotent inmates of a prison willing to suspend disbelief and live in the illusion of existing under the patronage of a benevolent master, and a Cordelia-like daughter who sees the emptiness of her father's words but pities and loves him anyway.

Mr. Merdle does not seem more malicious or fraudulent than Old Dorrit; by virtue of temporary financial luck, he has gathered about himself an audience of greater economic, political and social influence than that in the Marshalsea. Both Merdle and Dorrit are presented as pathetic victims trapped in counterfeit languages which they have coined and their audiences have too willingly "bought." Unlike Casby who is publicly denounced by his agent, Merdle and Dorrit ultimately expose and destroy themselves with no help from their children or followers. The most vital and dramatically vivid scenes involving these two are Dorrit's "prison speech" at Mrs. Merdle's, which has an electrifying effect on the dinner guests, and Merdle's suicide, which plunges the financial district into a panic. The fraudulent patriarchs display their greatest and most authentic power in the act of self-exposure which is inseparable from self-destruction.

The legacy of these fathers is not the memory of an absent authority but the presence of an empty one. Their offspring are in a sense orphaned, like Derrida's "writing" in relation to "speech," but in these cases the spoken word is also tainted. Speech itself has been broken into, interfered with, divided against itself by the written word. The patriarchs are perpetrators of forgeries, but they are also the victims of written language, of writs, and wills, bills of sale, codicils, contracts, account books, ledgers, vouchers. The "spoken" authority of the father is already bifurcated and weakened, invalidated, made *invalid* by the time it is repeated or represented by the child. Old Dorrit's favorite form of written communication is the IOU, an inscription with no basis in reality, a perfect lettered condensation of his speech and his relations with other people, an exact signature.

As the possessor of an "invalid" signature, Old Dorrit is himself lacking in substance and force. He is not an authority that generates energy in his offspring either by inspiring them or provoking rebellion. He is in himself inválid, an ínvalid in need of care. And that is what Little Dorrit offers him. She is not the Cordelia of Act i, scene i, but the Cordelia of the prison, ministering to and humoring her mad and weakened father and king. Though Dorrit has become a rich man, he dies imagining himself back at the Marshalsea: "They were in the jail again, and she tended him, and he had constant need of her, and could not turn without her" (ii, 236). Like Lear, Dorrit wants to strip off his clothing. "He sent off his sleeve-buttons and finger-rings"; "his clothes engaged his attention" (ii, 236). Amy survives her father though the text suggests an identification between father and daughter (his "face subsided into a far younger likeness of her own than she had ever seen" [ii, 236]) that calls into question the nature of such a survival.

Arthur Clennam, the other Cordelia, also survives his parents, including a mother who is inválid (not his true mother) and a seeming ínvalid, a person without force, who leaves her wheelchair when the situation requires it and exerts a negative power by concealing a document, a piece of writing, left by her husband's uncle for the benefit of Little Dorrit. As a figure of authority, Mrs. Clennam conceals strength of will behind physical weakness. But though her layering of fraudulence is a little more complex than that of Old Dorrit, she too is ultimately seen to be hollow and impotent. Her house and her plot collapse simultaneously. She too is an author with no substance and no generative possibilities. She can thwart, interrupt, delay, and undermine, but she cannot create.

In *King Lear*, when Kent intervenes on Cordelia's behalf, the King accuses him of trying "to come between our sentence and our power" (i, i). In a certain literal sense, Lear's allegation is accurate and it might be equally accurate as a description of Mrs. Clennam's suppression of her husband's uncle's will since by hiding it she prevents it from taking effect. But Lear's words have a resonance beyond the immediate situation. They provide a first glimpse of the crack which is about to widen into an abyss between the King' words and an effective magisterial authority. And though from Lear's point of view, Cordelia and Kent are the agents of this breach, subsequent developments in the play suggest that the split is within Lear and perhaps even within the nature of his language. Despite the detective-story elements in *Little Dorrit*, the solving of the mystery of the Clennam household and the missing will does not expose Mrs. Clennam as the single source of all obstruction but rather as a symptom of a pervasive infection.

Even Arthur's father, deprived of his son's true mother and banished to China, seems as much a victim of his own weakness as he is of Mrs. Clennam's revenge. Arthur's last memory of his father is of the older man trying and failing to put something in writing: "I saw him at the last with the pencil in his failing hand, trying to write some word for you to read, but to which he could give no shape" (I, 52). Arthur is the messenger and message of his father to Mrs. Clennam and the world. The problem is not simply that he has been separated from his father, like writing bereft of the authority of speech, but that he does not know and never knew his father's word. He delivers a gold watch with the inscription "DNF" to Mrs. Clennam. He thinks the letters may stand for "Do Not Forget," but does not know what it is that should not be forgotten. Arthur is part of a generation that has inherited IOUs and DNFs from their fathers. Their legacies are incomplete codes, letters that do not point ahead to new narrative possibilities but back to an absence of authority and power, an absence which they so thinly conceal as to seem almost transparent.

The children of such inválid/ínvalid elders are themselves disabled. They do not merely distrust language, they cannot speak without disclosing an emptiness within themselves, a gap between their sentences and power. Their efforts at forming an identity repeatedly remind them and the reader of their distance from reality. Like Sairey Gamp's Mrs. Harris, their every utterance declares their non-existence, their membership in the first category of "nobodies," that of the fictitious person. Simultaneously, and also like Sairey, they are forced at the end of the narrative to accept their status as nonentities without heroic standing in the plot or individual wealth or name in the social structure. It remains to be asked whether this signifies a final defeat or a transformation of an unexpected and hopeful kind.

At the end of the novel when Arthur and Little Dorrit are married, the couple emerge from the church and the text repeats "went down" without at first indicating a subject. Once again it is as though "nobody" "went down into a modest life"; "went down to give a mother's care . . . to neglected children"; "went down to give a tender nurse . . ." (II, 428). Not only are the couple not seen as if not really there, but they are not heard. They form a little invisible island of silence enclosed in the structure of a sentence that presents and conceals them as by the meaningless roar of the crowd: "They went quietly down into the roaring streets, inseparable and blessed; and as they passed along in sunshine and shade, the noisy and eager, and the arrogant and the froward and the vain, fretted and chafed, and made their usual uproar" (II, 428).

The image of two silent figures going "down" among an uproar where no coherent language is discernible seems more like death than survival, more like Sairey's descent into an inarticulate underworld than the beginning of a new life. Arthur Clennam and Amy Dorrit are not heroic characters who "leap into the breach." Their function is rather to suffer the breach, to embody and express it. In their absence from authority and in the absence of authority from them, they leave open a wound in the structure of society and language.

But it may also be that in "going down" from the egotism, false ambition, and empty talk of their elders, they exchange their inheritance – moral and psychological nothingness – for an unselfish identification with the collective. Insofar as the "descent" of Arthur and Amy is into a life of caring for the neglected, they become lost in the crowd and thereby join the fourth category of "nobody." Read in this way, the silent going down is also a kind of death, but it is final within the scope only of the kind of plot and world that privilege individual dominance and aggression. It may be a death, if we can believe in it, that promises an entirely new kind of life and story and conception of identity.

The example of Sairey Gamp (that is, of her class, and gender and imaginative nerve) may help us to believe, since though she and Mrs. Harris are sent out of the text by a rich old patriarch, there is no reason to assume that they are out for good. Dickens seems to have left Arthur, Amy, and us the mortified heirs of a mad Lear who has finally run out of empty words or the more hopeful inheritors of a shabby female Prospero whose inventions and interventions have only just begun.

NOTES

1 See especially chapter 8, "How Acts of Constitution are Stimulated," pp. 180–231, in Wolfgang Iser, *The Act of Reading: A Theory of Aesthetic Response* (Baltimore: Johns Hopkins University Press, 1978).
2 For a particularly stimulating discussion of "carnival" and "negation," see M. M. Bakhtin, *Rabelais and His World*, tr. Helene Iswolsky (Bloomington: Indiana University Press, 1984), pp. 410–15.
3 Charles Dickens, *Martin Chuzzlewit*, vol. I (of the novel), vol. x (of the series), p. 331 from *The Writings of Charles Dickens* (32 vols., Boston: Houghton Mifflin and Company, 1894). Further quotations from this novel will be cited in the text by volume (of the novel) and page number.
4 Bakhtin, *Rabelais and His World*, p. 413.
5 One of the most explicit references to the old man as Lear is made in a comment by Sampson Brass: "He quite realizes my idea of King Lear" (*The Old Curiosity Shop* in *The Writings of Charles Dickens*, VII, 438).
6 Charles Dickens, *Little Dorrit*, *Writings*, vol. I (of the novel), vol. XVIII (of the series), p. 14. Further quotations from this novel will be cited in the text by volume (of the novel) and page number.
7 Jacques Derrida, *Dissemination*, tr. Barbara Johnson (Chicago: University of Chicago Press, 1981), p. 77. This occurs in the section "The Father of Logos" in the chapter on "Plato's Pharmacy."
8 *Ibid.*, p. 77.
9 "I go to encounter for the millionth time the reality of experience and to forge in the smithy of my soul the uncreated conscience of my race" (James Joyce, *A Portrait of the Artist as a Young Man* [New York: The Viking Press, 1964], pp. 252–53).

5

Mr. Darwin collects himself

JOHN D. ROSENBERG

Late in life, from the chilling perspective of a posthumous self, Charles Darwin wrote a brief account of his own origins. "I have attempted to write the following account of myself, as if I were a dead man in another world looking back at my own life."[1] Darwin pushes the act of self-objectification to its theoretical limits: he gazes into the autobiographer's mirror and sees, staring back, not Charles Darwin but an aged instance of the species *homo sapiens.* Writing of himself as a dead man is not at all difficult, he tells us, "for life is nearly over with me."[2] The central activity of his life had been the collecting and interpreting of natural phenomena. Now, believing himself to be at life's end, he collects himself, a specimen dispassionately impaled on the keen pin of his self-observation.

Darwin began his *Recollections of the Development of my Mind and Character*[3] late in May of 1876, when he was sixty-seven years old. He wrote quickly and casually and, except for some later additions, completed the work in ten weeks. Twice in the opening paragraph he refers to the *Recollections* as a "sketch," with all the rapidity and informality the word implies. In no sense a full-scale self-portrait, the *Recollections* constitute a discontinuous narrative, by turns anecdotal and reflective, that captures the features of an old man in search of his formative self and desirous of preserving his past for his progeny. He had spent a lifetime studying sexual propagation and heredity. In the month in which he began his *Recollections* he learned that he was to become a grandfather for the first time,[4] and in the opening paragraph he tells us that it would have greatly interested him to read an

82

autobiographical sketch of his grandfather Erasmus. He is conscious of five generations of Darwins as he remarks, with habitual understatement, that the *Recollections* "might possibly interest my children or their children."[5] Not *my grandchildren*, the phrase we expect; in the more impersonal "my children or their children" we detect the characteristic estrangement from conventional associations that enabled Darwin to be both detached and loving. He must have known that, as a world-renowned scientist, his *Recollections* would be widely read. Yet the work was written not for the world at large but as an exercise in self-exploration for himself and his immediate family. The perspective is at once intimate and objective, quite like that in "A Biographical Sketch of an Infant," a pioneering study in child development based on Darwin's observations of, and benign experiment upon, his first-born son, William Erasmus.[6]

One of the as-yet-unborn grandchildren for whom Darwin wrote his *Recollections*, Nora Darwin Barlow, edited in 1958 the first unexpurgated edition in English. But Lady Barlow gave to her otherwise invaluable edition the unfortunate title *The Autobiography of Charles Darwin*.[7] *Autobiography* arouses in the reader false generic expectations, for it suggests a more self-consciously shaped and "literary" life than Darwin ever intended. The militantly prosaic opening, the disclaimer of any audience other than the family, the disavowal of any pretense to style, all make it clear that Darwin believed himself to be writing in spite of, rather than within, the quasi-novelistic conventions of English autobiography.

The most striking moment in the *Recollections* occurs on the willowy banks of the River Cam. Happier out of the classroom than in it, the young Darwin preferred the dank habitats of the local beetles, whom he hunted under the bark of the ancient willows that overhang the river between Cambridge and Grantchester. Sport, outdoor education, and innate passion all in one, the pursuit of beetles aroused in the young Darwin an eagerness that other undergraduates gave to horses or, more rarely, to books.[8] In proof of his "zeal," Darwin writes in the *Recollections*, he one day tore off some rotting bark, then

saw two rare beetles and seized one in each hand; then I saw a third and new kind, which I could not bear to lose, so that I popped the one which

I held in my right hand into my mouth. Alas it ejected some intensely acrid fluid, which burnt my tongue so that I was forced to spit the beetle out, which was lost, as well as the third one.   (*Autobiography*, p. 62)

Darwin remembered virtually everything he ever saw or touched (his mother is an arresting exception), and the "third and new" beetle remained fixed in his mind as an irksome absence for over fifty years. The pain, for Darwin, lay not in the burned tongue but in the lost treasure. No larger than a ladybug, with tiny jet-black head and jet-black cross emblazoned across its prickly orange back, *Panagaeus crux major* figures in Darwin's letters as *sacred*, his nightingale of insects, emblem of his lifelong pursuit of the elusive beauty of natural fact.[9]

The young Darwin felled birds with the same zeal that he hunted beetles. He awaited the start of the shooting season as the coming of "bliss on earth," and he placed his open hunting boots beside his bed at night, the better to reach the fields by sunrise.[10] In time the mockingbirds of the Galapagos Islands stirred within him intimations of transmutation,[11] and the thought of inflicting gratuitious pain became so painful that he could not bear to bait a live worm.[12] But before the voyage of the *Beagle*, before he had discovered his vocation, Darwin appeared in his pleasures to be something of an idler and barbarian. He behaved like what he indeed *was*, a genial, sports-loving youth of the provincial gentry. Only his slow-dawning genius set him apart from his peers, but it went unremarked by his teachers, by his family, and perhaps especially by himself. It remained the great bafflement of his later life, a bafflement recorded in the *Recollections* with a candor mistaken by his critics for mock-modesty, that the youth who chased beetles and downed whole flocks of birds – "very bad shooting this season, the first day I killed 10 brace"[13] – evolved into the Charles Darwin who forever altered our understanding of nature and of our place within it.

The grand organizing metaphor of autobiography, sacred or secular, depicts life as a journey, a voyage of discovery in which the old self gives birth to the new.[14] Darwin had the strange fortune of enacting the autobiographer's metaphor. For 1,737 cramped days and nights he circumnavigated the globe as naturalist aboard the HMS *Beagle*. Upon his return, his father remarked to his sisters, "Why, the shape of his head is quite altered."[15] Dr. Robert Darwin, who, according to his son, had "almost supernatural" powers of "reading the characters, and even the thoughts" of others,[16] saw at once that the voyage of the *Beagle* had been for Charles a voyage of discovery. Forty years after his return, Darwin wrote in the *Recollections* that his five years aboard the *Beagle* constituted "by far the most important event in my life and has determined my whole career."[17] One wishes that he had written more of his own evolution, but introspection was not his particular gift, and from the subdued perspective of old age in his country retreat-cum-laboratory at Down House, his realization of his life's work when exploring the tropical forests of Brazil and the frigid wastes of Tierra del Fuego must have seemed distant indeed. The mystery for Darwin's biographer is not the life-altering effect of his years aboard the *Beagle*. Rather it is that Charles Darwin, desultory student and medical-school dropout, was invited to serve as ship's naturalist on an important government mission of survey-ing and scientific research. Yet when the invitation reached him late in August of 1831, Darwin at age twenty-two was very likely the best-qualified young man for the job in England.

Even in his earliest days at school, Darwin tells us at the start of the *Recollections*, his enthusiasm for natural history, especially for collecting, was intense:

I tried to make out the names of plants, and collected all sorts of things, shells, seals, franks, coins, and minerals. The passion for collecting, which leads a man to be a systematic naturalist, a virtuoso or a miser, was very strong in me, and was clearly innate, as none of my sisters or brothers ever had this taste.   (*Autobiography*, pp. 22–23)

Misers not only hoard but love to count, and the passion for enumeration developed very early in Darwin, alongside the passion to hunt and to collect. After shooting his first snipe, his hands so trembled with excitement that he could scarcely reload his gun. Yet he paused long enough after each kill to keep an exact record of the scores of birds he felled each season.[18] "How I did enjoy shooting," he writes of his idyllic days on the estate of his Uncle Josiah[19] at Maer, "but I think that I must have been half-consciously ashamed of my zeal, for I tried to persuade

myself that shooting was almost an intellectual employment
... "[20] By "intellectual employment" Darwin has in mind the
discipline and energy of observation required of the hunter, the
same discipline that later enabled him to collect in a mere two
days, as he records in his *Diary of the Voyage of the H.M.S. Beagle*,
"all the animals, plants, insects & reptiles" on Charles Island, an
outlying link of the Galapagos archipelago some nine miles in
breadth.[21] At Maer Hall he kept track of his kills by knotting a
string tied to a buttonhole.[22] On the cramped, strewn deck of the
Beagle, and in his ten-by-eleven-foot cabin, which served him as
bedroom, livingroom, and laboratory, and which also housed
the ship's charts and library and, by day, two other officers, he
examined and classified each of his tens of thousands of specimens, ranging from minute *Cirripedia* to the huge fossil head of a
Megatherium, all of which he crated and sent back to England by
the shiploads, to the astonishment of those who viewed a
rodent-like head "the size of a Hippopotamus" and "an Ant-
Eater of the size of a horse!"[23]

The *Beagle* became Darwin's Ark. In nets dragged astern and
on expeditions up the High Andes, he gathered two of every
kind, male and female.[24] Twenty-eight years after setting sail, he
published *The Origin of Species*, an epic "deconstruction" of
Genesis in which he retells the story of our beginnings and erases
the Flood. Of the vast literature spawned by the *Beagle*, nothing
is stranger than the "Very Few Remarks with Reference to the
Deluge" which Robert Fitz-Roy, Darwin's brilliant and melan-
cholic Captain, appended to the 1839 *Narrative* of the voyage.
Later a fanatical foe of Darwin's unorthodoxy and finally a
suicide, Fitz-Roy in the "Remarks" delivers a sermon to his
young sailors, rebukes their feeble faith, imagines himself
calming the stormy waters of Galilee as he conjures up a
tremendous picture of Noah fronting the Flood and contends
that the gigantic fossil species unearthed by his shipmate Darwin
had failed to survive into modern times because they could not fit
into the Ark.[25] Fellow researchers on the same voyage, the
Captain and the ship's naturalist interpreted the same evidence
in opposite ways. Fitz-Roy foundered, as it were, on the shoals of
fundamentalism, while Darwin piloted the *Beagle* into the twentieth century. From our own secular perspective, the two men

appear to inhabit different universes. In fact they are antagonists by virtue of their very proximity, bound to each other as doubt is to faith, heresy to orthodoxy, science to myth. "Science is the criticism of Myth," Yeats wrote; "There would be no Darwin had there been no Book of Genesis."[26]

The child's compulsion to count, the miser's to hoard, the aboriginal urge to hunt, all drove the young Darwin in directions that he did not fully understand but that ultimately led to the publication of *The Origin of Species*. In the evolution of his own career he saw mimicked the larger evolution of the race, from the "primeval instincts of the barbarian" to the higher pleasures of observation and reason.[27] "I am become quite devoted to Nat: History," he wrote to his sister Caroline after nine months at sea; "you cannot imagine what a fine miserlike pleasure I enjoy, when examining an animal differing widely from any known genus. No schoolboy ever opened a box of plumcake so eagerly as I shall mine ... "[28] Years later the same image of acquisition recurs in a letter to William Fox, his boyhood tutor in entomology and a fellow beetlemaniac: "I am working very hard at my book [*The Origin of Species*] ... [and] am like Croesus overwhelmed with my riches in facts ... I shall not go to press at soonest for a couple of years."[29] Four months later, in June of 1858, he received from Alfred Wallace the remarkable letter on the trans-mutation of species that jolted him into publishing *The Origin* in the following year. Darwin's legendary thoroughness, his need to persuade incrementally through massive accumulation of fact, his wish to win the race as the tortoise and not the hare of science, doubtless delayed the publication of *The Origin* for at least a decade. But I suspect another, complementary motive. A boy's pockets are a private place; and misers count their hoard in darkened rooms. The most frank and open-natured of men, at the center of a world-wide network of researchers in a multitude of fields, all touching antennae at local scientific societies or through the penny post, Darwin was also, and paradoxically, a recluse. Hoarding and disclosing are curiously entwined; Darwin was at once gregarious and secretive in his disclosure of nature's secrets.

Darwin's childhood eagerness to collect and to classify coincided with what Gillian Beer calls his "passion for fabulation,"[30] a kind of natural magic of his own devising by which he sought to explain or control the world around him. At the Rev. Case's day-school at Shrewsbury, he told a classmate that he

could produce variously coloured Polyanthuses and Primroses by watering them with certain coloured fluids, which was of course a monstrous fable, and had never been tried by me . . . [31] [As] a little boy I was much given to inventing deliberate falsehoods, and this was always done for the sake of causing excitement. For instance, I once gathered much valuable fruit from my Father's trees and hid them in the shrubbery, and then ran in breathless haste to spread the news that I had discovered a hoard of stolen fruit.   (*Autobiography*, p. 23)

These scenes of childhood transgression are charged with a significance of which Darwin appears innocent, or perhaps chooses not to disclose. Yet it is difficult not to see in his theft of fruit from his Father's garden shades of the primal transgression in Eden. The young Darwin, however, feels not guilt but exaltation over the inventiveness of his deceits. A precocious and parodic Satan of a boy, he surmounts his Father's high garden wall in the cool of the evening, then plucks the fruit with a long stick rigged to a flower pot.[32] Like the young Augustine compounding his crime by its sheer gratuitousness, Darwin races off with the stolen apples only to give them away in a neighboring cottage. Ancient archetypes are embedded just below the surface of Darwin's narrative, as if in his own childhood he were naturalizing or secularizing our culture's central myth of guilt, as he was later to naturalize the central myth of our Beginnings in *The Origin*.

The most resonant of these early fictions touches on Darwin's mother and is preserved not by Darwin himself but by his son Francis in the *Recollections*. In a footnote William Leighton, the same schoolboy to whom Darwin told the tale about coloring primroses, recalls how Darwin brought a flower to school and said

that his mother had taught him how by looking at the inside of the blossom the name of the plant could be discovered. Mr. Leighton goes on, "This greatly roused my attention and curiosity, and I inquired of him how this could be done?" – but his lesson was naturally enough not transmissible.[33]

A haunting absence in Darwin's *Recollections* as in his life, Susannah Darwin figures more as a forgotten fragrance than a nurturing presence. Her son remembered her only by the bed in which she died, by the tears his father shed, by her black velvet gown and her work table. Susannah's voice, body, or touch are nowhere present in his writing. Yet from the same period of his life, and with ironic inaptness that suggests displacement, Darwin recalled with great clarity the burial of a total stranger, a brilliantly uniformed soldier at a nearby church:

... it is surprising how clearly I can still see the horse with the man's empty boots and carbine suspended to the saddle, and the firing over the grave. (*Autobiography*, p. 24)

Years afterward Darwin appears to have distanced himself even further from his mother's death by moving it back in time. "My mother died during my infancy and I can say hardly anything about her," he wrote in his sixty-fifth year.[34] Charles was in fact eight years and five months old when Susannah Darwin died. Unusually old for childbearing when he was born – she was forty-four – she seemed unusually young to those who mourned her death at fifty-two.

Darwin appears alienated not only from her memory but also from all consciousness of grief. In his mid-thirties he wrote a moving letter of consolation to his cousin William Fox upon the death of his wife:

I truly sympathise with you, though never in my life, having lost one near relation, I daresay I cannot imagine, how severe grief, such as yours, must be, & how little the longest expectation can resign one to the blow, when it falls.[35]

Only the clotted syntax, and the mistaken comma after "life", which momentarily reverses Darwin's intended meaning, suggest his latent awareness of a truth beneath the truth he denied: his anger at an absent mother. Susannah Darwin is never named in the *Recollections* or in the "Autobiographical Fragment" of 1838. Nothing is known of the cause of her death except that her illness was the kind known as "lingering," a condition calculated to vex a child in its combination of ungratifying presence and incomprehensible absence. Her poor health during

Darwin's early years, and the fact that she was old enough to have been his grandmother at his birth,[36] in part account for her absence from his memory. Yet the causes seem inadequate to the effect: almost total obliteration.[37] She comes to life only in the footnote on peering into flowers, as a girl astride a horse in a painting, and in a phrase from one of her few surviving letters. At the center of a portrait of the Wedgwood family she is an arresting figure, stylish, pensive, shapely, the eldest of the seven children ranged under the watchful eye of their parents.[38] In the letter, written in her early forties with a "prognosticating sigh," she tells her brother Josiah, "Every one seems young but me."[39] The footnote on looking inside a flower to discover a plant's name is especially enigmatic, for in the context of Darwin's confession of monstrous fables, the reader cannot tell if Darwin made up the story he told Leighton, if his mother was in turn telling a fable, or if the child gave a magical interpretation to his mother's otherwise plausible words. Nearly seventy years after hearing the story from Darwin, Leighton, who became an eminent lichenologist, speculated that Susannah Darwin might have been trying to introduce Charles to the Linnaean system of classification.[40] The surmise is less improbable than it seems, given her known interest in flowers and in the breeding of pigeons, two areas of her son's later research.[41] In the passage I have already cited on his miser-like passion for collecting, Darwin explains how as a very young child he "tried to make out the names of plants," an unusual locution in place of the more idiomatic "learn the names." Darwin's words seem to retain a vestigial memory of his mother's telling him to look inside the flower to discover a plant's name, as if the name were magically encoded within its corolla of petals and might by an act of Darwin's will be made to disclose itself. He did indeed spend much of his life studying plants, and in time they disclosed not only their names and natures but the remarkable ingenuities of their sexual adaptations. The result was a series of books on the contrivances by which orchids are fertilized, on the movements and habits of climbing plants, on cross-fertilization in the vegetable kingdom, together with a flood of articles on "Primula, and on their Remarkable Sexual Relations," "On the Action of Sea-Water on the Germination of Seeds," in addition to a host of other publications on botanical subjects, including forty-nine contributions to the *Gardener's Chronicle*.[42]

Darwin's apparent forgetting of his mother is the more remarkable in view of his virtually total recall of his father. "His recollection of everything that was connected with him was peculiarly distinct," Francis Darwin writes: "It was astonishing how clearly he remembered his father's opinions."[43] Of course, Dr. Darwin lived on well into his son's adulthood,[44] and, if only as a remarkable physical presence, he was impossible to forget. Enormous in build yet fine in feature, when Dr. Darwin last stepped on a scale he weighed 336 pounds, after which he grew considerably heavier and wisely abandoned the habit of weighing himself.[45] "He was the largest man I ever saw," Charles writes at the start of a fourteen-page verbal portrait of his father, a late addition to the *Recollections* that straddles, awkwardly and imposingly, the beginning of his own narrative.

Easy to caricature, grossly misunderstood, Robert Waring Darwin has figured as an ogre among Darwin's biographers, a misconception based in part of an oft-quoted passage in the *Recollections*, in part on the compelling power of the Oedipal myth, perhaps also on the folklorish associations of fathers with giants and giants with tyranny. Early in the *Recollections* Darwin writes that he was considered by all of his schoolmasters and by his father

as a very ordinary boy, rather below the common standard in intellect. To my deep mortification my father once said to me, "You care for nothing but shooting, dogs, and rat-catching, and you will be a disgrace to yourself and all your family." But my father, who was the kindest man I ever knew, and whose memory I love with all my heart, must have been angry and somewhat unjust when he used such words. (*Autobiography*, p. 28)

That Darwin retained his father's words with sufficient exactitude to put them in quotations after sixty years suggests something of the pain they inflicted. The timidity of the understated "*somewhat* unjust" preserves intact the child's fear of indicting a parent. The "somewhat" also casts doubt on Darwin's assertion of his father's kindness, as though he were atoning for even so mild an accusation by the hyperbole of his praise. Yet to appreciate the full force of the passage, we must recognize the fact of the father's kindness, the son's love of his memory, and his resentment of the indisputable cruelty and injustice of these particular words. They stand out so sharply in Charles's mind because they were so wrong in their prognostication and so *uncharacteristic* in their harshness and anger.

The misapprehension of Dr. Darwin as a domestic bully persists, despite its evident falseness. Psychoanalytic readings of Darwin's "case" assume a violent but repressed hostility towards a tyrannical father, a repression which produced the assorted illnesses – nausea, vomiting, palpitations, flatulence, boils, dizziness, eczema – which did in fact plague Darwin through much of his adult life.[46] Dr. Rankine Good is the most articulate advocate of the Oedipal thesis. According to Good,

a wealth of evidence ... unmistakably points to ... [Darwin's] symptoms as a distorted expression of the aggression, hate, and resentment felt, at an unconscious level, by Darwin towards his tyrannical father, although, at a conscious level, we find the reaction-formation of the reverence for his father which was boundless and most touching ... For Darwin *did* revolt against his father. He did so in a typical obsessional way (and like most revolutionaries) by transposing the unconscious emotional conflict to a conscious intellectual one – concerning evolution. Thus, if Darwin did not slay his father in the flesh, then in his *The Origin of Species*, *The Descent of Man*, &c., he certainly slew the Heavenly Father in the realm of natural history.[47]

Dr. Good assumes, erroneously, that Darwin's love of his father was a mere mask for the reality of his resentment; rather, the two emotions coexisted throughout his life, the one acknowledged, the other not. No reader of the Darwin family letters can fail to be struck by their extraordinary warmth and geniality, a familial high spirits irradiated by love. The letters to and from the Mount while Charles is aboard the *Beagle* comprise a kind of epistolary adventure story, with Charles providing the plot in the form of his daily discoveries, his sisters supplying the local news, and the whole presided over by the silent presence of "Papa." The aged scientist who opens his *Recollections* as if he were a dead man from another world seems light-years distant from the ebullient youth who describes his setting out from Plymouth harbor in a raging gale. "Papa's eyes were full of tears," Caroline writes on receiving Charles's account of his stormy embarkation, "when he thought first of your miserable night & then of your goodnatured Captain in all the confusion paying you a visit & arranging your hammock."[48] Charles learned of his father's tears of concern in a letter from Caroline he opened in April 1832, when anchored off Rio de Janeiro:

The sun was bright & the view resplendent; our little ship was working like a fish; so I said to myself, I will only just look at the signatures:, it would not do; ... I rushed below; there to feast over the thrilling enjoyment of reading about you all: at first the contrast of home, vividly brought before ones eyes, makes the present more exciting; but the feeling is soon divided & then absorbed by the wish of seeing those who make all associations dear. –

It is seldom that one individual has the power [of] giving to another such a sum of pleasure, as you this day have granted me. – I know not whether the conviction of being loved, be more delightful or the corresponding one of loving in return. – I ought for I have experienced them both in excess. –   (*Correspondence*, I, 220)

I find no repressed hostility in these words, only a remarkable ease in the expression and receipt of love. Years later Charles's sister Catherine wrote him of their father's last days, and again I find evidence not of tyranny but of the persistence of bonds of affection exceptional in a motherless family:

My father is perfectly collected, and placid ... so uncomplaining, so full of everybody else, of all the servants, the servants' children, etc. He attempted to speak about you this morning, but was so excessively overcome he was utterly unable; we begged him not to speak ... God comfort you, my dearest Charles, you were so beloved by him.

(Letter of 11 and 13 [?] November 1848, *Emma Darwin*, II, 119–20)

Yet Dr. Darwin's harsh words persisted in his son's memory, their power perhaps deriving from the fact that Charles seems to have shared his father's dim view of his prospects. So, too, did all of his schoolmasters, as he points out just before citing his father's words. In another incident the Headmaster of the Shrewsbury School dragged him before his classmates, held him by the ear, and declared, "This stupid fellow will attend to his gases and his rubbish, but not work at anything useful." Such tales of intellectual rags-to-riches have a certain charm, for they give hope to us all, but this one is very likely rooted in fact[49] and shares an important element with Dr. Darwin's accusation of caring for nothing but shooting and rat-catching. In neither is Charles accused of doltish sloth but of engaging in what appears to his elders – and doubtless also to himself – to be unprofitable activity. The "gases" for which the Rev. Butler chides the young Charles were very likely the products of his chemistry experiments with his brother Erasmus in a crude garden laboratory at the Mount, prototype of the rudimentary instrumentation and improvised equipment – saucers, tin biscuit boxes, bits of thread[50] – of his laboratory at Down House. The shooting and rat-catching that enraged Dr. Darwin were his early self-education in natural history. "I consider that all I have learnt of any value has been self-taught," he remarked late in life. Asked if his formal education had been of any value, he replied with bitter brevity, "None whatever."[51] It is not surprising that Darwin underestimated what he had learned, especially at Cambridge, in the course of his almost exclusively classical education, for his teachers, with the decisive exception of his botany professor, the Rev. John Henslow, badly underestimated him. He similarly, and perhaps for the same reason, underestimated his father's contribution to his intellectual culture.[52] His mentors and his father were justified in accusing him of idleness had he been preparing to become, as his father first hoped, a physician like himself or, failing that, a clergyman. They were wrong if he was in training to become the author of *The Origin of Species*, an outcome as unlikely to the young Darwin as learning he had been "elected King of England."[53] An idle schoolboy, Darwin was anything but an idle child. "Idleness" is a word he often uses but a state of mind he rarely experienced. He uses the word in the idiosyncratic sense not of "inactivity" but of "working fiercely at an activity that gives him pleasure,"[54] such as chasing beetles when he should be translating Vergil, or experiencing the great coruscation of ideas on transmutation that poured into his head and notebooks in 1838 when he ought to have been revising his notes on *The Geology of the Voyage of the Beagle*. "I have been sorely tempted to be idle," he wrote to Charles Lyell,

that is as far as pure geology is concerned, by the delightful number of new views, which have been coming in, thickly & steadily, on the

94

classification & affinities & instincts of animals – bearing on the question of species – note book, after note book has been filled, with facts, which begin to group themselves *clearly* under sub-laws.

(*Correspondence*, ii, 107)

In time, after accusations of childhood idleness lost some of their sting and Darwin had found his true vocation, he could play on the paradox of his working hard on research that the world at large considered idle. He apologizes to his sister Caroline for being a poor correspondent, for it is difficult "to write if one does not write often, and to do that is very hard work for a very idle yet busy man."[55] By the time he became the world-renowned author of *The Origin of Species*, the word "idleness" had lost much of its idiosyncratic flavor: "I cannot be idle, much as I wish it, and am never comfortable except when at work. The word holiday is written in a dead language for me."[56] Darwin had translated his childhood play into his life's work.

With the illusory clarity of hindsight, it is difficult for us to appreciate the fusion of uncertainty and apparent prescience that marks the slow unfolding of Darwin's career. Because he so altered the intellectual world we inhabit, including our conception of what a scientist is and does, we fail to appreciate how uncharted a course he followed. A trivial instance: during his engagingly prosaic courtship, filled with love-letters about pots and pans and the wages of London parlor-maids, Emma Wedgwood asks him to correct any flaws of style in her letters, for "in the wife of a literary man" such faults "wd not do you credit."[57] Darwin had already drafted his book on the formation of coral reefs and had twice been invited to read papers before the London Geological Society, yet Emma thinks of him as a *man of letters*, not a scientist. She does so not because of ignorance (she was a woman of keen judgment and intelligence) but because at the time she wrote – November 1838 – the word *scientist* did not exist in English. William Whewell, a philosopher of science and President of the Geological Society which Darwin had addressed, wrote in 1840, "We need very much a name to describe a cultivator of science in general. I should incline to call him a Scientist."[58]

Much later in the century, to judge from a curious sentence in Francis Darwin's *Life and Letters* (1887), the idea of science as an independent profession was not yet clearly established. Francis is unaware of the contradiction that immediately strikes the twentieth-century reader on either side of the colon following "Fitz-Roy":

> There is no evidence of any intention of entering a profession after his return from the voyage, and early in 1840 he wrote to Fitz-Roy: "I have nothing to wish for, excepting stronger health to go on with the subjects to which I have joyfully determined to devote my life."
>
> (*Life and Letters*, i, 243)

By "profession" Francis has in mind the traditional callings of cleric, physician, or teacher. The profession that Darwin so joyfully determined upon – that of "cultivator of science in general" – he in considerable measure created. Had he not lost his faith in Christianity (there was no sudden spiritual crisis, just a gradual falling away of convictions never passionately held), he would almost certainly have combined, as did his fellow beetle-chasers and his Cambridge mentor John Henslow, the profession of clergyman with his interests as a naturalist. Important science had of course been practiced for centuries, but after Darwin had abandoned medicine and the clergy, there was no organized profession of science for him to enter: no graduate schools to attend, no Guggenheim or National Science Foundation fellowship, no Woods Holes or Brookhavens or Institutes for Advanced Study, no vast scientific bureaucracy – academic, governmental, and private – to support and direct research.

Darwin was essentially self-trained. He mastered dissection, for example, by cutting up some ten thousand barnacles that passed in and out of Down House, briny mementos of his *Beagle* days. He was an amateur of science, but an amateur of world class, and some of his notorious diffidence[59] doubtless stems from the self-doubt of the self-taught. Yet the same self-education gave him an extraordinary freedom from pro-fessionally-conditioned presuppositions that enabled him to do major research in half a dozen different specialties. Turning understatement into something of a fine art, he maintained so low a profile that in time he all but vanished behind his bushy beard, or beneath the hedges of Down House, which he elevated into a protective vegetable shield by lowering the lane that passed in front of the grounds. Once settled into middle age and the raising of a family, he preferred the quiet local role of "squarson" – a kind of squire–parson–farmer[60] – to the dreaded exposure brought on by his world-wide fame. Among the householders of the village of Downe in Bagshaw's *Directory* of 1847, Charles Darwin is listed as "farmer," a credible designation given the time he spent with pigs, horses, breeding, and manure. When his childhood pockets became too small, his father bought him a specimen cabinet, and when his curiosity outgrew the vast tribe of *cleoptera*, he hired others to gather specimens and to teach him. As a medical student at Edinburgh he found the lectures "intolerably dull" and fled the operating room after seeing a child mangled in the days before anesthesia.[61] But he paid high wages to a former black slave who was resident in Edinburgh – "a very pleasant and intelligent man" – to teach him the taxidermy of birds.[62] He also stole time from the medical curriculum to sail with the dredgermen and oyster-fishers of Newhaven. The fruits of his researches issued in two scientific papers read to an undergraduate society. In one of the papers, with a boyish braggadocio that contrasts starkly with his later self-effacement, he lays claim to a discovery that "does not appear to have been hitherto observed either by Lamarck, Cuvier, Lamouroux, or any other author."[63]

For all the shooting, bug-hunting, and academic mediocrity at Edinburgh and Cambridge, Darwin was also reading. In the *Recollections* he mentions two books read at Cambridge that deeply influenced *The Voyage of the Beagle* and *The Origin of Species*. In the Rev. William Paley's *Natural Theology* (1802) he encountered the classic formulation of the "argument from design" that he later stood on its head, through the inverted and heretical teleology of Natural Selection.[64] He read Alexander von Humboldt's *Personal Narrative of Travels to . . . the New Continent* (1799–1804) with such enraptured attention that he in effect *dreamed* the voyage of the *Beagle* before he ever embarked upon it.[65] Darwin's sensibility had been formed on the modest hills and quiet rivers of Shropshire. Humboldt's fusion of exotic sublimity and scientific exactitude, his descriptions of tropical forests and frozen volcanic peaks, fired Darwin's imagination. What began as enthusiasm blossomed into obsession. In his final weeks at Cambridge, four months before the *Beagle* invitation arrived, he wrote to Caroline Darwin:

All the while I am writing now my head is running about the Tropics: in the morning I go and gaze at Palm trees in the hot-house and come home and read Humboldt: my enthusiasm is so great that I cannot hardly sit still on my chair . . . Henslow promises to cram me in geology. – I never will be easy till I see the peak of Teneriffe and the great Dragon tree; sandy, dazzling, plains, and gloomy silent forest are alternately uppermost in my mind . . . I have written myself into a Tropical glow.

(Letter of 28 April 1831, *Correspondence*, I, 122)

He taught himself Spanish, planned to book passage with some Cambridge friends to Teneriffe, and, of inestimable importance to his later work, began the systematic study of geology. Just after hastening back from a geological tour in Wales for the start of the shooting season at Maer, he was handed the letter from Professor Henslow that determined the future course of his life:

I have been asked . . . to recommend . . . a naturalist as companion to Capt Fitzroy employed by Government to survey the S. extremity of America – I have stated that I consider you to be the best qualified person I know of who is likely to undertake such a situation – I state this not on the supposition of yr being a *finished* Naturalist, but as amply qualified for collecting, observing, & noting any thing worthy to be noted in Natural History . . . Particulars of salary &c I know nothing. The Voyage is to last 2 yrs & if you take plenty of Books with you, any thing you please may be done – You will have ample opportunities at command – In short I suppose there never was a finer chance for a man of zeal & spirit.   (Letter of 24 August 1831, *Correspondence*, I, 128–29)

The timing must have seemed providential, for Darwin at twenty-two was still a believing if unzealous Christian. Had the invitation come a year or two earlier, he would have been an unnoticed and unpromising undergraduate. A few years later he would quite probably have been married and ordained, with responsibilities that would have precluded his accepting the offer, as they prevented his naturalist friend and senior, the Rev. Leonard Jenyns, who refused the position before it was offered to Darwin.[66] He was in a state of extraordinary intellectual receptivity and physical well-being that propelled him across seas and deserts and up the peaks of the High Andes, where he climbed above the frozen corpse of a horse with less endurance than he.[67] The timing in the larger intellectual world was as fortunate for Darwin as it was in his personal life. Professor Henslow's present to his young protégé was Volume I of Charles Lyell's just-published *Principles of Geology* (1830). Lyell's undermining of the Biblical account of Creation and of the Flood is implicit in his subtitle, if never stated in his text: *an Attempt to Explain the Former Changes of the Earth's Surface, by Reference to Causes Now in Operation.* Lyell made it possible for Darwin to interpret the significance of the geological evidence he found encoded high in the Cordillera or under the waters of the Keeling Islands. Perhaps more important, he alerted Darwin to physical processes that, over previously unimaginable aeons of time, account for great changes through gradual increments, processes that Darwin later extended from the province of geology to that of living things.

But Darwin's "authoritarian and tyrannical father,"[68] as legend has it, adamantly opposed the voyage. The fact is a good deal stranger, as we learn from the *Recollections*:

I was instantly eager to accept the offer, but my father strongly objected, adding the words fortunate for me, – 'If you can find any man of common sense, who advises you to go, I will give my consent.'

(*Autobiography*, p. 71)

As if the strain of disappointed expectation might be too great to bear, Darwin at first declined Henslow's invitation in a letter whose scrupulousness is as evident as its pain.[69] On the same day (30 August 1831), Dr. Darwin wrote to his brother-in-law Josiah that Charles had been invited to sail on

a voyage of discovery for 2 years. – I strongly object to it on various grounds, but I will not detail my reasons that he may have your unbiassed opinion on the subject, & if you think differently from me I shall wish him to follow your advice. (*Correspondence*, I, 132)

In this exchange of domestic civilities on a heroic scale, Dr. Darwin asked Charles to argue his eight objections to the voyage before his uncle at Maer. Charles did so, fairly and vigorously, stressing the dangers of the voyage and its possible damage to his future character as a clergyman. Uncle Josiah responded to

Charles Darwin in old age

each of his brother-in-law's objections, the last point in his letter serving as a virtual prophecy of Charles's future:

8– The undertaking would be useless as regards his profession [as a clergyman], but looking upon him as a man of enlarged curiosity, it affords him such an opportunity of seeing men and things as happens to few.   (Letter of 31 August 1831, *Correspondence*, I, 134)

Mr. Darwin collects himself

The flurry of letters between Maer Hall and the Mount ends with one of Dr. Darwin's few surviving letters (he disliked holding a pen, perhaps because of the girth of his fingers):

1 Sept 1831

Dear Wedgwood,
   Charles is very grateful for your taking so much trouble & interest in his plans. I made up my mind to give up all objections, if you should not see it in the same view as I did. –
   Charles has stated my objections quite fairly & fully – if he still continues in the same mind after further enquiry, I will give him all the assistance in my power.
   Many thanks for your kindness – yours / affectionly / R W Darwin
(Correspondence, I, 135)

   Dr. Darwin's promise of assistance was more than a gracious gesture. By virtue of his large medical practice and shrewd investments, he was a wealthy man. The post of naturalist aboard the *Beagle* was unpaid. Charles had no means of support other than his father's generosity, freely forthcoming even after he had abandoned Dr. Darwin's first preference of a profession and might well abandon his second. Assistance meant, in addition to moral support, paying for Charles's books, clothes, instruments, and food.

There followed what Stephen Jay Gould recently described as "perhaps the greatest intellectual adventure ever experienced by one man."[70] It is not my purpose to describe that adventure but to focus on the aging scientist who recalled it forty years later in the tranquility of Down House, a more commodious and anchored *Beagle*, where he slowly settled into the posthumous self that authored the *Recollections*. In his granddaughter Nora's edition, that posthumous self gazes at the reader from a photograph taken within a year of his death. He leans against a veranda pillar covered with the climbing vines he described in *The Power of Movement in Plants*. One of the tendrils touches the rim of his black, round-rimmed hat; another appears to grope for the collar of his black, clerical-looking cape. The tangled tendrils of the vine appear to mimic the bushy fringes of his beard. Darwin was an egalitarian across the whole spectrum of living things;[71] something of a crawler himself, he had a special sympathy for "lower," slow-moving creatures – worms, barnacles, creeping plants. The peculiarity of his genius is its slowness, thought without apparent motion, a quality rendered by the repose of the photograph, the cocoon-like enclosure of the cloak. We so habitually associate genius with quickness – the "Eureka!" of Archimedes or the acceleration of Newton's falling apple – that we cannot imagine a powerful mind that works slowly, but to stupendous effect. "He used to say that he was not quick enough to hold an argument with anyone," Francis Darwin writes; he then adds, without malice, "and I think this was true."[72] The eyes that look directly into the lens are kind but irremediably sad. The effect is haunting, a riddling portrait of a man who, quite to his own surprise and regret, found himself at the center of the fiercest intellectual and religious quarrel of the nineteenth century. At first glance the aged figure might be mistaken for a country parson. But the broad, round-brimmed hat gives him the look of a *padre*, one of the village priests he had seen fifty years earlier in the villages of South America.

All of his life Darwin had concentrated his intelligence on the observation of external nature. Of the world within the mind of Charles Darwin he was neither especially interested nor informative. He returned Francis Galton's questionnaire on mental traits with a characteristically self-effacing note: "I have answered the questions as well as I could, but they are miserably answered, for I have never tried looking into my own mind."[73] The note is doubly surprising, for it was sent three years *after* he wrote his *Recollections*.

The great, formative autobiographies of Western literature – the *Confessions* of St. Augustine and of Rousseau, the *Prelude* of Wordsworth, come to mind – were written by men who were by nature self-obsessed. Darwin is unique as an autobiographer in the degree to which he remained a stranger to himself. He was selfless in the double sense of exceptional generosity and exceptional elusiveness as a person, despite the openness and simplicity remarked upon by all who knew him. Highly idiosyncratic, eccentric to a degree unusual even for an Englishman, he remained a "character" without a self or, more accurately, he possessed so transparent a self that he never obtruded upon his own field of vision.[74] Such freedom from the distractions of self-consciousness gave him extraordinary analytic cunning whenever he chose himself as the object of his own observation. Seated before a mirror, he engaged in the uncanny act of self-objectification that enabled him to watch himself laugh, to persist in the laughter, and to hear that laughter with such detachment that it registered as *noise*:

> Looking at one's face whilst laughing in glass & then as one ceases, or stops the noise, the face clearly passes into smiles – laugh long prior to talking, hence one can help speaking, but laughing involuntary. –
> ("Transmutation Notebooks," N 6, in *Metaphysics, Materialism*, p. 71)

The self-enchantment that underlies all autobiography, and that lends the genre a fascination akin to that of watching another person asleep, is here totally absent. Darwin turns the defining act of the narcissist – gazing at one's own image – into an act of self-effacement.

There is a chilling element in such detachment, a coldness popularly associated with the objectivity of science. The *Recollections* reinforce the stereotype to the point of caricature: the scientist in so deep a freeze he has become "a dead man."[75] Darwin's metaphor is careless (dead men see nothing) and disconcerting, like the image at the end of the *Recollections* of his mind as an unfeeling "machine for grinding general laws out of large collections of facts."[76] From the perspective of his post-humous self, there had been an irrecoverable falling away from the youth who had once exclaimed, in anticipation of sailing on the *Beagle*, "Gloria in excelsis is the most moderate beginning I can think of!"[77] Yet despite Darwin's own disclaimers, acuity of mind and intensity of feeling persisted to the end. Four years after completing the *Recollections*, he crowds the words "astound[ing]," "remarkable," and "marvellous" into a few excited lines to Joseph Hooker describing the sensitivity of plants to gravity and light. At the time of his death he was still puzzling over the significance of "bloom," the frost-white coating on certain leaves and fruits.[78]

NOTES

1 *The Autobiography of Charles Darwin*, ed. Nora Barlow (New York: Norton, 1958), p. 21.
2 *Ibid.*, p. 21.

3 The title appears at the head of the autograph manuscript. Of the approximately one hundred editions in at least twenty-two languages, only one – that of the Soviet Academy of Sciences in 1957 – gets Darwin's title right. See R. B. Freeman, *The Works of Charles Darwin: an Annotated Bibliographical Handlist*, 2nd ed. (Hamden, CT: Dawson-Archon, 1977), pp. 172–80.

4 Ralph Colp, Jr., M.D., "Notes on Charles Darwin's *Autobiography*," *Journal of the History of Biography*, 18, no. 3 (Fall, 1985), p. 361.

5 *Autobiography*, p. 21.

6   When 110 days old he was exceedingly amused by a pinafore being thrown over his face and then suddenly withdrawn; and so he was when I suddenly uncovered my own face and approached his. He then uttered a little noise which was an incipient laugh. Here surprise was the chief cause of amusement, as is the case to a large extent with the wit of grown-up persons. I believe that for three or four weeks before the time when he was amused by a face being suddenly uncovered, he received a little pinch on his nose as a good joke. I was at first surprised at humour being appreciated by an infant only a little above three months old, but we should remember how very early puppies and kittens begin to play . . .

(In *Metaphysics, Materialism, and the Evolution of Mind: Early Writings of Charles Darwin*, ed. Paul H. Barrett, commentary by Howard E. Gruber [Chicago: University of Chicago Press, 1980], p. 209.) The paper first appeared in *Mind* in 1877 but was based on Darwin's much earlier notes of 1839–41. A thirty-eight-year interval between inception of an idea and its publication was not unusual for Darwin. His early research on worms produced papers in 1838 and 1840, but he worked at a pace mimetic of the creature in whose humble work-habits and intelligence he delighted, and who wrought such mighty effects from such minute causes, ultimately altering and fructifying the surface of the earth with each of its myriad and remembered turns. Darwin's four decades of worm-research culminated in 1881 in his last, highly popular work, *The Formation of Vegetable Mould, through the Action of Worms, with Observations on their Habits*. Darwin rehabilitates worms in the world of the lower animals as Wordsworth had rehabilitated Cumberland beggars and leech-gatherers in the human world. The suggestion of memory, and hence a degree of intelligence and even of shared culture, is implicit in the word *Habits*.

7 The work was published by Francis Darwin in 1887, five years after his father's death, in *The Life and Letters of Charles Darwin, Including an Autobiographical Chapter*. In deference to family opinion but in violation of his own, Francis deleted nearly six thousand words, most

importantly those expressing disbelief in the truth of Revelation and hostility to the "damnable doctrine" of eternal punishment for disbelievers (*Autobiography*, Preface, pp. 11–13, 86–87).

8 "I am dying by inches, from not having any body to talk to about insects," he wrote on his first long vacation from Cambridge to his cousin William Darwin Fox, a classmate at Christ's College (letter of 12 June 1828, *The Correspondence of Charles Darwin*, ed. Frederick Burkhardt and Sydney Smith [Cambridge University Press, 1985], 1, 56).

9 For the identification of the third beetle, see the anecdote, recounted fifty years after the fact, by Frederick Watkins, Archdeacon of York and undergraduate friend of Darwin, in *The Life and Letters of Charles Darwin*, ed. Francis Darwin (New York: Appleton, 1896), 1, 144. Darwin gives an account of the loss of the "sacred" *Panagaeus crux major* almost identical to the one in the *Recollections* in a letter of 1846 to the naturalist Leonard Jenyns. See *Life and Letters*, 1, 396.

10 *Life and Letters*, 1, 143; *Autobiography*, p. 54.

11 See Frank J. Sulloway, "Darwin's Conversion: The *Beagle* Voyage and Its Aftermath," *Journal of the History of Biology*, 15, no. 3 (Fall 1982), pp. 327–28, 345–48. Sulloway argues vigorously against the purported role of the Galapagos finches in effecting Darwin's conversion to transmutation.

12 *Autobiography*, p. 27.

13 Letter of 8 September 1830 to William Fox, *Correspondence* 1, 106.

14 I owe this point, as I owe so much else, to the Victorianist to whom this collection of essays is dedicated. "The ideal autobiography," Jerome H. Buckley writes in *The Turning Key: Autobiography and the Subjective Impulse since 1800*, "describes a voyage of self-discovery, a life journey . . . " (Cambridge, MA: Harvard University Press, 1984, p. 39).

15 *Autobiography*, p. 79.

16 *Ibid.*, p. 32.

17 *Ibid.*, p. 76.

18 *Ibid.*, pp. 44, 54.

19 Josiah Wedgwood II, son of the founder of the pottery works and father of Emma, Darwin's first cousin and wife. Maer Hall, in Staffordshire, was only twenty miles from The Mount, the late-Georgian house in Shrewsbury built by Darwin's father. There was much traffic between the establishments and much intermarriage among the inhabitants.

20 *Autobiography*, p. 55.

21 Entry of 26–27 September 1835, ed. Nora Barlow (Cambridge: Cambridge University Press, 1933), p. 336.

22 *Autobiography*, p. 54.

23 *Correspondence*, I, 386, 525. The *Beagle* hoard ultimately yielded for Darwin nine volumes of geological and zoological research, in addition to *The Origin of Species* and various collaborative publications by others on fossil mammalia, fish, birds, reptiles, flowers, plants, beetles, spiders, corals, crustacia, and so forth. A considerable number of specimens remain to be described after a century and a half of work in museums and laboratories all over the world. See *Correspondence*, II, xv, xvii, xxi.

24 "Throughout the voyage Darwin collected only a few specimens (usually a male and a female) of each species ..." Sulloway, p. 387.

25 (London: Henry Colburn, 1839), II, 671–72.

26 *W. B. Yeats and T. Sturge Moore: Their Correspondence 1901–1937*, ed. Ursula Bridge (London: Routledge, 1953), p. 154.

27 *Autobiography*, p. 79.

28 Letter of 24 October–24 November 1832, *Correspondence*, I, 278.

29 Letter of 8 February 1858, *Life and Letters*, I, 467–68.

30 "Darwin's Reading and the Fictions of Development," in *The Darwinian Heritage*, ed. David Kohn (Princeton: Princeton University Press, 1985), p. 558.

31 Dr. Edward Kempf, one of the more inventive analysts of Darwin's behavior, speculates in the *Psychoanalytic Review* that Darwin fancied he could alter the color of the flowers "after he had repeatedly urinated on them (not an uncommon experiment of boys) ... The urinating of the flowers probably had the value of being a fertilization curiosity." Dr. Kempf further speculates that Darwin suffered from repressed homosexuality, a surmise based on a misreading of the passage in the *Recollections* in which Darwin describes his uneasiness at dining alone in the same cabin with Captain Fitz-Roy, a man of irritable temper. Fitz-Roy was "extremely kind to me," Darwin writes, but "very difficult to live with on the intimate terms which necessarily followed from our messing by ourselves in the same cabin" (*Autobiography*, p. 73). Dr. Kempf appears to mistake *messing* for *groping*. See "Charles Darwin – The Affective Sources of His Inspiration and Anxiety Neurosis," *Psychoanalytic Review*, 5 (1918), pp. 156, 166–67. For an excellent discussion of Darwin's health, physical and mental, see Dr. Ralph Colp's *To Be an Invalid* (Chicago: University of Chicago Press, 1977).

32 *Autobiography*, p. 24.

33 *Autobiography*, p. 23n. Leighton later became an Anglican clergyman and botanist. The careers of many of Darwin's classmates and mentors combined in easy harmony the roles of cleric and naturalist. Darwin's Cambridge mentor, the Rev. John Stevens Henslow, Professor of Mineralogy and Botany, comes to mind, as do William Fox

and Leonard Jenyns. If to us the vocations of scientist and clergyman seem at cross-purposes, to the early Victorians they were complementary callings. As cleric, one was an exegete of God's "First Book," the Bible; on weekdays, as naturalist, one celebrated the intricate design of God's "Second Book," Nature. Darwin planned to pursue the tandem career of cleric–naturalist until quite late in the voyage of the *Beagle*.

34 Written in answer to a questionnaire on "English Men of Science, their Nature and Nurture." See letter of 28 May 1873 to Francis Galton, cited in Colp, "Notes on Charles Darwin's *Autobiography*," p. 364, n. 28. See also *Autobiography*, pp. 22, 24; "An Autobiographical Fragment" (1838), in *Correspondence*, II, 439; *Life and Letters*, II, 355.

35 Letter of 23 March 1842, *Correspondence*, II, 315–16. A year later Darwin wrote to the still-devastated Fox that he had had no comparable experience of losing a "cherished one" (*ibid.*, p. 352).

36 "Granny" was his pet name for his older sister Susan. His older sisters served in place of his mother at the Mount in the last stages of her illness and after her death.

37 Even on her tombstone she remains elusive. As if in token of her abbreviated life, her name is truncated to "Susan." See R. B. Freeman, *Charles Darwin: A Companion* (Hamden, CT: Dawson-Archon, 1978), p. 298.

38 Painted "in or about" 1780, after George Stubbs. Reproduced in *Emma Darwin: A Century of Family Letters 1792–1896*, ed. Henrietta Litchfield (New York: Appleton, 1915), I, facing p. 8; and in Alan Moorehead, *Darwin and the Beagle* (New York: Harper & Row, 1969), p. 29. See also the miniature of Susannah of 1792 by Peter Paillou, reproduced in Julian Huxley and H. B. D. Kettlewell, *Charles Darwin and His World* (New York: Viking, 1965), p. 9; and in Peter Brent, *Charles Darwin* (London: Heinemann, 1981), facing p. 120. Francis Darwin describes a miniature of Susannah with a "remarkably sweet and happy face," but if he writes of the Paillou portrait, the expression is more notable for its strength and intelligence than for its sweetness. See *Life and Letters*, I, 9.

39 Letter of June 1807, in Eliza Meteyard, *A Group of Englishmen* (London: Longmans, 1871), p. 357. The phrase "prognosticating sigh" is Meteyard's.

40 Brent, p. 24.

41 For her interest in pigeon-breeding and in flowers, see Meteyard, pp. 260–61. Francis Darwin (*Life and Letters*, I, 9) casts doubt on Meteyard's account of "the Mount pigeons," but Meteyard quotes letters of some length of 1807 and 1808 from Susannah to her brother Josiah promising him a gift of doves she has been breeding.

42 See *Life and Letters*, II, 533–41; and Freeman, *The Works of Charles Darwin*, pp. 194–207.
43 *Life and Letters*, I, 10.
44 Charles was in his fortieth year when his father died at the age of eighty-two. In the *Recollections* he misstates the year of death as 1847 instead of 1848 (*Autobiography*, p. 117), and in a letter to Joseph Hooker he writes that his father died "at eighty-four" (*Life and Letters*, II, 223), but one should resist the temptation to overinterpret such slips. Darwin was generally poor at remembering dates and anniversaries, perhaps because their random nature made them inhospitable to speculation. As a teenager he inquired of his sister Caroline, "I want to know how old I shall be next Birthday. I believe 17 ..." (letter of 6 January 1826, *Correspondence*, I, 26). His favorite child Annie, over whose death at the age of ten he grieved for the rest of his life, died at midday on 23 April 1851. In the *Recollections* he misstates the date as 24 April, although the 23rd – the birthdays of St. George and Shakespeare – is difficult to dislodge from English memory. Compare this passage from the *Recollections*: "My father possessed an extraordinary memory, especially for dates, so that he knew, when he was very old the date of the birth, marriage, and death of a multitude of persons in Shropshire" (*Autobiography*, p. 39).
45 *Autobiography*, p. 29.
46 The most astute comment on Darwin's health appears in one of his own letters: "I hope I may be able to work on right hard during the next three years ... but I find the noddle [*sic*] & the stomach are antagonist powers ... What thought has to do with digesting roast beef, – I cannot say, but they are brother faculties" (*Correspondence*, II, 85). His "Journal" shows a clear correlation between periods of illness and periods of stress associated with his work or, more rarely, with family calamities. Persistent vomiting and weakness reduced his normal workday to three or four hours, but within those hours his accomplishment was prodigious. His assorted illnesses were "adaptive," not in the sense of being imaginary or invented, but in sparing him, as he points out in the *Recollections*, "from the distractions of society and amusement" (*Autobiography*, p. 144). For Darwin's own litany of the maladies that plagued him for most of his adult life, see his "Medical Notes" of 1865 cited in Colp, *To Be an Invalid*, pp. 83–84. Colp surveys every scrap of medical evidence and speculation, ranging from arsenic poisoning to "neurotic hands" to "suppressed gout," and concludes that no single cause accounts for Darwin's many symptoms, although most "are indicative of psychic (as opposed to organic) causes" (p. 142). Darwin continued to work

productively into old age and died of coronary insufficiency at the age of seventy-three.

47 "The Life of the Shawl," *Lancet*, 9 (January 1954), p. 106. Dr. Good's ingenious thesis of patricide through publication has been frequently reiterated, among others by Ernest Jones in *Free Associations* and by Phyllis Greenacre in *The Quest for the Father*. In addition to "anxiety neurosis . . . much complicated by genius," Dr. Greenacre attributes to Darwin (without foundation) "severe attacks of malaria" (New York: International University Press, 1963, pp. 32–33).

48 Letter of 20–31 December 1831, *Correspondence*, I, 187.

49 Brent, p. 32. The incident is recounted by Darwin's son George, as told to him by his father.

50 *Life and Letters*, I, 122–23.

51 *Life and Letters*, II, 355.

52 "I do not think I gained much from him intellectually" (*Autobiography*, p. 42). Yet Robert Darwin's observations are cited more frequently in Darwin's early notebooks and manuscripts than those of any author except Charles Lyell. The intellectual interaction between father and son was especially intense during the most creative years of Darwin's life, those immediately following his return from the *Beagle*. Charles considered his father an authoritative observer of mental processes, especially of pathological states, and frequent queries to Robert find their answers in Charles's notebooks. See Edward Manier, *The Young Darwin and His Cultural Circle* (Boston: Reidel, 1978), p. 18; and *Metaphysics, Materialism, passim*.

53 *Autobiography*, p. 52. Darwin applies the analogy to his later becoming an honorary member of various royal societies.

54 See T. H. Huxley, Obituary Notice, *Proceedings of the Royal Society of London*, 44 (12 April 1888–21 June 1888 [London: Harrison, 1888]), p. xii, n. i.

55 Letter of May 1838, *Correspondence*, II, 85.

56 Letter of 4 February 1861, *Life and Letters*, II, 153.

57 Letter of 21–22 November 1838, *Correspondence*, II, 123.

58 *The Philosophy of the Inductive Sciences* (1840), I, 113. Cited in the *Oxford English Dictionary*.

59 The most striking instance is the last sentence of the *Recollections*:
With such moderate abilities as I possess, it is truly surprising that thus I should have influenced to a considerable extent the beliefs of scientific men on some important points.
It is not clear in this flattest of all valedictions if Darwin presumes to include himself in the genus of "scientific men." His surprise at the extent of his influence strikes me as wholly genuine – the dual

consequence of his having been intellectually slandered as a child and self-educated as an adult.

60 See James R. Moore, "Darwin of Down: The Evolutionist as Squarson-Naturalist," in *The Darwinian Heritage*, pp. 435–81.

61 *Autobiography*, pp. 47–48.

62 *Ibid.*, p. 51; and Freeman, *Charles Darwin: A Companion*, p. 133.

63 Ronald W. Clark, *The Survival of Charles Darwin: A Biography of a Man and an Idea* (London: Weidenfeld and Nicolson, 1984), p. 11.

64 The full title of Paley's book is *Natural Theology; or, Evidences of the Existence and Attributes of the Deity, Collected from the Appearances of Nature.*

65 For Paley, see *Autobiography*, p. 59; for Humboldt, pp. 67–68. In 1845 he wrote to Hooker, "[m]y whole course of life is due to having read and re-read as a youth his 'Personal Narrative' " (*Life and Letters*, I, 305).

66 On the timing of the invitation, see Brent, p. 209.

67 Entry of 21 March 1835, *Charles Darwin and the Voyage of the Beagle*, ed. Nora Barlow (New York: Philosophical Library, 1946), p. 234.

68 Dr. Douglas Hubble, "The Life of the Shawl," *Lancet* (26 December 1953), p. 1352. Cf. " . . . his father was always autocratic" (Huxley and Kettlewell, p. 66).

69 See letter of 30 August 1831 to Henslow, *Correspondence*, I, 131. Darwin actually wrote two letters of declination, one to Henslow and one to George Peacock, with whom the offer had originated. Further, he asked Henslow to send a second note to Peacock "in the chance of his not getting my letter." Temptation loomed so large, it seems, that Darwin felt compelled to burn his bridges thrice over, for he also asked Peacock to notify Captain Fitz-Roy of his decision.

70 "Young Darwin in Love and at Work," review of *Correspondence*, I, in *The New York Times Book Review*, 21 April 1985, p. 27.

71   Animals whom we have made our slaves we do not like to consider our equals. – ((Do not slave-holders wish to make the black man other kind)) animals with affections, imitation, fear of death, pain, sorrow for the dead – respect . . .
"Transmutation Notebooks," B 231, cited in *Metaphysics, Materialism*, p. 187.

72 *Life and Letters*, I, 117.

73 Letter of November 1879, *Life and Letters*, II, 414.

74 "He is the most open, transparent man I ever saw," Emma wrote on the eve of her marriage (*Emma Darwin*, II, 6).

75 Compare Einstein's "Autobiographical Notes," begun at exactly the same age Darwin began his: "Here I sit in order to write, at the age of 67, something like my own obituary." Cited in James Olney, *Meta-*

phors of Self: The Meaning of Autobiography (Princeton: Princeton University Press, 1972), p. 183, n. 3.

76 *Autobiography*, p. 139. The same self-reification attaches to his description of the huge portfolios into which he gathered and cross-indexed a lifetime's hoard of facts. Stacked high on shelves in an alcove adjacent to his study at Down, the portfolios served him as a kind of external brain (*Autobiography*, pp. 137–38).

77 Letter of 5 September 1831, *Correspondence*, I, 142.

78 *Life and Letters*, II, 511–12.

6

Lewis Carroll: "dishcoveries" – and more

MORTON N. COHEN

All biographers hope for good fortune. If we are lucky enough to find a cache of previously undiscovered material, we may reveal new facts, recount unreported adventures, or even pull a skeleton from a closet. With old material, we may make new and meaningful connections that help us see our subject better. But whether or not we find new facts or make new connections, we all hope, by staying with our subject long enough, to become sufficiently intimate with him or her to develop the kind of understanding that lets us illuminate the subtle, shadowy areas of personality.

With Lewis Carroll I have been fortunate in all three goals, discovering new material, making new connections, and achieving new insights, and I should like to recount how in three instances these avenues opened up to me and proffered the means of seeing my subject more clearly.

One of my earliest revelations – what Lewis Carroll might have called "dishcoveries" – concerned his diaries. We've known about Lewis Carroll's manuscript diaries for a long time. His nephew, Stuart Dodgson Collingwood, writing the official biography of his uncle in 1898, the year that Lewis Carroll died, had access to them. There were thirteen volumes in all. But we have also known that, somehow, after Collingwood finished his work, four of the thirteen volumes were lost. Also lost was another valuable piece of literary history to which Collingwood had access, Lewis Carroll's letter register, where he recorded every letter that he wrote and received during the last thirty-seven years of his life – for a grand total of 98,721. All missing: four volumes of the diaries and the entire letter register.

The diaries had been a concern of mine, naturally, from the first, when I decided to edit Lewis Carroll's letters. The Dodgson family and I talked about the surviving volumes when I discussed the future edition of the letters with them. Even though four volumes were missing, the nine that survived covered more than half of Lewis Carroll's sixty-six years. They are all important historically and, as the Dodgson family knew well, valuable commercially. At that time, they were in a bank vault in a London suburb. Roger Lancelyn Green's edition of the diaries, containing less than three-fourths of the manuscript text, had been published in 1953, but anyone working on an edition of Lewis Carroll's letters would benefit hugely from having access to the unpublished portions as well as the published volumes. In fact, ideally I would have a copy of the entire manuscript diaries to work with.

Others knew of the diaries, both scholars and collectors. For instance, the quest for copies of Lewis Carroll's letters had brought me an invitation to call on a well-known book and manuscript collector in New York. He expressed an interest in the edition of the letters that I was working on, but, over lunch, made it clear that he was even more interested in Lewis Carroll's manuscript diaries. He knew that the Dodgson family still owned them, he wanted to buy them, and he wanted me to help persuade the Dodgson family to sell them to him. In fact, he made it clear that he would like to have me serve as his emissary in the case. He also indicated, without much subtlety, that access to the hundreds of Carroll letters he owned would depend upon my full cooperation in securing those treasured notebooks.

"Mr. Collector," as I shall call him, was a highly successful businessman, and the grapevine had already passed the word that he was no great friend of scholars. It did not take me long to realize that if he acquired the diaries, he would put them into his own vault, as a financial investment, and leave them in the gloom to grow in dollar value. If he came to own the diaries, scholars would not have had a chance of seeing them in his lifetime, possibly even longer.

That lunch meeting was in the spring and soon I was back in

England for the summer, meeting again with members of the Dodgson family. I did not have to bring up the subject of the diaries. The family did and confided that the original volumes were a source of concern. The responsibility of simply possessing them was overwhelming. Was the bank vault sufficiently secure? Might the manuscripts deteriorate there? Should they be more accessible? Should they perhaps be sold? And if they were to be sold, should they go up for sale at auction, at Sotheby's or Christie's? They would probably bring a good price. But then the family would have no control over who bought them. Perhaps they would leave the country. My meeting with "Mr. Collector" haunted me. I knew that if the diaries went for auction, they would not have the same fate as that of the *Alice* manuscript. That text, having been sold at auction by Alice Liddell (Mrs. Hargreaves then), did come to the United States. But it was returned to London in 1948 and enshrined in the British Museum (now the British Library) as a gift from a group of public-spirited American bibliophiles by way of expressing their gratitude for Britain's courage during World War II.

Happily the Dodgson family accepted my suggestion that they get in touch with the Keeper of Manuscripts at the British Museum and see if the Museum would wish to purchase the diaries outright at a fair price, thereby avoiding the auction houses, book dealers, and book collectors. To their credit, the Museum's trustees recognized the importance of the diaries, made a handsome offer, and the notebooks went to their new home in Bloomsbury.

The Dodgson family generously permitted me to have a photocopy of every page in the nine surviving manuscript volumes to aid me in annotating the Carroll letters.

I immediately engaged a professional indexer to compile a complete index of the manuscript. He worked at it for a year, and when he presented his 210-page single-spaced index, he also gave me a page of his own notes. On his list he recorded some pages that the photocopiers had inserted twice, but, more important, he observed that some pages were missing. I didn't mind the duplicated pages, but I took myself immediately to the British Museum to check the missing pages. Indeed, he was right, pages were missing; quite a number of them had been cut out. Nor did it take me very long to infer a connection between the missing pages and the events and relationships in Carroll's life. In fact, I found that a distinct break in the friendship between Carroll and the Liddell family coincided with one of the missing pages and that the Liddells vanished from the diaries at precisely that point, not to reappear for a long time. Other pages were razored out as well, their nubs serving as telltale confirmations, and by checking Carroll's letters and the diary entries before and after the cuts, I could again deduce reasons for the dismemberments.

But who wielded the razor? Did Carroll himself have second thoughts about some of his entries and delete them in his later years? I knew instinctively that that was impossible. Carroll always held himself fully accountable for all he did, even for all his thoughts. He regulated his life and patterned his behavior in a manner that is almost unbelievable in modern times. Besides, his diary was not just an *aide-mémoire*; it was his means of justifying his life to God. He would never falsify it, mutilate it, or destroy a jot of it. How can one lie to God? Carroll never concealed the important facts of his life from that record, nor could he have destroyed a single page.

Then who did? Helmut Gernsheim, the photography historian, insists that two of the missing diary volumes were "destroyed by . . . [Carroll's] over-conscientious nephew–biographer, Stuart Dodgson Collingwood."[1] But the quality of Collingwood's work belies the Gernsheim assertion: Collingwood was scholarly and historical, never afraid to confront sensitive issues. The blame for the missing diaries cannot be laid at his door, and I know now where it belongs.

I believe that the four missing volumes have been lost by simple carelessness and neglect. There's a Dodgson family legend that for years the diaries were kept loosely in a box in the kneehole of a desk used by one of Carroll's nephews, not a Collingwood nephew but a Dodgson. The volumes that are lost probably got mixed in with other possessions and were either destroyed in error or discarded as unneeded remains when someone was moving house or disposing of the property of a recently deceased family member. We cannot be sure.

But I can tell for certain who snipped the pages from the

surviving diaries. From 1941 to 1960, the diaries were in the custody of Menella Dodgson, a Carroll niece. Unmarried, not well-to-do, Miss Dodgson lived in seclusion with other maiden sisters in Leamington Spa. In 1957, an American collector sent his son and daughter-in-law, who were visiting England, to call on the Misses Dodgson. The point of the visit was to determine whether the ladies had any Carroll memorabilia they cared to sell. The couple returned to London after the visit, and the daughter-in-law wrote a letter to her husband's father reporting the details of the visit. Her letter survives, and here is an excerpt from it: "Naturally [she writes] we asked . . . about the diaries. [Miss Dodgson] . . . said very emphatically that they were not for sale and will not be as long as the sisters are living. She is going to leave them to some cousins who undoubtedly will sell them . . . [We] asked if we could see them. She brought out a small brown cardboard box and in it were five or six books with ruled paper. We were told that some sections had been cut out. Miss Dodgson said she was going to cut out more before she died."

There it is. But why was niece Menella Dodgson so censorious? Probably because Dodgson had diligently recorded every new friendship with a child and, more to the point, set down a careful account of his meeting with his favorite child friends, especially the Liddell girls, and most particularly Alice. These accounts evidently were too vivid or too numerous for Miss Dodgson's Edwardian sensibilities, and she took the liberty of adjusting the record, leaving us to speculate about the facts recorded on those missing pages, about what must have appeared to Miss Dodgson as perhaps a violation of propriety that lay behind the break between Carroll and the Liddells. But you can't change a man's personality, character, motives or intentions by suppressing a few pages of his diary when so much else survives: with the help of the diary volumes that we still have and the mountain of letters that Carroll wrote, one can speculate, cautiously but with some confidence, about the Carroll–Liddell break, and I do that in some detail in my forthcoming biography of Carroll.

The "dishcovery" of the cut pages was serendipitous, to be sure, and every biographer must hope for similar good fortune. Making new connections depends less on luck, perhaps, but any biographer who tills his fields carefully and conscientiously can hope to establish them. My example relates to *The Hunting of the Snark*, a remarkable poem, the longest and arguably the greatest nonsense poem in the English language. Seekers after truth have, for a long time, sought to untie its knots and make sense of its nonsense. What does the *Snark* really mean, what inspired Carroll to write it? Carroll himself was taxed to answer these questions, and he simply couldn't. "I'm very much afraid I didn't mean anything but nonsense!" he wrote to some child friends in America. "Still, you know, words mean more than we mean to express when we use them," he went on, "so a whole book ought to mean a great deal more than the writer meant . . . The best [explanation] that I've seen is by a lady . . . that the whole book is an allegory on the search after happiness. I think this fits beautifully in many ways."[2]

The mysteries about motive and meaning persisted, of course, and were further complicated by the way Carroll was inspired to compose the poem. Here are the facts: on July 18, 1874, staying at his family home, The Chestnuts, in Guildford, Carroll went out for a breath of fresh air on the Surrey Downs, and on that solitary walk, a line of nonsense flashed through his mind, like a lightning bolt, unexpected and brilliant: "For the Snark *was* a Boojum, you see." Almost two years of gestation followed before Carroll published the poem.

A dozen or so years earlier, Carroll had invented *Alice's Adventures in Wonderland* in another spontaneous flash of inspiration. The spark then was provoked by the three Liddell children, sitting before him in the boat on the River Isis, all wanting him to tell a story. Logic and curiosity led me to wonder whether the *Snark* was not provoked by another person or persons in another demanding posture. I went to Carroll's letters and diaries to see if I could glean any clue to help solve the puzzle. I think I found it.

On the day before the memorable country walk in Surrey, Carroll had traveled from Oxford to Guildford expressly to help nurse "Charlie" Wilcox, his twenty-two-year-old cousin and godson whose family in Yorkshire had sent him to relations in the south hoping that a milder climate would ease his tubercular lungs. Charlie had taken a turn for the worse; Carroll, titular head of the family since his father's death, was notified, and he sped to the side of the desperately ill young man.

Arriving at The Chestnuts, Carroll took up a vigil on the evening of the 17th, and, after sitting at the bedside through most of the night and getting only three hours' sleep, he broke away and took that memorable walk. He had obviously been deeply moved by the sight of his dying cousin, and he must have been thoroughly exhausted after his journey and night-watch. Death, he knew, was near, and his heart was heavy with impending doom. The walk on the Downs was an escape – from the image of the dying godson, from the stuffy sickroom, from reality, even from reason and sense. And the flash of nonsense, that striking line of verse, must have been Carroll's own defense against his pain and morbidity. At the moment when life and good sense held no joy for him, his creative genius came to his rescue and transported him to a wonderland of imagination, to the world of nonsense. It brought diversion, relief.

Carroll returned to The Chestnuts to resume his nightly watches; very likely he toyed with the meaningless line that had come to him out of the blue and began to construct a long poem about the pursuit of a mythical beast. One can speculate that, as he built the verses one by one, he shared them with the ailing youth. Perhaps they even worked on them together, allowing the invalid, if only for a moment here and there, to forget about his approaching end. We cannot know how much the sick-room and the tragic facts of Charlie Wilcox's illness influenced the weird tale of adventure that became *The Hunting of the Snark*, but surely the subtitle of the poem, "An Agony, in Eight Fits," owes something to the young man's illness.

Even more gratifying for the biographer than making "dish-coveries" and new connections is arriving at a plane of intimacy with his subject, an intimacy that enables him to see subtler and more revealing character traits than he could see along the way. In Carroll's case, I have only recently come to realize that his relationship with his father was probably more complex than I earlier believed it to be.

The father, Charles Dodgson, was a formidable man. Articulate, healthy, vigorous, and apparently handsome, he was, by the time his first son was born, established in the Church. He had taken a double First at Christ Church, Oxford, and was thoroughly trained and proficient in the classics and in mathematics. An engaging, original lecturer and sermonizer, he was already on his way to becoming something of a force in the Church. Generous and charitable, he nevertheless emerges as formal and stern, especially in religious matters. In 1827, when he was twenty-seven, he married a cousin and then sired eleven children, seven girls and four boys. Lewis Carroll was born in 1832, the third child and eldest son.

As early as 1836 Dodgson *père* became Examining Chaplain to the Bishop of Ripon, and in 1837, his first sermon was published "by decree of the Lord Bishop." More published sermons followed, and when Lewis Carroll was ten, he held in his hands a copy of his father's translation of Tertullian. It was published with a preface by Dr. E. B. Pusey and sponsored by the advocates of the Oxford Movement as part of the ambitious *Library of Fathers of the Holy Catholic Church*. We do not know if the elder Dodgson had any say in the choice of Tertullian, but it is inconceivable that he would undertake so massive a labor on a writer with whom he felt no sympathy at all. Tertullian, born a pagan in the latter half of the second century, converted to Catholicism, lived an exceedingly ascetic life and preached strict personal discipline and restraint. That Charles Dodgson would be drawn to so stern a Church father is probably significant. Dodgson's position in the Church strengthened and his voice was heeded by High Church dignitaries. In 1852 he was made Canon of Ripon Cathedral and two years later Archdeacon of Richmond.

By all indications, the young Lewis Carroll fell under the spell of his father's powerful character. The father was "his ideal of what a Christian gentleman should be," Collingwood writes.[3] From an early age, the father was the son's tutor, and so successful was the father's instruction and the son's application in the home–rectory that when the boy went off to school for the first time, at age twelve, he was already proficient in Latin and mathematics and, by evidence aplenty, well read in a good many classics and in English literature. The father naturally imbued the son with his own religious principles, and the son, in these early years at least, dutifully accepted the parent's teachings, especially in matters of Christian doctrine, and sought to become a mirror image of his accomplished sire.

The record clearly reflects the son's devotion, respect, and love for the father – indeed, adulation is implied everywhere. Yet the record offers something more if one scans it carefully and examines a few neglected signposts. Indeed the father is a concerned parent always and the son reverential and conciliatory towards him. But the father was also stern, decidedly authoritarian, and any disagreement, any digression would not be acceptable. The son's heart must have harbored a corner of fear. "I have got a new hat," he wrote to his older sister from School House, Rugby, when he was seventeen, "which I suppose Papa will not object to, as my old one was getting very shabby; which I have had ever since the beginning of last holidays."[4]

We know, too, that as Carroll grew to manhood, he did not, perhaps could not, fulfil all his father's high hopes for him. Carroll was not, like his father, physically vigorous. He loathed sports at school, he was shy, withdrawn and solitary, he stammered, he was deaf in his right ear. He did very well academically at both Richmond Grammar School and at Rugby and then at Christ Church, his father's college. But he did not, like his father, make a double First. Like his father, he entered the Church, but was never ordained priest – he took only deacon's orders. He never assumed a curacy. Like his father, he wrote and published, first some mathematical works, and then, three years before his father's death, his *Alice*. But he was uncomfortable with the pomp and ritual of his father's High Church and turned to the simpler, unadorned ways of the Broad Church. Other areas of disagreement are evident. We have no record of a discussion between father and son, let alone a confrontation, on the subject of the theater, but it is clear that the son attended theatrical performances regularly and in fact defended the theater publicly as an uplifting force, with the full knowledge that his father would not countenance this behavior. Perhaps most disappointing to the father was the son's failure to marry and have children of his own, and when the father lay dying in 1868, he must have realized that the son, aged thirty-six, would never marry and produce the progeny he had hoped for.

If the senior Dodgson was less than elated with the path his eldest son was following – and he certainly must have been aware of his son's preference for female child friends above all others – Lewis Carroll must, in turn, have been aware of his father's discomfort and, being aware that he had caused disappointment, he felt some guilt. Guilt could come from an assessment of his condition and his efforts as well. He had tried to emulate his father, but he had only partially succeeded. Would not that partial success/partial failure bear in upon him and sow the seeds of inadequacy? He could not match his father's strength, his father's accomplishments as a man, a husband, a father, a churchman, a community leader, and the comparison must have dug into the son's consciousness. Might not the stern, authoritarian nature of the older man, his self-confidence, his vigor, been a source of some resentment in the younger?

How much discomfort, resentment, guilt the young man bore is not clear. We can't even be sure that he confronted the relationship's inadequacies consciously, coolly. But Lewis Carroll's diaries produce telltale signs of the younger man's deepseated difficult relationship with his father. For instance, in June 1855, Lewis Carroll, age twenty-three and already a don at Christ Church, left Oxford for the long vacation. Before joining his family in Yorkshire, he went to London to visit friends, to go to the theater and to the picture galleries. On Friday, June 22, he attended a performance at the Princess's Theatre in Oxford Street and saw Charles Kean and Ellen Tree in *Henry VIII*. He recorded the occasion in his diary and calls it "the greatest theatrical treat I ever had or ever expect to have." He was particulary moved by the final scene and Miss Tree's performance as Queen Catherine. "I never enjoyed anything so much in my life before," he concluded, "and never felt so inclined to shed tears at anything fictitious, save perhaps at that poetical gem of Dickens, the death of Little Paul."[5]

The reference to Paul's death in *Dombey and Son* is significant. Lewis Carroll read Dickens, liked Dickens, quoted Dickens. *Dombey and Son* was first published in twenty monthly parts between October 1846 and April 1848, and Lewis Carroll must have read it early on. The novel is extraordinary in its own right, of course, but it would have a special appeal for Lewis Carroll. *Dombey and Son* could easily become "Dodgson and Son," especially in Lewis Carroll's fanciful mind. And the novel is, after all, primarily about the relationship between a father and his two children, especially the son. It is, moreover, in the early chapters something of a *Bildungsroman* turned on its head, telling, as it does, the story of the birth and growth of the son, his education, his trials, and ultimately his death while still a schoolboy.

Paul's education is not like Lewis Carroll's in that he doesn't go off to schools like Richmond and Rugby. But in spite of the difference, Lewis Carroll would find many parallels between his own education and Paul Dombey's, many echoes in Dickens's pages of his own early years of tutelage.

When Mr. Dombey believes that his son needs instruction, he sends him off to a crammer, to Dr. Blimber's establishment in Brighton, to that

great hothouse in which there was a forcing apparatus incessantly at work. All the boys blew before their time. Mental green peas were produced at Christmas, and intellectual asparagus all the year round. Mathematical gooseberries ... were common at untimely seasons, and from mere sprouts of bushes, under Doctor Blimber's cultivation. Every description of Greek and Latin vegetable was got off the dryest twigs of boys, under the frostiest circumstances. Nature was of no consequence at all. No matter what a young gentleman was intended to bear, Doctor Blimber made him bear to a pattern, somehow or other.[6]

Imagine Lewis Carroll reading this passage:

Such spirits as he had in the outset, Paul soon lost of course ... he kept his character to himself. He grew more thoughtful and reserved, every day ... He loved to be alone; and in those short intervals when he was not occupied with his books, liked nothing so well as wandering about the house by himself, or sitting on the stairs listening to the great clock in the hall. He was intimate with all the paper-hanging in the house; saw things that no one else saw in the patterns; found out miniature tigers and lions running up the bedroom walls, and squinting faces leering in the squares and diamonds of the floor-cloth.[7]

The daily routine at Blimber's is enough to undo hardy, insensitive boys, and in gentle, delicate Paul's case, it wreaks havoc. It drains him of what little strength he has and ultimately saps his life away.

Lewis Carroll's reminiscences of his school days are not happy

ones. "During my stay [at Rugby] I made I suppose some progress in learning of various kinds," he wrote,

but none of it was done *con amore*, and I spent an incalculable time in
writing out impositions ... I made some friends there ... but I cannot
say that I look back upon my life at a Public School with any sensations
of pleasure, or that any earthly considerations would induce me to go
through my three years again.[8]

We know that at Rugby he was made to work from 7 a.m. to 10
p.m. six days a week, virtually a reification of Paul Dombey's
schedule. And we know too that he yearned for solitude and
privacy during those years, as did Paul. Lewis Carroll in fact
must have suffered Paul's every agony as he read through
Dickens's pages, must have deeply resented Mr. Dombey, the
tyrant who brought Paul's condition upon him, must have
shared all of Paul's desperation, his efforts to live up to his
father's expectations, his humiliation at failing.

Nor should we be surprised that the ending of Shakespeare's
Henry VIII provoked Lewis Carroll's diary reference to Paul
Dombey and brought Paul's plight and death to mind, for again
we have a gentle creature, Queen Catherine, victimized – neglected and rejected by the tyrant King. The cases are not precisely parallel. The elder Mr. Dodgson, Mr. Dombey, and King
Henry are enormously different from each other, as different as
Lewis Carroll, Paul Dombey and Queen Catherine are from one
another. But we do have parallels. The latter three each sought
to please the former, and each failed.

"The greatest blow that has fallen on *my* life was the death ...
of my own dear father," Lewis Carroll wrote when he himself
was approaching his end.[9] One is inclined to take that statement
at face value. But perhaps it conceals as much as it reveals.
Surely his love and gratitude were genuine. But what other
emotions came to the fore when his Olympian model was
silenced and removed? How did Lewis Carroll feel when he
suddenly found himself titular head of the family with the care
and welfare of a gaggle of sisters and brothers laid on his
shoulders? Did his father's death leave him with an unreconcila-
ble guilt, guilt that accrued through the years when he suspected that his father found him inadequate? Guilt at his

resentments over his father's superior strength and accomplishments?

Perhaps not so curiously, a number of arrogant fathers appear in the works of Lewis Carroll, and we have instances where a son rises up and crosses the father's wishes or takes vengeance on a father. Who was the "beamish boy" that slew and who the Jabberwock that was slain? And why do we have, albeit in jest, the young man berating the older in "You are old, Father William"? Father-grumbling is not the most persistent theme in the works of Lewis Carroll, but it is there, and it is there for a reason.

If I am right in my reading of these subtle signs and significations, I trust that they, along with the "dishcoveries" and the new connections are leading me to a closer and more intimate recreation of the remarkable man we know as Lewis Carroll.

NOTES

1 *Lewis Carroll: Photographer* (revised ed.; New York: Dover Publications, 1969), p.v.
2 *The Letters of Lewis Carroll*, ed. Morton N. Cohen with the assistance of Roger Lancelyn Green (London: Macmillan, 1979), I, 548.
3 Stuart Dodgson Collingwood, *The Life and Letters of Lewis Carroll* (London: T. Fisher Unwin, 1898), p. 131.
4 *Letters*, I, 11.
5 *The Diaries of Lewis Carroll*, ed. Roger Lancelyn Green (London: Cassell & Company, 1953), I, 53–54.
6 Chapter XI.
7 Chapter XII.
8 Collingwood, p. 30.
9 *Letters*, I, 121.

7
Prosopopoeia and Praeterita

J. HILLIS MILLER

Most people who know anything about John Ruskin know he abominated the pathetic fallacy, or said he did. He forcefully said that he did in a section of *Modern Painters*, Volume III, "Of the Pathetic Fallacy." Trees, rocks, flowers, and the sea are not animate, said Ruskin. Any poet who ascribes animation to them is falsifying the facts. Of Holmes's lines, "The spendthrift crocus, bursting through the mould / Naked and shivering, with his cup of gold," Ruskin scornfully asserts, "This is very beautiful and yet very untrue. The crocus is not a spendthrift, but a hardy plant: its yellow is not gold, but saffron."[1] Of a passage from Kingsley's *Alton Locke*, "They rowed her in across the rolling foam – The cruel, crawling foam," Ruskin asserts, "The foam is not cruel, neither does it crawl. The state of mind which attributes to it these characters of a living creature is one in which the reason is unhinged by grief. All violent feelings have the same effect. They produce in us a falseness in all our impressions of external things, which I would generally characterize as the 'pathetic fallacy'" (v, 205).

Ruskin knew that in renouncing the pathetic fallacy in the name of truth-telling literal accuracy of language, he was also renouncing the fundamental resource of romantic poetry, perhaps even of poetry in general. All poetry, of whatever time or culture, depends on the pathetic fallacy, in spite of Ruskin's claim that the greatest poets, Homer or Dante, are not guilty of it. Moreover, as I have argued in another essay, the pathetic fallacy is no more than a dyslogistic word for the trope of personification or prosopopoeia.[2] If prosopopoeia, as Paul de Man has observed,[3] is the basic trope of lyric poetry, even more basic than metaphor, Ruskin's rejection of the pathetic fallacy is also a rejection of poetry as such in the name of truth and truthtelling. Most people would agree that if one had to choose between poetry and truth, in the end one would have to choose truth. To put this another way, if poetry must ultimately be seen as no more than a complicated species of lying, then poets ought indeed to be banished from the commonwealth. At any rate it becomes exceedingly difficult to make a persuasive argument for keeping poets around. Only by overcoming in one way or another the distinction between trope and truthtelling can this impasse be avoided. All Ruskin's thinking about poetry and about art turns around and around this issue.

Nor is the issue absent from *Praeterita*, that latest of Ruskin's works. Ruskin's description, in *Praeterita*, of his own essential character emphasizes his extraordinary powers of close and patient observation and his inaptitude for storytelling, in both senses of the word. As he tells the reader several times, his true vocation was for geology. That profession would best have used his "patience in looking, and precision in feeling": "I have literally never known a child so incapable of acting a part, or telling a tale. On the other hand, I have never known one whose thirst for visible fact was at once so eager and so methodic" (xxxv, 51; further references to this volume will be by page numbers only). Readers of *Praeterita* will know that the adult Ruskin, at least, had a great gift for telling a tale, for example in the narration of the death of his cousin Charles at the end of the seventh chapter of the first volume, "Papa and Mama" (135–37). Nevertheless, the essentials of the argument against the pathetic fallacy, without the use of the term, are repeated in the praise of Byron even over Homer and Shakespeare in Volume I, Chapter 8, of *Praeterita*, "Vester, Camenae":

But the thing wholly new and precious to me in Byron was his measured and living *truth* – measured, as compared with Homer; and living, as compared with everybody else. My own inexorable measuring wand, – not enchanter's, but cloth-worker's and builder's, – reduced to mere incredibility all statements of the poets usually called sublime. It was of no use for Homer to tell me that Pelion was put on the top of Ossa. I knew perfectly well it wouldn't go on the top of Ossa. Of no use for Pope

to tell me that trees where his mistress looked would crowd into a
shade, because I was satisfied that they would do nothing of the sort . . .
Shakespeare said the Alps voided their rheum on the valleys, which
indeed is precisely true, with the final truth, in that matter, of James
Forbes, – but it was told in a mythic manner, and with an unpleasant
British bias to the nasty. But Byron, saying that 'the glacier's cold and
restless mass moved onward day by day,' said plainly what he saw and
knew, – no more."   (148, 149)

What Ruskin here calls "sublime" or "a mythic manner" is not
explicitly limited to the pathetic fallacy or prosopopoeia, but
contains it as an essential ingredient. Two of the three examples
Ruskin gives are prosopopoeias. The example from Pope's *Pasto-
rals* (II, 74) had already been cited by Ruskin as another horrid
example in "Of the Pathetic Fallacy," and the example from
Henry V, Act v, scene iii, line 5, is a nasty (and grotesque) British
version of personification: the Alps blow their noses on the
valleys. The praise of Byron as one who says "That *is* so; – make
what you will of it" directly echoes the phrasing in "Of the
Pathetic Fallacy" of Ruskin's praise for Casimir de la Vigne's
ballad, "La Toilette de Constance." Though Ruskin does not
even allow himself Casimir's brief justified lapse into the
pathetic fallacy, his narrative of the death of his cousin Charles is
not unlike Casimir's poem in its plain stating of the truth: "every
soul was saved, except Charles, who went down like a stone"
(137).

Just as the examples from Homer and Dante given in "Of the
Pathetic Fallacy" of noble poetry eschewing prosopopoeia in fact
contain submerged prosopopoeias and prove the impossibility
of expunging it even from the most direct and truthtelling language,[4] so here when Byron calls the glacier "restless" he is just
as surely personifying it, so indulging in the sublime and
mythic, as is Pope when he personifies the trees or Shakespeare
when he makes the Alps a giant with a headcold. As in "Of the
Pathetic Fallacy," so here Ruskin's examples prove the opposite
of the overt conceptual argument they are meant to support.
They demonstrate, that is, that there is no poetry, perhaps no
language at all, without prosopopoeia. Nevertheless, the section
in *Praeterita* praising Byron shows that Ruskin in his old age
remained true to his commitment to his cloth-worker's or build-

er's measuring stick of literal truthtelling as against any sort of poetic lie, especially the lie of prosopopoeia.

But Ruskin's continued rejection in *Praeterita* of personification of nature as a species of tale-telling and play-acting is not my main subject here. Here I want to observe and follow up the implications of the fact that Ruskin's rejection of the pathetic fallacy implies a rejection of autobiography as well as of poetry. This is so because autobiography is as much as lyric poetry a species of prosopopoeia and impossible without it.[5] This fact may be formulated in a number of ways.

Prosopopoeia: the word comes from the Greek *prosopon*, mask or face, and *poien*, make, confer. The trope of prosopopoeia uses language to ascribe a voice or a face to the absent, the inanimate, or the dead. It personifies what does not in fact have personality. Prosopopoeia is a trope of address, a species of apostrophe. By speaking to what has no life, face, or voice, it invokes an answer and presupposes the possibility that what is addressed may answer back, as in Wordsworth's "ye knew him well, ye Cliffs / And Islands of Winander!" (*Prelude*, Book Fifth). In the case of an autobiography, the absent, inanimate, or dead that is resurrected (assuming it ever had the unified life of a single "I") is the past self of the autobiographer. This occurs by a curious species of "Lazarus, come forth!" The invocation of the past self in autobiography strangely combines the myth of Pygmalion with that of Narcissus. As Pygmalion fashioned Galatea of stone and then fell in love with her, the autobiographer fashions out of language an effigy of his or her past self and then, like Narcissus, may fall in love with that image, ascribe it life, and idolize it as his or her true self: "That is I."

Autobiography, as many commentators have recognized, is a transaction between two "I"'s, the "I" of the present who speaks in the present and writes the autobiography, and the "I" of the past self whom the autobiography brings back to life through language. In a successful completion of the autobiographical project, the two "I"'s ultimately merge. This twoness becoming a oneness may be observed in a sentence in the first chapter of *Praeterita*, Volume II: "For as I look deeper into the mirror, I find myself a more curious person than I had thought" (243). Here the "I" who speaks or writes in the present is at once distinguished from the "I" in the mirror of memory and at the same time *not* distinguished, in a constant wavering of the personal pronoun: "I find myself." The "I" in the mirror is the same as the present "I," as the image of mirror imaging suggests, nor does the present "I" do anything other than describe a self already there. At the same time the "I" who writes is not the same as the mirror image and has at least the power of looking at it objectively and describing it.

As a matter of fact, of course, neither one's past self nor language itself has life, any more than the foam is cruel or the crocus spendthrift. Autobiography is active, constructive, performative. It is a way of doing things with words, not a passive description of something already there. The fundamental tool of autobiography, as the sentence just quoted from Ruskin attests, is prosopopoeia, in this case the ascription of life to an effigy made of words. Ruskin's anathemas against the pathetic fallacy would therefore apply equally well to autobiography.

Does Ruskin in *Praeterita* simply ignore or forget this fact, or does he devise strategies to avoid committing in this new way the crime he so forcefully condemns in "Of the Pathetic Fallacy"? There is no evidence, that I know, that Ruskin explicitly made the connections between his autobiographical project and the prohibition against the pathetic fallacy I have traced out. Nevertheless, many aspects of the narrative strategy of *Praeterita* indicate Ruskin's implicit recognition of the problem. In *Praeterita* Ruskin tried to write a strange kind of autobiography that would, against impossible odds, avoid committing the sin of prosopopoeia. I call it a sin because another name for it is idolatry, the worship of graven images. Idolatry as such is condemned elsewhere by Ruskin, as Gary Wihl has observed, with the same scorn with which he condemned the pathetic fallacy.[6] Such condemnation is appropriate for someone brought up, as Ruskin was, in a sternly fundamentalist Evangelicalism. It also forms a curiously twisted link with the European tradition of thinking about the sublime, Ruskin's word, in *Praeterita*, as I have noted, for false poetry. If Ruskin condemned the sublime as lie, Kant, on the other hand, affirmed that "Thou shalt not make unto thee any graven image," is the most sublime passage in the Hebrew Bible, the condition of the most sublime poetry, the poetry of the Hebrew Bible. But the implications of this chiasmus cannot be followed up here.

The most economical and the most overt places to see Ruskin's strategies for avoiding idolatrous prosopopoeia in his auto-biography are the title, the subtitle, and the preface of 1885. The preface was dated May 10, 1885, two months, that is, before the first chapter of *Praeterita* proper was published, though the early chapters of the autobiography are no more than slight revisions of material already published in *Fors Clavigera*. The preface of 1885 is the outline of Ruskin's project for *Praeterita* rather than, like many prefaces, something written last as a description after the fact of work already accomplished. Whether he succeeds in carrying out that project is another question, to which I shall return briefly at the end of this essay.

How then does Ruskin propose to write an autobiography that will avoid committing the pathetic fallacy in that particular form of it I put under the double aegis of Pygmalion and Narcissus? Autobiography is the making of an effigy out of words, not stone, that is hailed as oneself. In this greeting the past "I" and the present "I" join in a recognition of the self, deep in the mirror. Such a recognition is a new mirror stage, not that Lacanian one at the beginning of life, where the man child sees himself in the mirror as others see him, and says, "That is I," but the mirror scene near the end of life, in which the aging man sees his own image in the mirror of memory, an image he momenta-rily forgets he has himself constructed out of the resources of language, and says, "That is I."

Praeterita: the word is one of the ordinary Latin terms for the past, but it has a triple connotation. The word is the plural past participle of *praetereo*, to pass over or pass by. To call the past, the personal past of the autobiographer, *praeterita*, literally "things passed over," both shifts the definition of that personal past from people to things and at the same time emphasizes its miscell-aneous, plural, multiple nature. The past of the autobiographer is made of a series of detached things that do not necessarily hang together to form a whole. Moreover, the word *praeterita* suggests that this past is not only made of manifold, perhaps disconnected, things, but also made of things that have been passed over in the sense of not recorded, forgotten. If the autobiographer does not record them in language now, before he dies, they will be permanently forgotten, passed by, *praeterita*. The work of the autobiographer has nothing to do with the preservation of the self or with the fashioning of an image of the self. It is a work of memory, of preservation. Autobiography is archival rather than self-analytical, self-confrontational, or self-fashioning.

The subtitle then asserts that what is recalled to be stored in written form ready to be called forth again and remembered again by any reader are scenes and thoughts "perhaps worthy of memory." Ruskin will not say that they are worthy or that they are not worthy. They perhaps may be or they perhaps may not be. He implicitly leaves it to the reader to decide. The phrase "worthy of memory" suggests that there may be some scenes and thoughts from Ruskin's past life that are not worthy of memory. Such unworthies may be allowed to drop forever into the abyss of things that have passed by or been passed over. In fact *Praeterita* is punctuated by hints of things Ruskin says are not worthy to be remembered. The reader may ask, "Worthy in what sense? Good for what?" The preface gives the answer and also gives the criteria by which some things may be passed over in total silence. They are the traditional criteria, pleasure and utility: "I have written them therefore, frankly, garrulously, and at ease; speaking of what it gives me joy to remember at any length I like – sometimes very carefully of what I think it may be useful for others to know; and passing in total silence things which I have no pleasure in reviewing, and which the reader would find no help in the account of" (11).

The full phrasing of the subtitle spells this out and makes it clear just what Ruskin meant by calling his autobiography by the odd name of *Praeterita*: "Outlines of/Scenes and Thoughts/Perhaps/Worthy of Memory/In My Past Life." The formulation suggests that the scenes and thoughts, the objective and subjective aspects of Ruskin's past life, are just hanging around somewhere waiting to be remembered. They are not attached to any unified and unifying "I." This shift from the single "I" of the autobiographer to "scenes" and "thoughts" is reinforced, within the body of the text, by the fact that so many of the chapters are named for places. Examples of this in the first volume of

Praeterita are "The Springs of Wandel," "Herne-Hill Almond Blossoms," "The Banks of Tay," "Schaffhausen and Milan," "The Col de la Faucille," "Christ Church Choir," "Roslyn Chapel." No doubt the actual chapters are as much about people as about places and as much about Ruskin himself as about the other people who shaped his life, but the titles metonymically shift from the people and what they did and felt to the scenes in which that happened, as though a given locus had some determining effect on what could happen in that locus and as though it were therefore perhaps most worthy of memory. The chapter titles also reinforce the implication that the book is the memorial record of a series of disconnected and self-enclosed places.

This implication is fulfilled in the way Ruskin organizes the book as a sequence of detached segments, each published separately. He asserts overtly that he has left out much and is making no attempt to tell everything in an unbroken sequence. And of course *Praeterita* is unfinished. It was broken off by the madness of Ruskin's last decade that made it impossible for him to work any more, as the storm cloud settled down for good. That might be said to be an accidental incompleteness, from which no conclusions can be drawn. It could, however, just as well be argued that *Praeterita* is in principle unfinishable. *Praeterita* is a potentially endless sequence of scenes and thoughts from Ruskin's past life perhaps worthy of memory. The autobiography is constructed on principles that intrinsically lack *telos*. It is just "scenes and thoughts perhaps worthy of memory in my past life," not any form of "the story of how I came to be what I am." This is so, at least in what Ruskin says he intends to do, because the link of those scenes and thoughts to any integral or integrating "I" is carefully cut by the formulation of Ruskin's autobiographical project.

The first word of the preface is "I." The word occurs again and again throughout the three brief paragraphs of the preface. The strategy of the preface is to affirm the present "I" of the writer, that of the garrulous old man speaking at ease of whatever it gives him joy to remember, while on the other hand systematically depersonalizing his past self, in a scrupulous avoidance of the pathetic fallacy. On the one hand, Ruskin says, "*I* have written these sketches of effort and incident ... *I* have written them, therefore, frankly, garrulously, and at ease; speaking of what gives *me* joy to remember at any length *I* like – sometimes very carefully of what *I* think it may be useful for others to know; and passing in total silence things which *I* have no pleasure in reviewing ..." etc. [my italics]. On the other hand, Ruskin speaks of his record of his past life not as the resurrection of another "I," the "I" he once was, but as "outlines," "sketches" of past "scenes and thoughts," of "my described life," of "long past scenes," and of his desire to give his readers "knowledge as complete as I can give them" of his "personal character," as though he were describing a mountain or a flower with appropriate scientific objectivity.

Only once does this scrupulous depersonalizing of the past self for the sake of affirming the living presence of the speaking self and its mastery over the past as an objective source of amusement and instruction break down in an effaced prosopopoeia of the past: "My described life has thus become more amusing than I expected to myself, as I summoned its long past scenes for present scrutiny ..." True to his project of depersonalizing his past self, Ruskin speaks here not of summoning another "I" but of bringing back long past scenes in a kind of interior theater that he can scrutinize at leisure, as a student of film studies a stopped frame in a film clip. But the word "summoned" suggests, against Ruskin's apparent intent, that the long past scenes are called forth by means of an imperative command. This would be another form of "Lazarus, come forth!" or of calling spirits from the vasty deep. One speaks a summons only to what is thereby implicitly granted the power to speak back, as in the example from Wordsworth cited earlier: "ye knew him well, ye Cliffs / And Islands of Winander!" Just as Wordsworth's sentence is a prosopopoeia of the cliffs and islands, fulfilled of course in the description of the boy's conversation with the owls, in "mimic hootings," so Ruskin's phrase, though it speaks not of the past self but of past scenes, is a prosopopoeia of those scenes that is hard to distinguish from the prosopopoeia of the past self who was the main actor in those scenes. To put this another way, the work of memory is never impersonal, whatever Ruskin may wish to say of it. Memory always goes by way of an obscure and effaced personification of the past self who was witness to the scenes that are remembered. One must summon up the past "I" in order to reach the scenes that past "I" witnessed, the thoughts he thought. The role of prosopopoeia in memory is so natural and so universal as to be taken for granted and to pass unnoticed, unless it is present, as here, in a word like "summoned" that betrays, against the grain of Ruskin's attempt to write an autobiography without prosopopoeia, that such a project is impossible. There can be no autobiography without prosopopoeia.

But what is Ruskin's reason for wanting to accomplish this impossibility? I have said that it is a desire to avoid committing the sin of idolatry, but there is more to say about this. The final paragraph of the preface gives the clue. Idolatry, one might say, is a sin not just because it is worship of a graven image, lacking life, as though it had life, whereas the life has been ascribed to a stock or stone (or effigy in words) by a fallacious figure of speech. Idolatry is also a sin because it arrogates to man a power that properly only belongs to God. Just as only God properly can be said to be a person, or just as God is the original person, so any man or woman is a person only because God has granted him or her the privilege. God made man in his own image. This means that human personality is secondary, derived. We hold it only on sufferance from God, as a possession that may be revoked at any moment. Prosopopoeia is a sin because in it man imitates God, puts himself in the place of God. In prosopopoeia man performs an act of ascribing life and personality only God can do with impunity, as when He fashioned Adam of "the dust of the ground," breathing life into him, and then made Eve of Adam's rib. The Lord giveth and the Lord taketh away. God's creation of Adam and Eve is a continuation of his divine imperative, "Let there be Light." It is an imperative, not a performative, since God already foreknows what his words will call forth, whereas a true performance is not divine but human, all too human. A performative is a way of doing things with words that is always to some degree (which means to an infinite degree) unpredictable and uncertain, whereas God always knows exactly what will happen. Or, since God does not speak Adam and Eve into existence, but breathes life into them, it might be better to speak of the creation of man under the rubric and within the problematic of the gift, in this case the gift of life. It is a gift God can give, withdraw at any time, and give again when the dead are reborn in heaven or at the general resurrection at the last trumpet. But in this case it is a gift that can in no way be returned by any commensurate gift from man to God. In that sense the gift of life is outside the circuit of normal giving and receiving. It is a gift without gift, as Maurice Blanchot might say, that is, a gift that generates an infinite and unpayable debt. It might be said that the uttering of prosopopoeias by poet or autobiographer is a sinful error because it acts as though man too could enter into the circuit of the giving and receiving of life, whereas that is a game he is forbidden to play: "Thou shalt not make unto thee any graven image."

All this complex system of thought underlies the last paragraph of Ruskin's preface. Here the language shifts suddenly to one of those curious "here and now" locutions: "I am writing this here in such and such a place and now at such and such a time." What is odd about such written expressions is that like any dating they are at once unique, valid for one time and place only and in one unique inscription, and at the same time, since they are language, are infinitely repeatable, for example in every copy of *Praeterita* ever printed. "I write these few prefatory words," says Ruskin, "on my father's birthday, in what was once my nursery in his old house, – to which he brought my mother and me, sixty-two years since, I being then four years old." The preface ends with the place and the date: "Herne Hill,/10th May, 1885." Such expressions work to shift attention away from the matter that is written or written about, referred to ("my described life"), toward the physical act of writing, the place and time of writing and the actual presence of the writer, the "I" who writes "I am writing this." It could be argued that this assertion of the present existence of the "I" of the writer is the most important function of autobiography, more important than the rescue and ratification of the past "I." But at the same time, of course, these words in the present tense, "I write these few prefatory words," the place (Herne Hill) and the date (10th May, 1885) are for a modern reader full of the poignancy of the irrecoverable past. In fact they were thrown into the irrecoverable past at the instant they were written or even by the act of writing them, since the "I," the present tense verb "write," the place, the date, are part of the general repeatability of all language. Anyone can write "I write." The words are, as soon as they are written, anonymous and belong to no one, nowhere. Even the place, Herne Hill, can, as Ruskin himself asserts, remain the same for sixty-two years, and it is of the essence of 10ths of May to return every year, as Ruskin implicitly recognizes when he observes that the today on which he writes is an anniversary, his father's birthday.[7]

Writing kills the "I" who writes. It renders him or her anonymous and universal, a mere function of grammar, a "shifter," as the linguists call the first-person pronoun. Ruskin implicitly proposes to escape this remorseless process by the procedure he describes in the remarkable last sentence of the preface: "What would otherwise in the following pages have been little more than an old man's recreation in gathering visionary flowers in fields of youth, has taken, as I wrote, the nobler aspect of a dutiful offering at the grave of parents who trained my childhood to all the good it could attain, and whose memory makes declining life cheerful in the hope of being soon with them." A complex set of moves is made simultaneously in this sentence. The act of summoning back scenes and thoughts of his past life through memory is once more defined in a depersonifying figure. This memorial act is a gathering of visionary flowers in fields of youth, not by any means the resurrection of his dead self through an act of language. Therefore it is not by any means a sinful prosopopoeia. The memories are not even real flowers but mere visionary ones, phantasmal, unreal. Ruskin here remains true to his resolute desire to tell the truth and to do without lying poetic fictions. If *Praeterita* were no more than that, however, it would do no more than affirm the sad fact that the past is dead. For us the readers of *Praeterita* today this dictum would apply as much to the garrulous old Ruskin writing in his nursery at Herne Hill on the 10th of May, 1885, as it would to those scenes and thoughts of his past life he summons up for present scrutiny and description.

But Ruskin then goes on to describe that visionary bouquet as a dutiful offering at the grave of his parents. Flowers put on a grave are a promise of resurrection. They promise the resurrection both of the one buried there and, implicitly, of the one who places the flowers. As the flowers live, so the buried loved ones somewhere live on and so I can hope not to die wholly but to rejoin them after death in a general reunion. The memories of the past and the self that experienced those past scenes and thoughts are depersonified in the name of an optative future resurrection, the hope of being soon again with the dead parents, after death. The scenes and thoughts perhaps worthy of memory are flowers gathered for the parents' grave as a figurative anticipating of a future joining with them by that present "I." The depersonification of the past "I" not only avoids idolatrous prosopopoeia. It also functions as a necessary preparation for the personification of the present speaking and writing "I" and its mastery over the dead "I" of the past: "Unless the grain die . . ." *It*, my past self, is dead, therefore "*I*," my present self, is alive. But that relation of death and life, in turn, is a proleptic representation of the hoped-for resurrection after death. Only God can give life back after He has taken it away. The prosopopoeia of the present "I," that writing "I" so insisted on in the present, is justified as an allegory of God's real act of prosopopoeia to come, the unfathomable mystery of the resurrection into the life after death. Ruskin, it will be remembered, allows, in "Of the Pathetic Fallacy," for the necessity and propriety of prosopopoeia on only one occasion, that is, in speaking of what is immeasurably above man, the mystery of God and of his transactions with the world, as in the prosopopoeias in the Bible: "all the trees of the field shall clap their hands." We, you or I, anticipate this resurrection whenever we read *Praeterita* and bring back to life in our mind's eye and ear not so much the young Ruskin as the one who wrote the book, the garrulous old man scribbling on the edge of madness and death, writing against death, and failing, silenced by madness before he could finish the outline he had planned.[8] Our act anticipates God's act, but only at the cost of falling into the error Ruskin so carefully avoids, the error of taking a prosopopoeia literally, giving a face, a voice, and a soul to the dead letters on the page.

NOTES

1 John Ruskin, *Works*, Library Edition, ed. E. T. Cook and Alexander Wedderburn (London: George Allen, 1902–12), v, 204. Further quotations from Ruskin will be from this edition, identified by volume and page numbers, or in the case of vol. xxxv, which contains *Praeterita*, by page numbers only, after the initial citation.

2 See my "Catachresis, Prosopopoeia, and the Pathetic Fallacy: The Rhetoric of Ruskin," *Poetry and Epistemology*, ed. Roland Hagenbüchle and Laura Skandera (Regensburg: Verlag Friedrich Pustet, 1986), pp. 398–407.

3 See "Hypogram and Inscription," *The Resistance to Theory* (Minneapolis: University of Minnesota Press, 1986), p. 47. After showing the connection between apostrophe, the figure of address, and prosopopoeia, de Man here goes on to say: "Now it is certainly beyond question that the figure of address is recurrent in lyric poetry, to the point of constituting the generic definition of, at the very least, the ode (which can, in its turn, be seen as paradigmatic for poetry in general)."

4 As I have argued in the essay refered to in note 3, the example from Homer implicitly personifies the earth in calling it "life-giving," as Ruskin makes explicit when he paraphrases Homer as calling the earth "our mother still, fruitful, life-giving," and the example Ruskin quotes from Dante obscurely personifies the leaves in the reflexive "si levan" ("take themselves off"), while the lines in Dante just after those Ruskin quotes contain an explicit personification: "fin che' la ramo / vede a la terra tutte le sue spoglie" ("till the bough sees all its spoils upon the ground").

5 As Paul de Man also affirmed. See "Autobiography as De-Facement," *The Rhetoric of Romanticism* (New York: Columbia University Press, 1984), p. 76: "Prosopopoeia is the trope of autobiography, by which one's name . . . is made as intelligible and memorable as a face."

6 See Gary Wihl, *Ruskin and the Rhetoric of Infallibility* (New Haven: Yale University Press, 1985). When Marcel Proust renounced Ruskin he did so by accusing him of "idolatry" (Proust's word) in the specific form of ascribing to works of art the intrinsic possession of beauties that were in fact imported into them by the critic. Whether or not Ruskin actually did that is the basic question any reading of Ruskin's works must ultimately confront, but it could be argued that Proust was turning against Ruskin a tool of rhetorical analysis that he had learned or could have learned from Ruskin himself, for example from the denunciation of the pathetic fallacy. To put this another way, the contradiction within Ruskin is repeated not only within Proust's own

works but also in the relation between Ruskin's text and Proust's reading of Ruskin. For a good discussion of the latter see Dana Brand, "A Womb with a View: The 'Reading' Consciousness in Ruskin and Proust," *Comparative Literature Studies*, 18, no. 4 (December 1981), 487–502.

7 For an admirable analysis of this peculiarity of pronouns, proper names, signatures, placenames, and dates, see Jacques Derrida, *Schibboleth/pour Paul Celan* (Paris: Editions Galilée, 1986).

8 See xxxv, 632–38, for Ruskin's plans for the rest of *Praeterita*, III.

8

Patterns in time: the decorative and the narrative in the work of William Morris

NORMAN KELVIN

Wherever William Morris as a young man looked he seemed to see that true art, or the best art, was decorative, and more often than not was also narrative. What he saw corresponded to the shape his imagination had already embraced and to the direction his mind and feelings were already taking. By the age of seven he had read all the Waverley novels. By fifteen, his idea of boyish, intimate correspondence with his favorite sister Emma was to describe decorative architectural detail: "I . . . saw a very old church [at Abury]," he wrote, "the tower . . . had four spires on it of the decorated order and there was a little Porch and inside the porch a beautiful Norman doorway loaded with mouldings the chancel was . . . paved with tesselated pavement."[1] At Exeter College, Oxford, a few years later, he read Ruskin. It would be difficult to say how much enthusiasm for medieval decorative art he brought to his reading by this time, how much he took from it. Whatever the answer, as an undergraduate he steeped himself in medieval manuscripts at the Bodleian, and in the long vacations of 1854 and 1855 he toured the cathedrals of northern France, where he gloried in the carving and the stained glass, and indeed in every decorative component of Gothic architecture: structures which were not only ornamental but which, like the novels of Scott and illuminated medieval manuscripts, told a story.

What was early pleasure became later in Morris's career a commitment. The decorative and narrative, as practice and metaphor, came to inform his work as poet, designer, and writer of romances and to mark his vision of history and politics. But a

La Belle Iseult, painting by William Morris (1858) (Tate Gallery)

third concept also began early to inform his work and mark his vision. That concept is the frame. As a structure it is ubiquitous in Morris's work, and as an idea it is an organizing principle for viewing both his life and art. The narrative, the decorative, and the making of frames together form the pattern that connects his life and art.

We can begin to see the first two, and at the same time briefly take a wide view of his entire career, if we consider his early and sole surviving easel painting, *La Belle Iseult*,[2] completed in 1858, and juxtapose it with what he wrote, late in his life, about early illustrated printed books.

In painting *La Belle Iseult*, Morris invented the pattern on Iseult's dress – the bunches of pomegranates looking as if done in an ogival stitch. Jane Burden as model wore a white dress, and Morris painted on the embroidery pattern. Similarly he made up designs for the pattern on the carpet and on the cloth draping the table that Iseult faces.[3] And it is of course a narrative to which these decorative details are integral: in all probability the painting depicts Iseult just risen from her sickbed in the tower to which she had been confined by King Mark when she tried to kill herself upon hearing false rumors of Tristram's death. Given this probability, the wreath of rosemary that we see is worn in remembrance for the Tristram Iseult believes to be dead. But whatever the possible symbolism of the details within the painting, the largest "statement" of the work is an aesthetic one. It is not a rejection of the symbolism that informs medieval and Pre-Raphaelite use of natural forms but an emphasis on something else: on making the painting testify in the first place to the visual pleasure Morris took in observing how the painters he most admired made decorative detail integral to the depiction of a moment in a story.

As for illustrated books, in his essay of 1895, "Some Woodcut Books of Augsburg and Ulm," he said: "I claim the title of works of art both for these picture-ornamented books as books, and also for the pictures themselves. Their two main merits are first their decorative and next their story-telling quality; and it seems to me that these two qualities include what is necessary and essential in book-pictures."[4] His admiration for the "books themselves," as well as for the "story-telling" pictures within them, implies praise of narrative itself in these books, and though he settled into a discussion of the pictures alone here, his insistence on the importance of narrative recurs throughout his essays and lectures of the 1890s, as in his earlier talk (1892) on "Woodcuts of Gothic Books", in which, in the course of praising books of the fifteenth century, he moved without pause to art in general, asserting that the two functions of "*[a]ll* organic art [italics mine]

... are the telling of a story and the adornment of a space or tangible object."[5] Narrative was in fact a defining characteristic not only of a book but of much else. Like ornament, it was for him a structure and an organizing principle of whatever had large meaning.

As for the importance to him of a story-telling picture, it is useful to recall that such a picture has a double status always. In the mind and feelings of the viewer the image generates events that occurred before the moment depicted and led up to it, and events in an extrapolated future that familiarity with the story also creates. It generates, that is, a chronology in words. On the other hand, the eye of the viewer also comprehends the composition – the forms and their arrangement, whatever the subject matter – as a single visual event. Similarly, the decorative forms Morris loved – acanthus leaves, flowers, bunches of fruit – can be seen in this double perspective. Like narrative pictures, they can be regarded as images that represent a moment in the process of germination, growth, and decay; and they can also be comprehended as forms transfixing the moment seized upon, as patterns in which time functions as simultaneity only.

It is useful also to see Morris's pattern designs as *framed* by what went before and what will follow, i.e., by generation and growth, and then decay; and to see "story-telling" illustrations and pictures, such as the fifteenth-century German woodcuts he admired or his own painting *La Belle Iseult*, as similarly framed by what went before in the tale and what follows. Regarding Morris's sense of the visual as a sense of the moment framed opens a way for seeing his love of the decorative-narrative not only as his preference in art but as a metaphor encompassing his activities and interests beyond art. For this framing of a moment in time, a moment in his own art most often derived from nature, also describes his approach to history. Moreover, the most obvious occurrences of frames in Morris' work, the decorative borders characteristic of the Kelmscott Press books, remind us that in Morris's work the frame is nearly always in juxtaposition with a narrative moment and that the frame is nearly always highly decorative. The question to ask is, how does this frame relate to the narrative?

There is strong evidence to help answer the question in

Morris's early experiment in making illuminated manuscripts. It is a good place to begin, because Morris, in his self-dedication to the book arts, oddly recapitulated the historical movement from illuminated manuscripts to printed books.

In 1856, he made for Robert Browning and Elizabeth Barrett Browning a manuscript of two stanzas of a song from *Paracelsus*, in which there is a decorative background and also, on either side, "solid columnar borders which maintain the color scheme." In the same year he prepared for Georgiana Macdonald (who was to marry Edward Burne-Jones in 1860) a manuscript of his own poem "Guendolen" that contains a decorative frame in which several colors including gold are used.[6] These examples may seem innocuous, but they set the stage for others in the 1870s; and these can best be discussed in connection with two uncompleted ventures (in 1867 and 1871) at producing illustrated printed books as well, both in collaboration with his closest friend, Edward Burne-Jones.

The surviving woodcuts by Burne-Jones for the first, an illustrated edition of *The Earthly Paradise* – the "book that never was"[7] – give no evidence of how important the decorative frame was to become for Morris. But what remains from the second uncompleted collaboration, an illustrated edition of Morris's masque, *Love is Enough*, does. Morris designed several borders (and two initials) before the project, like the previous one, was abandoned. A trial page survives. As a "text" this page can be read as an early statement of what happens when Morris's decorative patterns are brought into conjunction with Burne-Jones's drawings: a central matter in any discussion of the Kelmscott *Chaucer*, the great culmination of Morris's career as a maker of decorative frames. In the surviving trial page of *Love is Enough* a pattern based on fruit and leaf forms constitutes a vertical border the length of the text on the left-hand side. On the right, a border of the same dimensions depicts four cherubs in an ascending column, repeating or paralleling the sinuous curve of the leaves in the left hand border. And although Georgiana Burne-Jones, recalling the plan for the book, says that all the borders completed were by Morris[8] the figures on the right were most decidedly drawn by Burne-Jones,[9] as a comparison with some of his known drawings, his caricatures for example, makes

Love is Enough.

THE MUSIC.

OVE is enough: though the world
be a-waning,
And the woods have no voice but
the voice of complaining;
Though the sky be too dark for
dim eyes to discover
The gold - cups and daisies fair
blooming thereunder,
Though the hill be held shadows,
and the sea a dark wonder,
And this day draw a veil over all deeds passed over,
Yet their hands shall not tremble, their feet shall not falter;
The void shall not weary, the fear shall not alter
These lips and these eyes of the loved and the lover.

THE EMPEROR.

The spears flashed by me, and the spears swept round,
And in war's hopeless tangle was I bound,
But straw and stubble were the cold points found,
For still thy hands led down the weary way.

THE EMPRESS.

Through hall and street they led me as a queen,
They looked to see me proud and cold of mien,
I heeded not though all my tears were seen,
For still I dreamed of thee throughout the day.

THE EMPEROR.

Wild over bow and bulwark swept the sea
Unto the iron coast upon our lee,
Like painted cloth its fury was to me,
For still thy hands led down the weary way.

Trial page for a proposed illustrated and decorated edition of
Love is Enough (1872) (William Morris Gallery)

evident. Moreover, Morris would have been incapable of drawing infant forms with the suppleness and easy movement that characterize these figures.

What makes the probability that the borders are in fact by Morris *and* Burne-Jones, rather than Morris alone, of interest is that they in fact compete. It is not only, as Joseph Dunlap has written, that the "thin types" Morris had to use for the verses comprising the text of the page "cannot support the strength and vitality of the decorative initials and borders."[10] There is a competition, too, between the leaf and fruit forms on the left and the cherubs on the right, and if only because the left-hand border (and the decorated initial – clearly Morris's work too) is more abstract, *its* strength, in terms of its function as a border, is more apparent, while the right-hand border falls somewhere between an illustration and a decorative border. There is at best a strenuous dialogue here rather than a simple contrast between "passive" forms by Morris and "active" figure drawings by Burne-Jones, and it anticipates more interestingly what occurs on the pages of the Kelmscott *Chaucer*, as well as the significance of these pages in a discussion of framing in Morris's work.

The competition with Burne-Jones's drawings reappears only with the Kelmscott Press. But in the 1870s there is further evidence that something other than inadequate type caused Morris to make decorated borders that overwhelm the text. Several of the illuminated manuscripts he made during this period point to a different cause, and it is worth turning to the first of the book arts for him again.

In 1870, Morris collaborated with friends on an illuminated manuscript, *A Book of Verse*, fifty-one pages in length and consisting of his own poems, and prepared as a gift for Georgiana Burne-Jones. The decorative patterns for the first ten pages were done by George Wardle, one of Morris's associates in the work, and Morris took over at page eleven, drawing all the rest. Strikingly, the decoration, starting with page eleven but not before, strongly competes with Morris's own words and calligraphy. From page eleven on, the decoration "tends to be of primary concern" and "it is not unusual for words at the end of the longer lines to burrow into it"[11] – that is, into the broad vertical border that the decoration along the right side constitutes. In 1871, for an illuminated manuscript of *The Story of the Dwellers at Eyr*, also made for Georgiana Burne-Jones, Morris created on the first page a frame that is simply massive; or, in Dunlap's more qualified view, the "stems, fronds, blossoms, fruit, and acorns, which [fill] the margins ... are barely restrained from overwhelming the text by a frame of blue poles."[12] And in the following year Morris made for Georgiana Burne-Jones an illuminated *Rubáiyát*, in which "on most of [the twenty-three vellum pages] foliage, flowers, fruit, and vines *aggressively* [italics mine] crowd about the small roman letters in the central triangle."[13]

As early examples of Morris's illuminated manuscripts, these three show that it is impossible to speak of his decorative borders as supplementing in an inconsequential way the narrative texts or pictures they frame.[14] In general, a frame can be said to arrest the text, to contain it and cut it off for a brief moment from the page that precedes and follows, for the sake of the aesthetic pleasure that viewing frame and text as a single form gives. But it does not only do this. What Morris's early illuminated manuscripts show in the extreme is that any frame or border has its own energy. It cannot merely decorate and it does not only contain narrative movement. By relating aesthetically to the image of whatever kind it contains, it enlarges the image to include itself. It creates a relationship between itself and what it frames that is never static. The aggressiveness with which Morris's early decorative borders enter into that relationship exaggerates the ever-present dynamic. But like all extreme cases, they enable us to understand the "normal" ones: those in which the frame and content are so successfully related that the energy of the first seems wholly supportive and dedicated to containing the image, in which the frame seems passive even though a transaction with the image is continuously occurring.

The frame is never passive; at the very least it pushes against the movement of the image into past and present, or what is the same thing, it interrupts the movement from the preceding to the following page. Morris's decorative borders in these early illuminated manuscripts at times invade the text, which is unsatisfactory. But in art peaceful separation is not the antithetical and desired condition: a better balance of forces is. The question is whether the decorative in Morris's work ever does coexist in harmonious exchange with the narrative fill: whether the decorative, so often seen as the very incarnation of passivity (when for example it is contrasted with the fine arts), can, in Morris's use of it, quietly connect with the narrative it encloses to form a single balanced pattern.

It is a question to be pursued by widening our view. In Morris's work, the frame appears not only as a border surrounding drawings or pages of text but as a functional presence in much of his narrative writing.[15] And the major early instance of this is of course *The Earthly Paradise*, 1868–70.

In overall structure it is, like *The Canterbury Tales* of which Morris was so admiringly aware, a "frame" story, containing narrators, whose presence makes up the "frame," and a "content" composed of the stories these narrators tell. A group of fourteenth-century Norsemen, fleeing the plague, are washed up on an island somewhere in the Atlantic, inhabited by a Greek people; and each of the two groups agrees to tell one story a month. Each group draws upon its own heritage (this is roughly true with respect to the Norsemen), agreeing in effect to exchange medieval and classical tales: in effect to juxtapose them.

Since the Norsemen and the Greeks both live in the fourteenth century and the stories are an extension of those who tell them – the Greeks come into being almost exclusively by narrating – the gap in time between the classical and the medieval tales is reduced. Voiced by people of the fourteenth century, the classical tales lose some of their antiquity. And finally, since all the stories in the content are an extension of the consciousness of the figures in the frame, an exchange between frame and content occurs, aided by the weakening of the time barrier described, that causes a continuous reduction of the separateness of frame and content. We are finally left, when we elect the retrospective view of the entire work, with a pattern: one in which frame and content have been transfigured into elements in a single completed form.

Moreover, there are actually two frames to *The Earthly Paradise*: a series of monthly lyrics, and the frame figures of Greeks and Norsemen. Their function is complementary because both include visual phenomena whose effect is temporal.

The poems, which constitute together an inner frame, introduce a lament for a lost love and, more important, descriptions of natural forms, as the lyrics move through the seasons. The natural detail invoked from poem to poem is not only characteristic of the decorative detail of Pre-Raphaelite poetry but connects the monthly poems together into a circling limit. The limit is a temporal one. The time they occupy, one year, can be grasped in a way that mythic time in the narrative fill cannot, and the poems thus function in relation to the content by pulling toward the present, arresting the plunge into the infinity of mythic time that the tales invite.

As for the decorative quality of the two sets of narrators, both, during an entire year, engage in no important physical action in contrast even to Chaucer's pilgrims. Their physical presence is a kind of embroidery bordering the sound of their voices, for their speaking voices create the *action* of the content.[16] But these speaking voices cannot of course be located spatially in either the frame or the content to the exclusion of the other. Speaking characterizes the figures in the frame; and speaking carries forward the action of the content. The speaking voice is at once part of the "decoration" of *The Earthly Paradise* and *is* the medium of the fill. Even more than the natural detail of the lyrics, effective as these are in creating a circle of finite time to arrest the straight line of infinity, the speaking voice unifies the entire work. It creates the "organicity" that Morris admired in art or, in the terms we are using here, governs both finite and infinite time by being the voice of both. Through its own continuous presence the speaking voice joins frame and content into a single pattern.

"Organicity" of frame and content, as a concept, invites us to consider two early works of Morris in which frames are not an obvious feature: the painting *La Belle Iseult* and the narrative poem *The Life and Death of Jason*. With respect to *La Belle Iseult*, the issue is ambivalent. On the one hand, there is so much of the decorative in the painting itself as to make a highly decorative frame – if we regard it as a possibility – redundant or overwhelming; as to make it seem implausible that Morris may ever have planned such a frame. The shapes in the pictures are bound together by the overlay of connecting decorative patterns and constitute a single, strong, self-delimiting form for which the unornamented frame as we have it seems appropriate. On the other hand, given the history of the painting – the possibility that Morris parted with it before he deemed it complete[17] – there is a strong probability that Morris at an early stage did plan a highly decorative frame for the picture when finished. Whether or not such a frame would have pleased viewers today, its absence – the presence in its place of a plain one – creates a movement inward from the edge of the canvas rather than an equal exchange between the picture image and the frame. It gives the interior decorative detail precisely the force that the decorative has when it is an aspect of a frame. It relates to the narrative in the content in a double way: as part of the embroidery or symbolic detail of that narrative itself and as the limiting decoration which opposes the temporal movement which is the essence of narrative.

As for *Jason*, it is an ever clearer case of the decorative impulse moving inward in the context of the frame-as-missing, for *Jason* was begun as a tale intended for *The Earthly Paradise* but by its separate publication in 1867 was cut off from the enclosing and decorative presence of the Northern wanderers and their Greek hosts (an impersonal third-person narrator tells the story). About its decorative substance, Graham Hough has written, "Jason is not padded or inflated, but every scene and every incident serves Morris as a theme for profuse descriptive embroidery . . . deliberately elaborated like a Pre-Raphaelite painting."[18] Or, in my view, because of the "presence" of the absent frame, the decorative has moved inward, memorializing what is missing rather than simply permitting it to disappear. A contrast helps us to see this: though decorative detail in the stories of *The Earthly Paradise* is never so sparse as to cause the poem to be mistaken for the work of someone other than Morris, neither is it as abundantly present as in *Jason*. This argument may seem to reverse cause and effect. It is true that *Jason* was kept out of the larger work for which it was originally intended because it had become too long. But part of what makes it "too long," i.e., for inclusion in *The Earthly Paradise*, is that Morris in writing *Jason* indulged the impulse to decorate already directed in theory to the frame story only; and the result is similar to what occurred in *La Belle Iseult*: a pattern of interior decoration that not only supports the "action" it overlays and decorates but also in its self-consistency opposes the action, precisely as an outer frame would.

My point is that framing is nearly always important and integral for Morris, that it is usually associated for him with the highly decorative, and that in those early works in which a decorative frame is absent, notably the painting *La Belle Iseult* and the narrative poem *The Life and Death of Jason*, the decorative has moved inward, away from the "absent" decorative frame. Moreover, in at least the second of these two instances, and possibly in both, the inward movement occurs in the "presence" of an absent frame we know Morris had initially planned to provide. Even in its absence the frame in these works speaks of its necessity and function: its necessary function in relation to narrative.

The term *narrative* in his work and among his interests encompasses myth, history, and romance. He often equates it with "epic," by which he means "full of incident," whether historical or fictional. Whatever its form, when Morris writes narrative or enjoys it as a reader, struggle, conflict, and violence usually mark the action. It is not the "action" of a lament or an *aubade* that characteristically attracts him in medieval literature but the action in works like Malory's *Morte Darthur* and Froissart's *Chronicles*. Moreover, the best poems in Morris's own first collection, *The Defence of Guenevere* (1857), are "King Arthur's Tomb," "The Haystack in the Floods," "Sir Peter Harpdon's End," "Concerning Geffray Teste Noire," "The Eve of Crecy," "The Judgment of God," and the title work itself. Most of these being directly indebted to Morris's reading of Froissart, they are poems in which violence or the threat of violence is a strong presence, and significantly they are often cited as evidence of Morris's "vigor" or "realism," sometimes to contrast him with Tennyson. As for the Icelandic saga literature, which early became an enthusiasm of his and remained one, the centrality of struggle, conflict, and violence needs no gloss.

And yet there is an ambivalence in Morris about their centrality – about the persistence and endurance of struggle, conflict, and violence and about the ability of history or time-locating to transform their psychological meaning. The three are the ground of existence, he believes, but when psychological immediacy obliterates historical context, in his work sometimes and in his life most usually and naturally, he sees that they exhaust life, that they do not renew it. Working with received material, he could redeem violent life by creating the tragic stature of protagonists who die, and this Morris does best in his use of Icelandic literature, as in his *Sigurd the Volsung*, published in 1876. But for a life like his own, which was in some ways a continuous denial of the tragic or an effort to limit the effects of what a tragic vision made evident, a force that contains or counterpoints violence was essential. It is apposite to think of Morris's temper, which most recently has been described by Jan Marsh, whose interest is in Jane Morris's life and William Morris's effect upon it: "He had a ferocious temper," Marsh writes, "which might be harmless as his friends knew, but was nevertheless not pleasant to witness."[19] Marsh goes on to recount an incident, first reported by Rossetti, in which Morris threatened to throw from a window a piano whose arrival had delayed his dinner. And many actual physical outbreaks – putting a fist through a wall, biting into wood – became the stuff of other anecdotes about Morris and found their way into the reminiscences of those who knew him. Yet equally important was his revulsion from his own violence. The shame he felt may have contributed to his life-long feeling of apologetic concern for Jane, but more important it made him seek in both his life and work an alternative. He found one, or the ideal of one, and the word that for most of Morris's life and work describes the opposite of violence is rest. Rest, not gentleness. Rest became, for most of Morris's career, the alternative to violence and, as such, its frame.

It is not trivial that the subtitle of *News from Nowhere* is "An Epoch of Rest" or that in the ideal society Nowhere, which comes into being through civil war, none of the arts requiring aggressive energy are practised, as Lionel Trilling has observed.[20] Significantly, there is scarcely any story-telling in Nowhere, and the arts practiced are almost exclusively the literally decorative ones.[21] "Rest" is signified most fully, articulately, and indeed profoundly by the practice of these arts, and they are a frame about the absent narrative. There is also an outer frame: the consciousness of Guest, which registers with stage wonder and fear (themselves in context decorative) all that the inhabitants of Nowhere describe and which finally breaks through stage-fear to take pleasure in this discovery of rest, as the explanation of the way of life continues and Guest's attachment to the inhabitants grows.

Violence as content, rest as frame. This is, I submit, though it is first made explicit in the late work *News from Nowhere*, a way of approaching much of Morris's work before and after 1890, if aggressive energy be seen as the general concept of which violence is a particular form, and if we keep in mind that in Morris's work and life narration is everywhere and always inseparable from aggressive energy, and often from violence itself.

We can view Morris's career as a political activist, particularly as a socialist, as a "violent-narrative" content, fixed in specific time and framed by his coincident career as a designer of wallpaper and textile patterns. During the years of his most active participation in radical politics, 1883 through 1889, he produced an impressive number of patterns for wallpapers and textiles, and indeed, some of his best. And if we include the earlier years of political involvement, 1876 through 1882, when Morris was first active on behalf of the Eastern Question Association and then briefly for the future of the Liberal Party, the period in which he produces patterns for domestic use and simultaneously engages in polemical action become nearly coextensive.[22] In the years, that is, in which Morris continuously denounces capitalism; in which his letters speak of the possibility, sometimes the necessity, of political violence; and in which anger, conflict and struggle – with the police and with fellow socialists and in behalf of faraway events like the Sudan War (1885) and the effort to prevent the execution of the Chicago anarchists (1887) – are the mark of his feelings and consciousness and structure the narrative of his public life, there is an accompanying and continual making of patterns for Morris & Co., an apparent seeking and finding of rest from the meaning and activity of that public narrative.

We can apply this paradigm also to the last years of Morris's life, the period 1890 through 1896, the years of the Kelmscott Press and the late prose romances. The entire period is relatively one of rest for him because these are the years of the Hammersmith Socialist Society, in which Morris freed himself from warfare with fellow socialists if not wholly from political effort. But it is also the period in which he concentrated great energies on the book arts. These arts become the narrative content of his existence, and the continuing but diminished engagement in political lecturing and writing exchanges place with the decorative art of printing and becomes the frame.

We must, to see this, think of Morris's energetic commitment to the Press. He became absorbed in designing type. He reviewed the work done by others, particularly the cutting of typefaces and wood-blocks. He located paper and ink that met his exacting standards and then arranged for their purchase. He sought and acquired medieval manuscripts and early printed books, if for pleasure then also, as he avowed, to study and use as models in his practice of the book arts. And finally he kept up a business correspondence and lengthy negotiations with Bernard Quaritch, who sold, distributed and sometimes published the books printed at the Kelmscott Press.

Morris's letters, from 1890 through 1896, are a record of all of the above. But his letters also support my other view of these years, that although his political activity continued it did so without the intensity that marked the late 1880s, the period in which his absorption in politics (including strenuous efforts to block the move of fellow socialists toward parliamentarism) was marked by the exercise of what can be called his aggressive will. To insist that socialism only "embroiders" or "borders" his "real" life in the 1890s would be to misrepresent Morris terribly; yet there is no escaping the shift in emphasis. Politics moves from the center to the outside, to make room for a new focus. In that sense socialism becomes a frame, "decorative" in that it moves at a slower pace, embraces a circle of colleagues narrowed to one of friends and congenial associates, and takes on, in the planning and conduct of the weekly meetings, a distinct feeling of ease. Details such as concerts, dramatic readings, and picnics, as well as serious lectures, acquire meaning as gestures of a congeniality that was usually absent during the contentious 80s.

But there is a basic instability of any division of Morris's work into frame and content. The making of Kelmscott Press books is not only a "narrative content" of Morris's life in the 1890s. It is a process producing works of art that ask to be considered in and for themselves.

Nearly every one of the Kelmscott Press volumes contains pages that are in effect images made up of frame and content, the content consisting either of text or of a drawing by someone other than Morris and the frame invariably a patterning of leaves, fruit, flowers and vines cut on a woodblock from Morris's design. As we saw earlier, almost as soon as his interest in making

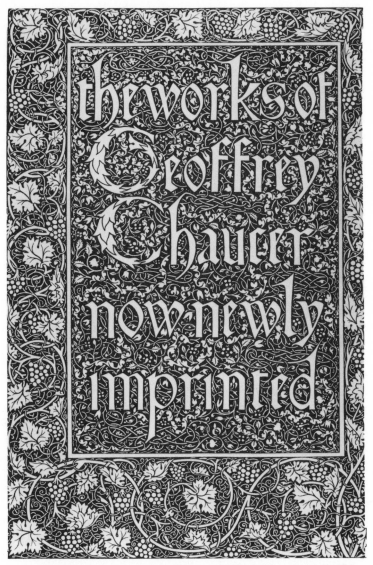

The engraved title page of the Kelmscott Press edition of *The Works of Geoffrey Chaucer* (1896) designed by Morris (reproduced with permission of the Syndics of Cambridge University Library)

illuminated manuscripts and illustrated books began, Morris's borders began to compete in strength and vitality with the typeface, with the calligraphic representation of his own words, and in one instance with a drawing by Burne-Jones. It is only when the decorative can legitimately triumph, when its pattern becomes internal or coextensive with content and border, as in *La Belle Iseult*, *The Life and Death of Jason*, and *The Earthly Paradise*, that the competition disappears. It disappears also, it should be stressed now, in tapestries and carpets of Morris's own design, notably the *Woodpecker* tapestry and *Holland Park* carpet. It disappears because the decorative establishes a hegemony throughout the image or pattern.[23]

If we open the books of the Kelmscott Press what we see is the instability of function caused by the intrinsic nature of Morris's decorative borders. But we see also examples of aesthetic success that remind us of the tapestries and rugs, of *Jason*, and possibly of *La Belle Iseult*. A glance at the Chaucer, the culminating production of the Press, will strongly suggest this. On any page containing a Burne-Jones woodcut drawing and Chaucer's text, Morris's borders compete with both in strength and energy and thus raise a question of how, in terms of the major premises of this discussion, we are to think of them, since Chaucer's text is quintessentially the kind of narrative which signifies action, energy, and central position; and Burne-Jones's drawings are the kind of narrative drawings that seize upon a moment and generate their own past and future. Morris's borders should provide rest, a kind of escape from narrative time, a withdrawal from the aggressive action of the text and even of the pictures. They of course do nothing of the kind, and although they do function as frames they do more even than partake in the exchange between frame and content that worked successfully in *The Earthly Paradise*. The competition is so vigorous as to suggest again the "primacy" of decoration over text,[24] frame over content: as to create that instability of distinction that accompanies most of Morris's division of images, verbal narratives, and experience into frame and content.

However, there is a page in the Kelmscott Chaucer that does something quite different, and there are pages like it in other Kelmscott volumes: *The Story of the Glittering Plain*, *The Recuyell of*

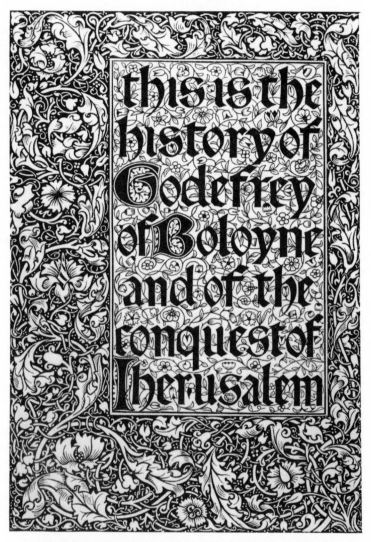

The engraved title page of the Kelmscott Press edition of
The History of Godefrey of Boloyne (1893), designed by Morris
(reproduced with permission of the Syndics of Cambridge
University Library)

the Historyes of Troye, Tennyson's *Maud*, *The History of Godefrey of Boloyne*, *A Dream of John Ball*, and *News from Nowhere*, to name several important examples. In each of these volumes, the page to which I refer is the title page or frontispiece. And what they all have in common is the absence of ordinary type. Whatever words there are are cut from woodblocks, as is all the "accompanying" ornamentation. The decorative patterning, as in the tapestries and carpets, in *La Belle Iseult*, and in *Jason*, is continuous. It is as strong a presence in the content as in the frame. There is no competition: there is a balancing of the strength of lines and forms. Alive, vigorous, splendid, lavishly decorative, they create a magnificent wholeness on the page, a splendor indeed architectural and "organic," for even as the forms assert their individuality they work together. Action is in the strong lines of the flowers and leaves cut in woodblocks, rest in the less aggressive letters and words also cut from blocks. But all are decorative, and this reduction of words to a component of a decorative whole signifies rest in the largest sense: rest from meaning, not from all meaning but from the meaning of the narrative of the nineteenth century, as Morris's decisive use of the word "rest" in the subtitle of *News from Nowhere* makes clear.

There is, finally, one other kind of border-and-content composition that by Morris's own definition is architectural. This is the image presented when two adjacent unillustrated pages in a Kelmscott Press book are perceived as a unit. In "The Ideal Book," his lecture of 1893, Morris insists on the importance of proportion in the margins in any book – the inner margin to be the smallest, the margin at the top next in size, followed by the outer one, and the bottom to be largest of all.[25] He observed these proportions in the books he printed, and if his rigorous requirement is not mandatory for us today, if other proportions also give us pleasure, those he insisted on (and which he regarded as commonly accepted before the eighteenth century) are very effective. They create around the text precisely that condition of rest that a border promises. Indeed, it is more than rest. It is silence, signifying absolute rest.

Furthermore, Morris says that a properly proportioned white space around a text can function in the place of ornament itself.[26] We can add that when that white space stands in the place of ornament around a *narrative* text, it becomes, uniquely, total relief from the action. It does not oppose the energy of the action, nor does it balance it. Nor is it the primary frame, for in the absence of a decorative frame, the massed type on the page creates its own border by the regularity of the left and right edges of the block of text. But the white margins are a space in which the text can exist. As pure space, in which no energy of the decorative is concentrated, these margins provide that absolute rest of which I spoke. However, because the margins have their own limits and vary in size, they import into the idea of background space the qualifying attribute "proper" or "appropriate." They convert space into an extension of the architecture that Morris, in "The Ideal Book" and elsewhere, insists should go into the design of individual letters, spacing of words, and leading between lines. In their proportion, finally, they signify the intervention of an artist to give meaning to pure undecorated space, which is potentially meaningless. As a result, in any Kelmscott Press volume, to cite the most apposite example in this discussion, when two pages having neither illustrations nor decorated borders are opened to form a single unit, pure space is seen combined with the type it encloses to provide, through architectural proportion, aesthetic gratification different from that afforded by the organic decorative page but analogous to it. It demonstrates that when architectural principles are followed, the unornamented becomes a special case of the ornamented, that what appeared at first to be a contrast is an alternate expression of a steady concept, and, in this case, an expression of it that is aesthetically successful.

If a page on which words have been converted into their forms as letters of the alphabet is a triumph of the aesthetic in a rest from narrative meaning, if a page on which a pure white border properly proportioned creates an architectural pleasure that is a rest from the narrative within the border, a Kelmscott Press volume in its entirety is similar in meaning to both but finally more complex than either. Morris intends it to be an object signifying rest: contemplation and pleasure in the decorative. Because it has these attributes, it is, finally, associated by Morris with the domestic. And the "domestic" is a concept so large for him that it could be viewed as governing the others discussed here rather than amplifying them. It pertains to the particulars of his work and also to a vision rooted in desire that shapes his general discourse in many areas.

News from Nowhere, that "epoch of rest," is a good paradigm for the matter. The protagonist, "Guest," journeys by water from London to Lechlade; and the destination reached is Morris's own beloved home at Lechlade: Kelmscott Manor. Like Huck Finn's voyage (in one of Morris's favorite novels), Guest's journey to the headwaters of the Thames is an occasion indirectly to interpret and judge nineteenth-century civilization, and Guest like Huck concludes with a distrust and dislike of that civilization. But in addition to Guest's and Huck's traveling in opposite directions along their rivers and the visual absence in *News from Nowhere* of what is condemned (the "action" occurs in the twenty-first century), there is a large difference between the two works. In the quest for an escape from nineteenth-century civilization, the goal to which Guest is led is not, like Huck's, an escape from houses; the goal *is*, in fact, a house. The final moment in Nowhere, in which Guest's desire becomes focused, is a glimpse of the interior of another house – the church at Kelmscott converted into a dining hall and referred to as a "biggish house". Within it, Guest sees an idealized domesticity, fused with fellowship in this instance, though he reaches only to the threshold before the vision fades for him.

If it fades for Guest, the idea never did for Morris, and throughout his career it gave focus to his own desire. Significantly, regarding himself as a man who longed to be firmly rooted on earth, he reminded Georgiana Burne-Jones in a letter that the root meaning of *world* is home of humankind.[27] It is not pedestrian, moreover, to note that the largest part of the effort of Morris & Co. was devoted to decorating domestic interiors: to furnishing and enhancing homes. And a domestic image is by intention in the nineteenth century an image of rest.

In this consideration of rest in association with the decorative, and both as a "border" upon "narrative" or historic activity, we have Morris's own words making the connection in a remarkable way. In his 1892 essay, "Some Thoughts on the Ornamented Manuscripts of the Middle Ages," he wrote:

If I were asked what is at once the most important production of Art and the thing most to be longed for, I should answer, A beautiful House; and if I were further asked to name the production next in importance and the thing next most to be longed for, I should answer A beautiful Book. To enjoy good houses and good books in self respect and decent comfort, seems to me to be the pleasurable end toward which all societies of human beings ought now to struggle.[28]

"A beautiful house," and "a beautiful book," both to be enjoyed in "decent comfort" seem an oddly precise and limited goal for historic struggle in 1894, when, Morris insisted, he was as much a socialist as ever. Yet this is but a recapitulation of what he had told us four years earlier: that the goal of historic struggle is "an epoch of rest." He can think of no contemporary struggle more grand than the international socialist effort to change society, but for this global epic he can think of no *telos* more grand than a beautiful and comfortable house, wherein the main source of pleasure is reading and aesthetically enjoying a physically beautiful book.

But there is further meaning in all this. The "beautiful book," as Morris conceived it, is medieval in inspiration. The "beautiful house" is a structure of no particular date (so long as it is not of the eighteenth century) but is one that has been properly furnished: one in which the dweller has nothing that he or she does "not believe to be beautiful and know to be useful."[29] Implicitly too, and this is not meant as irony or satire, it is a house that Morris himself might have furnished, for though genuinely modest in many areas (notably the writing of poetry), he was quite confident of his taste and general ideas in interior decorating. In this sense, a beautiful house would be "modern," that is, nineteenth-century in its potential or in its best realization.

This is important because the main "texts" for Morris were the Middle Ages and the late nineteenth century, whenever, at least, his subject of inquiry or praise was art. Despite his reading of Marx and Engels and his familiarity apparently with Hegel too,[30] despite his intellectual acceptance of the idea that history is an uninterrupted dialectical process, when Morris writes about history in his essays and letters and the matter at hand connects with art, he silently refuses the dialectic vision. He refuses the vision of history as a gratification of a desire to understand each period in its own terms. Like Ruskin's, his vision is moral-aesthetic. The aesthetic gives rise to the moral and governs it: the centrality of the aesthetic, finally, makes history for Morris a dialogue between the Middle Ages and the nineteenth century and causes the Middle Ages and the nineteenth century in his characteristic reference to be juxtaposed.[31] They are cemented together like two forms in a mosaic, or like leaded panes in a medieval – or Morris & Co. – stained-glass window.

Medieval-modern *and* socialist, for the mosaic contains all three. Morris's socialism as a struggle to provide beautiful books inspired by medieval book arts, to be enjoyed in the comfort of beautiful homes draped with the fabrics of Morris & Co., or to liberate energies for making beautiful and useful objects, is finally not absurd. It expresses concretely his commitment to the aesthetic as the true life of the senses that socialism promises to fulfill.

But it was a commitment that alienated him from the main socialist activity in the late nineteenth century, from the movement that stressed unionism and parliamentarism and was about to establish the Independent Labour Party as an historic force and direction. He only partly confronted his alienation, because he was obliged in his own mind to see his medievalism-modernism as committing him to the same broad idea of social revolution – basically, removal of class divisions – that was held by those whose immediate political agenda was more strategic than his own. His lack of an immediate political agenda, coupled with his insistence that "education" was the only true definition of "political action," placed him in an unstable role among socialists. He could never fully make common cause with the union organizers and parliamentarists nor define for himself a position that would at the time be publicly, that is nationally, viable. The result was alienation without separation. Finally, the power and energy with which he confronted his alienation generated in turn, in this mode of perceiving Morris, a bordering, decorative response to the public narrative he believed himself to be helping to forward. That response was the writing of his late prose romances, which constitute the one large body of his work so far unnoticed here. Interestingly, these romances provide a border in time on either side of the medieval–modern–socialist "content"; for they first reach back to a period before the Middle Ages, and then forward, beyond the nineteenth century.

A Dream of John Ball (1886–87), arguably not a romance but a political text – a part of the medieval–modern–socialist narrative of Morris's career[32] – is set in the fourteenth century and can be regarded in this discussion as a point of departure. *The House of the Wolfings* (1888) and its pendant *The Roots of the Mountains* (1889) are set earlier, at the time when the Gothic tribes first encountered the Romans. The romances Morris next wrote move forward, first to the twenty-first century, in *News from Nowhere* (1890), which is a synthesis of the fourteenth century and the epoch of "pure" communism promised by Morris's reading of Marx and Engels; and then, into a *timeless* world, in the series of works beginning in 1891 with *The Glittering Plain* and concluding with *The Water of the Wondrous Isles* (begun in 1894 and posthumously published in 1897). Like the world of *News from Nowhere*, this timeless world is furnished with dress and decoration taken from the Middle Ages, but it is outside of history altogether. And like Morris's borders for Burne-Jones's woodcuts in the Kelmscott Chaucer, borders in which leaves and flowers and fruit are stylized and curve perpetually as the vine that joins them curves, so these romances are stylized. Hung on a sinuous thread of repeated adventure are images that assemble the attributes of Gothic leaders, medieval knights, and saga warriors.

Superficially, all this *is* rest. It is rest from the struggle in *John Ball* (from the battle that will have to be fought again) by reaching back to the age when egalitarian barbarism was strong. It is rest also from the conflicts of the nineteenth century, achieved by reaching forward to the twenty-first. However, this final frame to Morris's career, this final search for repose, is once again subverted. As the aggressive energy of the borders to Burne-Jones's illustrations submerges the pictures, and overwhelms also the narrative text of others, so the energy of these late prose romances invades the socialism which on the conscious level Morris still regarded as his own.

In these fantasies, kings, princes, and war heroes rescue women from forest-dwelling evildoers and establish primitive (if perfect) social organizations at the end of their quests. It may be too facile to describe the very act of writing these romances as aggressive. But the use of magic in them to bring social order and a kind of egalitarianism out of chaos, in true mythic fashion, can most appropriately be called aggressive. This employment of magic aggressively rejects the historical–moral stance, the materialism and rationalism, of Morris's fellow socialists in the last decade of the nineteenth century.

Once again a seemingly passive border is unstable in its role, invading the subject it frames, in this case equally aggressive socialism. There is no balance of forces as in the pages of the Kelmscott Press books which are wholly decorative, in pages bordered by white space in proper proportion, in tapestry or carpet designs, in *Jason*, or indeed in *The Earthly Paradise*. This is not only because the life and work, rather than two parts of a work, are juxtaposed here. It is because Morris, this time, in the final romances, is seeking a way out of the nineteenth century.

The contest finally is between the Morris who has John Ball say that the thing fought for by one generation must be fought for again under a different name by the next generation, that there is no escape from history; and the Morris seeking rest in magic who does not find rest in it but who does in the process shift the social–political struggle to a timeless land, thus repudiating John Ball's commitment to the ongoingness of historic time. In this last image, the Morris who seeks to renew the world through magic frames the Morris for whom life was either a narrative of human wills in conflict or an imposition of artistic will upon inert matter.

Morris was incapable of the interior monologue, of the exploration of consciousness that in modernism, in the novels for example of Virginia Woolf, are a radical extension of the naturalism to which he so long had held. Unerring, nevertheless, in his focus on the individual as the final object of historical concern, as the intelligible focus of ideas of liberation and reformation, he intuitively saw that the way to affirm the individual was to affirm the primacy of the imagination, feelings, and desires. These he perceived rightly were not dependent on time, and this perception permitted him to fall away into a world in which time is not a dimension. It was his alternative to a naturalistic psychology of self.

He had spent a lifetime using medievalism as a critique of the nineteenth century. Medievalism provided him with an aesthetic more than anything else and so his critique was an aesthetic one, in which society was judged by its capacity to produce and recognize beautiful and useful objects. In the prose romances, he again uses the furniture of medievalism, but there is nothing now to criticize. There are only palpably evil human figures to be overcome by courage and magic: there is, so to speak, no problem of aesthetic environment. A remarkable thing occurs as a result. More so than anywhere else in Morris's work, beauty in these stories-out-of-time becomes beauty of personal form and of personal relationships.

As a further result, Morris expresses and develops physical love in a way different from its presentation in his earlier works. It is no longer now in his art a fragile event functioning in subordinate manner to prepare the way for violence or tragedy. It is an effective presence, unfrustrated by events, and the descriptions of it have a lyricism remarkably anticipating the prose of D. H. Lawrence's novels. In the process of writing this way, Morris revaluates aggressive narrative, as he does in *News from Nowhere*, but discovers in these romances-out-of-time that the opposite of aggression need not be rest but can be another action: desire begetting consciousness of the other; and generating its own frame, the embrace of a human couple. This image is not a full political answer to the problems of the nineteenth century, but as a goal for social struggle it vastly enlarges on a beautiful house and beautiful books by redefining the human beings who will read the books and live in the house.

NOTES

1 Norman Kelvin (ed.), *The Collected Letters of William Morris*, I (Princeton: Princeton University Press, 1984), p. 7.

2 The painting has at various times been called *Queen Guinevere* and *La Belle Iseult*. I believe that the evidence for regarding the work as a depiction of "Iseult in the Tower" (Malory, Book IX, chapter 19), an interpretation suggested by Christine Poulson, is very strong. For a good discussion of the matter, see Joanna Banham and Jennifer Harris (eds.), *William Morris and the Middle Ages* (Manchester: Manchester University Press, 1984), pp. 114–16 and Plate IV.

3 I am grateful to Ray Watkinson for calling my attention to many of the details in the painting discussed here.

4 *Bibliographica*, I (1895), 444–45; reprinted in William S. Peterson (ed.), *The Ideal Book: Essays and Lectures on the Arts of the Book by William Morris* (Berkeley: University of California Press, 1982), p. 50.

5 In Peterson (ed.), *The Ideal Book*, p. 26.

6 For a discussion of both manuscripts, see Joseph R. Dunlap, "William Morris: Calligrapher," in Paul Needham (ed.), *William Morris and the Art of the Book* (New York: The Pierpont Morgan Library, 1976), p. 49.

7 The title Joseph Dunlap has given his work devoted to the never-completed illustrated edition of *The Earthly Paradise*. See Joseph R. Dunlap, *The Book that Never Was* (New York: Oriole Editions, 1971).

8 Georgiana Burne-Jones, *The Memorials of Edward Burne-Jones* (London: Macmillan, 1906), II, 24.

9 S. C. Cockerell notes that one "marginal ornament was engraved by [Morris] from a design by Sir E. Burne-Jones" but does not say which. See his essay "A Short History and Description of the Kelmscott Press, in *A Note by William Morris on His Aims in Founding the Kelmscott Press* (London: Kelmscott Press, 1898), p. 8; reprinted in H. H. Sparling, *The Kelmscott Press and William Morris: Master Craftsman* (London: Macmillan, 1924), p. 139.

10 Dunlap, *The Book that Never Was*, p. 47.

11 Dunlap, "William Morris: Calligrapher," in Needham (ed.), *William Morris and the Art of the Book*, p. 57.

12 *Ibid.*, p. 57.

13 *Ibid.*, p. 59.

14 For an extended discussion of this matter, see E. H. Gombrich, *The Sense of Order: A Study in the Psychology of Decorative Art* (Ithaca, NY: Cornell University Press, 1979).

15 Mary Ann Caws has demonstrated what can be seen when the concept of the frame is applied to certain nineteenth- and twentieth-century novels. See her book, *Reading Frames in Literature* (Princeton: Princeton University Press, 1984). I am indebted to this work, as I am to essays by my colleague Gerhard Joseph on Tennyson, Browning and Arnold, for my initial realization that the concept was a promising one that could be further explored and applied.

16 Rolph, the leader of the Norsemen, does recount the wanderers' actions prior to their arrival at the Greeks' island, but this does not change the fact that in the narrative present there is no large action.

17 Whatever Morris's final plans for a frame for the painting, the present relatively plain one may well have been regarded by him and even by early subsequent owners as temporary. Ford Madox Brown had given Morris some assistance with the work, and at some point before Morris regarded it as complete he gave it on request to Oliver Brown, Madox Brown's son. D. G. Rossetti then obtained it from "Nollie" Brown and it remained with him until his death, when it passed first to W. M. Rossetti and then to Jane Morris. It is probable

that either Morris or Rossetti provided what was intended as a temporary frame. At any event, the unadorned frame on the painting, as it now appears in the Tate Gallery, is probably the first and only one it ever had. For sharing with me the information given here and the conjectures based upon it, I am grateful to Ray Watkinson.

18 Graham Hough, *The Last Romantics* (London: Gerald Duckworth and Co., 1949), p. 130.

19 Jan Marsh, *Jane and May Morris: A Biographical Story 1839–1938* (London and New York: Pandora Press, 1986), p. 63.

20 See Lionel Trilling, "Aggression and Utopia: A Note on William Morris's *News from Nowhere*," *The Psychoanalytic Quarterly*, 42, no. 2 (April 1973), 214–25.

21 For a more extended discussion of my view of the decorative arts in *News from Nowhere*, see "Introduction," *The Collected Letters of William Morris*, II (Princeton: Princeton University Press, 1987), pp. xxvii–xxviii; xxx–xxxii.

22 Between 1876 and 1889, Morris designed forty-five textile patterns, including "Strawberry Thief," "Windrush," "Medway," "Compton," "Larkspur," "Acanthus," "African Marigold," "Honeysuckle," "Vine and Pomegranate," "Bird and Vine," "Bird," "Brother Rabbit," and "Bird and Anemone," to name some that are among the best in his entire career as a designer. In the same period, he produced eighteen wallpaper patterns, including "Sunflower," "St. James's," "Wild Tulip," "Lily and Pomegranate," "Bruges," "Willow Boughs," and "Fritillary," again to cite patterns that are among the best in his life's work. Moreover, if there is a slight falling off in sheer number during the intense socialist years as compared to the earlier political period (twenty-nine textile patterns between 1876 and 1882, sixteen from 1883 to 1889; ten for wallpaper between 1876 and 1882, and eight from 1883 to 1889), the decline is offset by the production of Hammersmith rugs and tapestries, which begins in 1879. Although Burne-Jones and others designed some of these in the period 1883–89, Morris produced two of the finest patterns, those for the *Holland Park* carpet (1883) and for the *Woodpecker* tapestry (1885).

23 For a relevant discussion of Persian carpets, see Gombrich, pp. 79, 101, and *passim*.

24 Morris of course intended balance, integration, and harmony of elements on all pages of a printed book. For a discussion of his guiding principles, see the essay "Printing," signed by both Morris and Emery Walker, in *Arts and Crafts Essays* (London: Longmans Green and Co., 1903), pp. 128–33. See also note 25.

25 See "The Ideal Book," in *William Morris: Artist, Writer, Socialist*, I, ed.

May Morris (Oxford: The Shakespeare Head Press, 1936; reprinted New York: Russell & Russell, 1966), p. 315.

26 "The Ideal Book", p. 317.

27 *The Collected Letters of William Morris*, II, 52.

28 Peterson, p. 1.

29 See Morris's essay, "The Beauty of Life," XXII, *Collected Works*, ed. May Morris (London: Longmans, Green, 1915; reprinted New York: Russell & Russell, 1966), p. 76.

30 For a discussion of evidence strongly suggesting that Morris was familiar with Hegel's writings, see Mark Swenarton, *Artisans and Architects: The Ruskinian Tradition in Architectural Thought* (London: Macmillan, 1988), pp. 91–93.

31 For a discussion of Morris's work in the context of that of other Victorians who related the medieval past and the nineteenth-century present, see Jennifer Harris, "William Morris and the Middle Ages," in Joanna Banham and Jennifer Harris (eds.), *William Morris in the Middle Ages: A Collection of Essays* (Manchester: Manchester University Press, 1984), pp. 1–17. See also Alice Chandler, *A Dream of Order: The Medieval Ideal in Nineteenth-Century Literature* (Lincoln, Nebraska: University of Nebraska Press, 1970; and London: Routledge & Kegan Paul, 1971), pp. 184–230.

32 For other purposes, I have elsewhere viewed *A Dream of John Ball* as taking its place among the romances and as initiating a quest of Morris's that begins with *John Ball* and concludes with *News from Nowhere*. See "Introduction," *The Collected Letters of William Morris*, II, xxvi.

9
Life's "half-profits": writers and their readers in fiction of the 1890s

MARGARET DIANE STETZ

All which details, I have no doubt, JONES, who reads this book at his Club, will pronounce to be excessively foolish, trivial, twaddling, and ultra-sentimental. Yes; I can see Jones at this minute (rather flushed with his joint of mutton and half-pint of wine) taking out his pencil and scoring under the words 'foolish, twaddling', etc., and adding to them his own remark of *'quite true'*. Well, he is a lofty man of genius, and admires the great and heroic in life and novels; and so had better take warning and go elsewhere.[1]

A novelist of the 1890s, looking back upon these words of the narrator of *Vanity Fair* (1847–48), might well have felt a forgivable spasm of envy. To have known so much – the sex, social class, level of education, and taste – about the reader of one's work; to have understood in advance what such a man expected of literature and so the point at which he would become hostile; and to have been free, moreover, to dispense with that reader in the first chapter of the novel, confident that there was another, more sympathetic, one ready at hand: here was luxury indeed! Still more enviable perhaps, from the viewpoint of half a century later, would have been the invulnerability of Thackeray's "Manager of the Performance" to verbal abuse or physical attack from the other side of the footlights. "JONES," whether because he was a true or merely a would-be gentleman, could be counted upon to remain ensconced in his armchair and to confine his offensive remarks to scribbled marginalia. He did not even represent a danger to the author's income; for if he were reading the monthly number of *Vanity Fair* at his club, then chances are the club itself had made the purchase and would continue to buy all twenty parts.

How different the relationship between artist and audience looked to "Anthony Hope" (pseudonym of Anthony H. Hawkins), writing *A Change of Air* in 1893. In that novel, Dale Bannister, a London poet who has made his reputation with revolutionary odes of a Shelleyan kind but who has lately begun to express more conservative sympathies in his work, finds himself stalked by a half-crazed reader. For "Doctor" James Roberts, a self-educated country physician, Bannister's political shift represents the dashing of his own hopes for the reformation of society: "He expected Dale to do all he would give his life to see done, but could not do himself ... He regarded the poet much as a man might look upon a benevolent volcano ... And the volcano would not act!"[2] The poet's own position, however, is that he owes nothing to his readers, insisting that "'I always write to please myself,'"[3] and that the relationship between literature and life is not his concern. His reader has other ideas. Upon hearing that Bannister is about to issue a pro-monarchical poem, Roberts becomes an avenging force:

His head racked him more and more. Connected thought seemed to become impossible; he could do nothing but repeat again and again, 'The traitor! The traitor!' ... [The] moon shone placidly down on the solitary figure of the maddened man, wrestling with his unconquerable rage. He could not stem it; yielding to its impulse, with quivering voice and face working with passion, he stretched fist to the sky and cried,
    'By God, he shall pay for it!'[4]

Unlike "JONES," the reader of mid-century who was content to vent his spleen quite harmlessly, Roberts arms himself and sets out to ambush the writer whose work has let him down. Nothing but pure chance prevents him from killing the poet, as the shots meant for Bannister hit a female companion instead.

Though Anthony Hope's version of the encounter between writer and reader may be a somewhat extreme and sensationalized one, it is certainly not unique in its decade. It comes amid a flood of fiction that dramatizes what can only be called terrorist attacks – shootings, burnings, and verbal snipings – inflicted both upon authors themselves and upon their manuscripts by angry readers. It comes, too, as part of a body of less melodramatic stories and novels that show authors thrown, often unwillingly, into social contact with their own readers, contact that is problematic and uncomfortable, at the least, on both sides. In the course of some of these encounters, writers become the victims of their readers' desires, as the passions awakened by the published texts are translated into a longing for spiritual or even erotic possession of the creators behind the works. In a few of these cases, the writers flee; in others, they are drawn into the temptation of allowing intimacies purely for literary purposes, in order to turn their readers into new "copy," but then are left afterwards with the responsibility for models who refuse to vanish from the scene when their artistic usefulness has ended. Sometimes, death is the only escape from the pursuing reader.

The frequent intrusion into these imaginative works of readers as characters offers concrete evidence of contemporary uncertainty about the boundaries between Art and Life, and contemporary fear of the effect upon the former of the latter. For fiction writers of the 1890s, reality, clearly enough, could not be trusted to keep its place, even if one could define satisfactorily what that place might be. And the fictional portrayal of readers as violent, judgmental, and demanding – often, as Avenging Angels, out to rectify some perceived wrong committed by the artist-figures – seems indicative of a widespread anxiety, even a sense of guilt, on the part of the writers themselves, troubled about the degree to which they were going to Life for the material of their Art, while denying that they owed any duties to the world in return. Far from having worked out a consistent theory of the proper relations between the actual and the imaginary, or between the artist and society, aesthetes, realists, New Women novelists, and naturalists alike were plagued by doubts as to how these elements were to be integrated. Their confusion, in turn, left them feeling intellectually defenseless against assaults from representatives of Life, unable to tell such critics to "take warning and go elsewhere." When let loose upon the imagination, such doubts also generated nightmarish pictures of authors at the mercy of imminent attack.

Not all these intrusive reader-figures can be dismissed as products of paranoid fancy. Certainly, there were concrete changes in the climate of late-Victorian publishing that made it increasingly difficult for authors to know how to define themselves in relation to the world around them or how to anticipate what their audiences might require of them. Writers at the end of the century were indeed vulnerable to the invasion by Life of their personal domains in a way that their earlier Victorian counterparts had not been. The disintegration of the circulating libraries at the start of the nineties, and with it the loss of a dependable market for fiction, forced publishers to come up with aggressive techniques for generating public interest both in literature and in its makers. Under these new conditions, anonymity and privacy were all but impossible to retain, as publishers released photographs of authors, used details of their lives as part of normal publicity campaigns, and pressured them to talk to journalists. Such methods were by no means confined to the presses catering to "mass" tastes. Beginning with Volume IV (January 1895) of the *Yellow Book*, John Lane ran as a feature in that esoteric periodical a series called "Bodley Heads" – portraits of writers with books on the lists of his Bodley Head firm. That these portraits had been commissioned from the likes of Walter Sickert and William Rothenstein softened, but by no means obscured, the commercial intent of the enterprise.

Among the "trade," as opposed to "art" publishers, of course, undisguised efforts to lure readers with the promise of possessing images of their favorite authors abounded. T. Fisher Unwin issued *Dreams* (1891) with a reproduction of a signed photograph, inscribed "Yours faithfully," of Olive Schreiner; Chatto & Windus sold Mark Twain's *Pudd'nhead Wilson* in 1895 "With Portrait"; and Ward, Lock, Bowden & Co. reissued George Meredith's *The Tragic Comedians* in 1891 "With a Photogravure Portrait of the Author" and "Two other Portraits Engraved on Wood," while also producing a large paper edition of *The Tale of Chloe* (1895) "containing a recent photogravure portrait of Mr. Meredith . . . [and] a photogravure of the Chalet at Box Hill," as the advertisements stated. Readers of Thomas Hardy, meanwhile, were offered the luxury of a "Photogravure Portrait of the Author" in each of the volumes of the Wessex Novels series done by Sampson Low, Marston & Co. in the early nineties.

An author who managed to keep his or her image out of print still had to face persistent requests by journalists for personal interviews and public statements. The proliferation in the nineties of such new magazines as the *Bookman* and the *Book Buyer*, wholly given over to the subject of authors and authorship, meant that writers and their lives were under perpetual scrutiny by professional gossip-mongers. As the hero of Henry James's "John Delavoy" (1898) explains to a naive woman being pumped for details about her late brother, an author, for a piece in a literary journal:

'Don't you know what he [Mr. Beston, the journal's editor] means by wanting you to be personal?'

In the way she looked at me there was still for a moment a dim desire to spare him – even perhaps a little to save him. None the less, after an instant, she let herself go. 'Something horrible?'

'Horrible; so long, that is, as it takes the place of something more honest and really so much more clean. He wants – what do they call the stuff? – anecdotes, glimpses, gossip, chat; a picture of his 'home life,' domestic habits, diet, dress, arrangements – all his little ways and little secrets, and even, to better it still, all your own, your relations with him, your feelings about him, his feelings about *you*: both his and yours, in short, about anything else you can think of. Don't you see what I mean?'[5]

The industry of literary biography had been gearing up throughout the 1880s. There had been a steady flow of biographies produced in the traditional way – that is, by the relatives or friends of dead writers; into this category fell J. W. Cross's *George Eliot's Life* (1885), Sir Francis Darwin's *Life and Letters of Charles Darwin* (1887), and W. M. Rossetti's *Dante Gabriel Rossetti as Designer and Writer* (1889). But the eighties had also seen the growth of a new phenomenon started by publishing houses: the biography series, committed to turning out a certain number of "lives" a year, under the guidance of an editor who matched the recently dead subject with a hack willing to undertake the work. Among the more distinguished examples of the type were Macmillan's "English Men of Letters" series, Walter Scott's "Great Writers" series, and W. H. Allen's "Eminent Women." In the early nineties, with these and similar ventures thriving and with volumes of the *Dictionary of National Biography* also appearing at the rate of one every three months, the earlier perception of writers' lives as belonging to the public domain but as open only to posthumous inspection began to alter. If information about authors could be made into popular entertainment and sold for a profit after the subjects were dead, then why not while they were still alive? The result of this shift in the nineties toward invading the privacy of living writers was a collection such as Helen C. Black's *Notable Women Authors of the Day*, published by Bryce in January of 1893. For the sum of ten shillings and sixpence, the reader could, as the advertisements promised, satisfy his or her curiosity about the "personal characteristics and the drawing-rooms of various writers" from Eliza Lynn-Linton to Edna Lyall, while gazing upon their accompanying portraits.

Middle-brow journals of the nineties were filled with features such as "The Writing of 'Dodo.' A Talk with Mr. E. F. Benson," which appeared in the *Bookman* of November 1893. The article in question is a typical one, not just for its attempt at describing "domestic habits," but for its effort to connect the characters in Benson's novel, *Dodo*, with actual figures from the author's life. Indeed, at one point in the piece, the author is cornered into insisting defensively that his heroine "is not the portrait of any one person. More than half of it was written before I ever met the lady who was stated to be the original of the character. Dodo is – to put it briefly – a compound of many characters blended in one type."[6] Journalists of the nineties must bear more than a little blame, not only for increasing the writers' sense of exposure to a prying public, but for confusing the already blurry demarcations between their lives and their fiction which novelists were so desperately trying to make.

Photographs, not merely of faces, but of residences and their interiors, portrait drawings, articles and interviews all gave the audience a new sense of access to writers, while heightening the writers' own sense of impending invasion. Perhaps most insidious was the founding, at the end of the decade, of Herbert Morrah's *The Literary Year-Book*, an annual purportedly produced for the benefit of writers themselves, with lists of typists, explanations of proofreaders' marks, and tables for calculating royalties. In fact, however, its main feature was its Directory of Authors, in which pseudonymous identities were exploded and home addresses were published. Authors who offered only the name of a publisher or of a club as an address were scarcely better protected; for the *Year-Book* also included the locations of these institutions.

Throughout the nineties, the movement in England was toward greater and greater exposure of the artist, so it should not surprise us to find a sense of vulnerability to the public working its way into fictional situations. In Richard Le Gallienne's "The Woman's Half-Profits" (1894), for instance, the new publicity techniques are the means by which a discarded lover catches up with the poet who has used their affair to inspire his work:

Rondel, however, had for some time kept his address a secret from Annette. But the candle set upon a hill cannot be hid: fame has its disadvantages. To a man with creditors or any other form of 'a past,' it is no little dangerous to have his portrait in the *Review of Reviews*. A well-known publisher is an ever-present danger. By some such means Annette had found her poet.[7]

Similarly, the lovestruck protagonist of Thomas Hardy's "An Imaginative Woman" (1894) is able, by using her contact with a newspaper editor, to track down and nearly to contrive a meeting with the man whose poetry obsesses her. Although Oscar Wilde had inaugurated the nineties with his confident assertion that "To reveal art and conceal the artist is art's aim,"[8] with each passing year of the decade it became clearer that art would not offer a very effective hiding-place from the determined reader. Even Wilde himself would discover the bitter truth of this after the stoning of his publishers' offices provoked by his arrest in 1895.

Compounding the sense of defenselessness felt by authors of the nineties was a justifiable uncertainty about the composition and character of the audience receiving their works. No longer was the average reader a "JONES" at his club or a clergyman's daughter. Indeed, there did not appear to be an average reader. The polite middle-class public which had dictated taste and conduct for much of the Victorian age was being infiltrated by a great unknown, the "Populace" of Matthew Arnold's *Culture and Anarchy* (1869). As Nigel Cross notes in *The Common Writer: Life in Nineteenth-Century Grub Street*, "The literary market-place amounts to the number of people able and willing to read. By the

1890s there was a general belief that the 1870 Education Act (which extended state education at primary level) had trebled the reading population and created a monstrous half-educated audience for new, lighter, cheaper reading matter."[9] Certainly, if there was much speculation as to what this new audience would ask of literature, there was little doubt among contemporary observers as to what it would reject. H. G. Wells's account, in *Experiment in Autobiography*, of this period emphasizes the reading public's impatience with anything but truth to life, and that life its own:

The habit of reading was spreading to new classes with distinctive needs and curiosities. They did not understand and enjoy the conventions and phrases of Trollope and Jane Austen, or the genteel satire of Thackeray, they were outside the 'governing class' of Mrs. Humphry Ward's imagination, the sombre passions and inhibitions of the Brontë country or of Wessex or Devonshire had never stirred them, and even the humours of Dickens no longer fitted into their everyday experiences.[10]

On such an audience, any fine distinction between literature as a transcription of fact and literature as a transmutation of fact through the medium of artistic invention would be lost, as would all notions of "conventions," of "poetic license," or of what we would now call narrative strategies. The writer could expect to suffer the consequences of being identified with his or her own protagonists or personae by the sort of "innocent reader" whom Henry James described in "Glasses" (1896) – one "for whom the story is 'really true.'"[11] And such a reader might well direct feelings aroused by a text, whether of hatred or of love, toward the unwitting author.

Thackeray's "JONES" of the 1840s, comfortably settled in his club, knew better than to bridge the physical distance between himself and the writer of the novel he was reading. But there were indeed reports current in the nineties of actual readers in this new literate class forcing themselves upon authors. Perhaps the most notorious example was the treatment of Kipling, who, fed up with persecution by unmannerly admirers, was driven to flee Rottingdean in 1902 for a more secluded village. As Angus Wilson has recorded in *The Strange Ride of Rudyard Kipling*,

It was a remove from increasing involvement with the masses to near-isolation, for even in the five years of their stay at Rottingdean, changes in social habit had brought ever more horse-bus loads of holidaymakers from Brighton two and a half miles away to what had so little time before been a quiet village green. More and more people were taking holidays and asking more from them. Kipling was now a very famous man and it was a natural part of some Brighton holidays to go out and see where he lived. This prying and peeping led to much disagreeableness – Naulakha with trippers rather than reporters – and anyway, the house was right beside the green and the high walls did not preserve the family privacy.[12]

To middle-class writers of the nineties, the literary enthusi-asms of this new group of readers seemed as immoderate, and as potentially threatening, as their dislikes. George Gissing's "Spellbound," published in the *English Illustrated Magazine* of October 1897, is a fictional portrait of just such a crazed, ill-educated graduate of the recently established National Schools – a young draper's assistant being driven mad by his passion for print:

As it happened, his route led him past the doors of a newly-opened Free Library. It was like the sight of a public-house to the habitual drinker; he quivered under the temptation, and whipped himself forward; but his weary legs were traitorous. The reading-room, with its smell of new print, once more drugged his conscience, and there he sat until nightfall.

After this he yielded utterly to his vice . . . No matter the subject, its display in fresh-smelling print sufficed to interest him, or, at all events, to hold his eyes; there he stood, spellbound, unresisting, oblivious of everything save his gratification in the mere act of reading.[13]

Fortunately, it does not occur to him, as it did to the holi-daymakers in Brighton, to go off in pursuit of the authors whose works hold him in subjection. This, however, is the purpose in life of another Gissing character, the relentless Linda Vassie of "At High Pressure," which appeared in the *Sketch* of February 1896. Linda, the product of a family attempting to raise itself "above the lower middle-class degree in which they began,"[14] bombards helpless writers with a rain of opinions and requests: "Scarcely a book, magazine, or newspaper came into her hands which did not suggest a letter of inquiry, criticism, or sympathy;

her collection of autographs was very large, and she rejoiced loudly over every important addition to it."[15] But letters alone will not content her, and she violates the distance between writer and reader whenever she can. As the narrator says ironically, "Her desire to form intimacies with people of name sometimes led her into an unpleasant situation. Civil coldness did not discourage her, and to the hints which would have rebuffed a sensitive woman she was, happily, obtuse."[16]

The woman reader in general, regardless of her class, appears to have been another source of anxiety for fiction writers of the nineties. Women had traditionally composed much of the market for literature throughout the nineteenth century, but statistics indicate that the share of female readers among the book-buying public was greater than ever at the end of the Victorian period. Nigel Cross attributes this development to "the impact of the Board schools" established by the Education Act, which expanded "equal educational opportunities for girls. After 1870 the literacy rate . . . increased from 80.6 per cent of men and 73.2 per cent of women in 1871 to 93.6 per cent of men and 92.7 per cent of women by 1891."[17] Of these readers, an unknown number could be expected to belong, unlike their earlier Victorian counterparts, to the growing ranks of the "New Women" who had broken with stereotypes of feminine docility and adopted instead a questioning, critical stance toward all demonstrations of male authority, including male authorship. Even Gissing's Linda Vassie, that voracious cultural magpie, has picked up, we are told, an interest in the "cause of 'womanhood.'"[18] That some of the most hostile and violently dangerous reader-characters in nineties fiction – such as Annette in Le Gallienne's "The Woman's Half-Profits" and Letty Moore of Hubert Crackanthorpe's "A Conflict of Egoisms" (1893), who shreds the only copy of a manuscript – turn out to be strong-willed and independent women does suggest a correspondence between the increasing visibility of the "emancipated" female and the increasing nervousness of the male writer.

Male fear of the "New Woman," however, will not in itself account for the full range of fictional situations in works of the nineties showing writers impinged upon or imperilled by their readers. Although Annette comes stalking the poet–protagonist with a gun in "The Woman's Half-Profits," so too does the title character of *The Lady Charlotte* (1898), a novel by a woman, who could scarcely have had reason to fear assaults by her own sex. In Adeline Sergeant's tale, Lady Charlotte, a conservative aristocrat who is by no means the sort to have "views" on the "Sex Question," coolly packs a revolver when she calls on the author who has drawn upon some of her family history without permission in his latest book. Her warning to the trembling Arthur Ellison – "'Now, look here. It sounds melodramatic, but it isn't, it's deadly earnest. You will do what I tell you, or I shall shoot you dead'"[19] – is a chilling one, but without any feminist message whatever about the status of women. Lady Charlotte's only crusade is to hold the author accountable for his unacknowledged borrowings from life and his distortions of fact. As she says while pointing her weapon at his head, "'You will write down, on this paper, that you told a deliberate lie, and that you humbly beg my pardon for it, and for the other lies and slanders contained in your vile and abominable book.'"[20] In Adeline Sergeant's work, at least, dread of the reader who refuses to honor the excuse of "poetic license," or to separate literature from life, cuts right across the lines of sex.

Indeed, any simple equation between the emergence of the "New Woman" in British society and the appearance of aggressive, dominating reader-figures in fiction breaks down in the face of numerous examples of male characters who pursue or threaten artists of both sexes. One of the most fascinating instances in this period of just such a reader-character stalking an author involves a predatory man and a beleaguered female poet. Gertrude Warden's *The Sentimental Sex* (1896) begins as a comic novel, but turns into a new sort of tragedy – a tragedy of misreading, in which misinterpretation of a literary text ruins two lives and causes one death. The reader is an unsophisticated Australian colonist, Niel Vansittart, who becomes obsessed with *Rainbow Lights*, a volume of poems by an Englishwoman using the pseudonym "Iris." Warden cleverly opens the novel with one of these verses – an overheated collection of erotic clichés about "pulses throbbing at the memory alone of your touch" and "burning ... lips upon my own" – to show us how far off the mark Vansittart is in seeing them as innocent love lyrics and in expecting their author to be the girl of his Angel-in-the-House fancies:

'[S]he is my ideal of womanhood: intellectual, refined, and lovely, full of sympathy, full of soul, brimming over with feeling and poetry and beautiful thoughts – a creature far too delicate and high-strung and sensitive to endure rough contact with the world.'[21]

He constructs his own version of the poems themselves, then of the author responsible for them, his passion fed by the promotional campaign of the volume's publishers, who have tried to compensate for the bad reviews of *Rainbow Lights* by issuing a new edition with a glamorous photograph of "Iris" as the lure. Ownership of her image increases the reader's sense of ownership of the unknown author, while also turning all other purchasers of the book into rivals. As Niel himself explains,

'I bought up all the copies of "Rainbow Lights" which contained the portrait. I didn't want other men to be looking at her, and then giving utterance in my hearing to such sacrilegious sort of remarks as that she was "confoundedly pretty." I had the picture copied on ivory by a miniature painter and placed in a locket which I wore on my watch-chain.'[22]

Sure that the moods of loneliness and of longing he has found in the text are transcriptions of autobiographical fact – "'The whole scene came before me just as though I had been a witness of it . . . that lovely, fragile girl, sighing her heart out amid such unresponsive surroundings'"[23] – Niel decides that he is the answer to "Iris's" *cri de cœur*. He sends an offer of marriage in care of her publishers and is undeterred by the publishers' reply, informing him that his is the thirty-fourth such proposal. In fact, he sets sail for England and does at last corner "Iris," a.k.a. Isabel Lambert, an experienced, cynical, very "modern" young widow to whom writing poetry is merely a way of supporting herself. Wilfully blind to the difference between his image of "Iris" and the author herself, he insists upon possessing her anyway. His argument is that the powerful effect of her art upon his life has created a bond between them and, therefore, given him the right to claim her in return: "'You have shaped my life for more than two years; you have drawn me over the sea like a magnet; you want me, you belong to me, just as I belong to you and want you.'"[24]

The relentlessness and fervor of his pursuit does eventually wear her down; she marries him, saying openly that she does so for his money, so that she can afford to stop writing for a living. After their marriage, however, the ardent reader becomes a controlling reader, who not only demands that the author go on producing literature, but that all future work must reflect and validate his own sense of reality. "Iris" records, with mixed sarcasm and horror, how

that same afternoon he suggested to me in all seriousness that as we had now been married five months, it was quite time that I composed another 'Rainbow Lights' volume all about my love for *him*.

'Love ennobled by the holy sacrament of marriage,' he explained. 'The only love worth having.'

I had to swallow down an irreverent desire to break into Book of Nonsense rhymes on the spot. Fancy my writing 'to order' about my feelings for Mr Vansittart!

> 'I once had a husband named Niel,
> Who talked of his soul a good deal.'

Or,

> 'I had a little husband: his height was
>   six feet four,
> He talked about his feelings till he became
>   a bore.'[25]

Inevitably, the relationship between writer and reader comes apart, making the latter ever more desperate and violent. This time, however, the murderous impulse vents itself in suicide; Niel turns the gun upon himself. The suicide note he leaves – addressed not to Isabel, but to "Iris" – could serve as a coda to any one of dozens of stories or novels of the 1890s about monomaniacal readers out to possess and to reshape both texts and authors according to their own desires, to bring Art and Life into alignment with each other: "Oh Iris, if it could have been real and you could have loved me!"[26]

The encroachment of journalism and advertising upon the world of publishing, changes in the composition of the reading public, even the rise of unfamiliar social and sexual types – all were, to the imaginations of writers of the 1890s, unsettling developments. Some of these do help to account for what one might call the "Orpheus Complex" of so many novelists and short story writers of the period. There had been, moreover, an actual band of maenads at work in England since the late 1880s in the form of the National Vigilance Association, ready to tear both "pernicious" literature and its offending creators limb from limb. Fear of censorship and brickbats from such an organization contributed to the nervousness of already nervous authors, particularly after the jailing in 1889 of Henry Vizetelly for publishing Zola in translation and after the Oscar Wilde trials in 1895.

Yet the range and variety of the bullying, grasping readers who appear in 1890s fiction, and the breadth and diversity of their demands, suggests that no single environmental factor, and indeed no set of such factors either, can really be held up as the cause of this phenomenon. Too many of these avenging reader-characters are quite literally close to home; they are not merely members of the public at large, but also of the author-characters' own domestic circles. The writer-figures have chosen them in marriage or chosen to maintain familial ties with them, despite their evident hostility to Art for its own sake. In "William Foster," a short story from Robert Hichens's *Tongues of Conscience* (1900), a wife murders her husband, because he refuses to write " 'a good book, a book to make people better and happier' "[27] and continues instead to publish amoral, "poisonous" fiction, the product of a " 'black imagination ... that will come like a suffocating cloud upon the imaginations of others ...' "[28] In *The Murder of Delicia* by Marie Corelli (1896), a husband drives his novelist–wife to an early grave through his combination of flagrant adultery and carping criticism of her work for its lack of " 'a proper sense of delicacy.' "[29] Mr. Gresley, beloved brother of the writer Hester Gresley in Mary Cholmondeley's *Red Pottage* (1899), burns the only copy of the manuscript of her second novel when he finds, after a surreptitious reading, that " 'She has entirely disregarded my expressed wishes' " in it: " 'I told her after the "Idyll," that I desired she would not mention the subject of religion in her next book, and this is worse than ever,' " he says peevishly before lighting the bonfire.[30] Mrs. Chantry, of Rhoda Broughton's *A Beginner* (1894), buys up from the publisher and destroys the entire edition of her niece's three-volume novel, because it contains "advanced" scenes which she misreads as shameful proof of the girl's fall: "'They do not read like second-hand!'" she accuses, deaf to the author's plea that they are merely the products of "'imagination and intuition.'"[31] The criminal assaults in these works, whether upon the lives of the authors or upon the integrity of their creative endeavors, are all what we might call "inside jobs," accomplished by readers close to the artist-figures. But they also become "inside jobs" in another sense. In the latter two cases, where only the manuscripts perish, the author-characters themselves go on to forgive their attackers; in Broughton's novel, the fledgling artist even learns to internalize her aunt's standards and so to forswear writing entirely, transforming her anger at conventional barriers into guilt at having dared to transgress them.

Guilt is the buried emotion that surfaces throughout imaginative works of the nineties. To find the root of these recurring nightmares of exposure, of entrapment, and of violence being done both to the artist-figures and to their manuscripts, one must discard the popular notion of the late-Victorian writer. The pose of the self-confidently "advanced" Artist, dedicated to Art alone and either careless of the judgments of others or taking pleasure in shocking and outraging them was merely that – a pose or, to use a more Wildean term, a "mask." Behind it lay a complicated and confused sensibility, peculiar to the decade, that revealed itself in fictions of artists hunted down and punished. Far from being at war merely with middle-class mores, or with journalists, or with a socially and culturally uneducated reading public, the writers of the nineties were at odds with themselves, advocating total freedom for Art from the tyranny of Life on the one hand, yet bound to Life for their subject matter and inspiration on the other. These avenging readers who pursued the male and female artist-heroes in fiction were the phantoms unleashed by the authors' own consciences.

For the average author whose career began in the nineties, the transition from being a Victorian reader to becoming a late-Victorian writer was by no means smooth. Such writers, born between 1850 and 1870, had grown up with the works and ideals of Dickens and George Eliot as influential presences (at least one of these later writers, George Gissing, never abandoned his youthful loyalty to Dickens, despite his rejection of Dickens's social aesthetic). Long before Zola, whose works were not published in England until the 1880s, and other European realists arrived to inform them that artists owed no responsibility to the society they dissected, George Eliot had impressed upon them that fiction should "give the loving pains of a life to the faithful representing of commonplace things";[32] that fiction must, moreover, be grounded in the artist's own sympathy for his or her characters, must generate further sympathy in the reader, and must spread sympathy from the text outward into the world.

Abandoning this notion of a "loving" connection between Art and Life was surely as wrenching for some late-Victorians as giving up Christianity had been for their predecessors. And what succeeded it was the bleak prospect of viewing experience – social ties, erotic and romantic encounters, and losses – as nothing more than insignificant threads to be woven into the pattern of a literary work, the condition described by a character in Broughton's *A Beginner* of feeling oneself "bound to regard the whole of creation as 'copy.'"[33] The new aesthetic of the 1890s made writers cynical; as the narrator says of the artist-heroine in *A Writer of Books* (1898) by "George Paston" (pseudonym of Emily Morse Symonds), "She had learnt sharp lessons in the book of life during the past year, and they would make useful copy; that was all that they were good for."[34] But the new aesthetic also left writers feeling guilty; as we are told about Cosima Chudleigh, heroine of *A Writer of Books*, at the instant when her future husband proposes,

Even at that agitating moment she could not help taking mental notes of his manner and appearance. He was the first man who had made genuine love to her, and the experience was much too valuable to be lost ... She felt suddenly ashamed of her cold-blooded observation of these details at such a time, and with an effort forced her attention to the consideration of his hurried, broken words.[35]

Cosima's penitence and remorse increase a hundredfold after the wedding. She realizes that she has married to be able to "treat adequately of the elemental passion of love" in her work – "to gain the knowledge and experience which are necessary for success in the art of fiction" – but that no divorce is possible once the "experience" has been acquired.[36] The benefit to her art brings no corresponding improvement to life, her own or anybody else's. Indeed, as the novelist-figure in Ellen Thorney-croft Fowler's *Concerning Isabel Carnaby* (1898) also learns, turning one's acquaintances into fiction merely breeds resentment and increases the hostility between artists and society; for the models become readers of the published text and, unable to believe in the notion of composite types, "see" themselves in it. As Lady Farley, in *Concerning Isabel Carnaby*, says acerbically of the author of a fictional treatment of her social circle, "It was somewhat ill-bred of Mr. Seaton to abuse our hospitality by making copy of our faults . . ."[37]

The reader as Avenging Angel, then, represents the flip side of the figure of the exploited model – a subconscious acknowledg-ment by writers of the 1890s that art could neither be produced in a vacuum nor received in one. To behave as though one's literary imagination and the fruits of it where wholly autonomous was to invite the appearance of Nemesis, armed with a revolver, a marriage proposal, or both. Just when Hyacinth Rondel, the self-satisfied poet in Le Gallienne's "The Woman's Half-Profits," begins gloating over the commercial success of his love lyrics, "one of those discarded Muses who sometimes remain upon the poet's hands as Fates" invades his study.[38] Annette Jones has read his volumes and, despite Rondel's own insistence that "As a matter of fact, several ladies had 'stood' for the series," she has "with burning cheek and stormy bosom, recognized herself in many an intimate confession."[39] The battle between them that follows, waged at the point of her gun, is both comical in dramatic terms and serious in its aesthetic implications:

'Man! are you so *great* that you have lost the sense of pity?' . . . she continued, 'an artist pays his model at least a shilling an hour, and it is only her body he paints: but you use body and soul, and offer her nothing . . .'

'I give you immortality. Poor fly, I give you amber,' modestly suggested the poet.

But Annette repeated the word 'Immortality!' with a scorn that almost shook the poet's conceit, and thereupon produced an account [for half-profits on his royalties] . . . 'Either the money or the marriage. Personally, I prefer the money . . .'[40]

Despite their professions of having rejected the moral imperatives of earlier Victorian authors and despite their pose of writing solely for themselves, fiction writers of the 1890s remained haunted by doubts about the choice of Art for its own sake. Publicly, they espoused a philosophy of the superiority of Art over Life and complained bitterly whenever Life, whether in the form of inquiring journalists or overeager fans, appeared to intrude upon their domains. Yet as the recurring confrontations between author-figures and reader-characters in their work show, the novelists and short-story writers of the nineties could not shake the feeling that Life, too, deserved its "Half-Profits" and would someday come to claim them.

NOTES

1 William Thackeray, *Vanity Fair*, ed. J. I. M. Stewart (London: Penguin Books, 1968), pp. 43–44.

2 Anthony Hope, *A Change of Air* (London: Methuen, 1893), p. 71.

3 *Ibid.*, p. 133.

4 *Ibid.*, p. 175.

5 Henry James, "John Delavoy," in *The Complete Tales of Henry James*, ed. Leon Edel (London: Rupert Hart-Davis, 1964), IX, 428.

6 Raymond Blathwayt, "The Writing of 'Dodo.' A Talk with Mr. E. F. Benson," *Bookman*, November 1893, p. 51.

7 Richard Le Gallienne, "The Woman's Half-Profits," in *Prose Fancies* (London: Elkin Mathews & John Lane, 1894), p. 39.

8 Oscar Wilde, "The Preface," in *The Picture of Dorian Gray* (London: Ward, Lock and Co., 1891), p.v.

9 Nigel Cross, *The Common Writer: Life in Nineteenth-Century Grub Street* (Cambridge: Cambridge University Press, 1985), p. 205.

10 H. G. Wells, *Experiment in Autobiography* (London: Victor Gollancz, 1934), II, 506–7.

11 Henry James, "Glasses," in *The Complete Tales of Henry James*, IX, 329.

12 Angus Wilson, *The Strange Ride of Rudyard Kipling: His Life and Works* (New York: Viking Press, 1978), p. 260.

13 George Gissing, "Spellbound," in *A Victim of Circumstances and Other Stories* (London: Constable & Co., 1927), p. 265.

14 George Gissing, "At High Pressure," in *Human Odds and Ends: Stories and Sketches* (London: Lawrence and Bullen, 1898), p. 277.

15 *Ibid.*, p. 278.
16 *Ibid.*, p. 282.
17 Cross, p. 206.
18 Gissing, "At High Pressure," p. 279.
19 Adeline Sergeant, *The Lady Charlotte: A Novel* (London: Hutchinson & Co., 1898), p. 290.
20 *Ibid.*
21 Gertrude Warden, *The Sentimental Sex* (London: John Lane, 1896), p. 57.
22 *Ibid.*, pp. 22–23.
23 *Ibid.*, p. 20.
24 *Ibid.*, p. 110.
25 *Ibid.*, pp. 148–49.
26 *Ibid.*, p. 225.
27 Robert Hichens, "William Foster," in *Tongues of Conscience* (London: Methuen, 1900), p. 151.
28 *Ibid.*, p. 143.
29 Marie Corelli, *The Murder of Delicia* (London: Skeffington & Son, 1896), p. 129.
30 Mary Cholmondeley, *Red Pottage* (1899; reprinted London: Virago Press, 1985), p. 260.
31 Rhoda Broughton, *A Beginner* (London: Richard Bentley and Son, 1894), p. 41.
32 George Eliot, *Adam Bede*, ed. Stephen Gill (London: Penguin Books, 1980), p. 224.
33 Broughton, p. 41.
34 George Paston, *A Writer of Books* (London: Chapman & Hall, 1898), p. 272.
35 *Ibid.*, pp. 144–45.
36 *Ibid.*, p. 43.
37 Ellen Thorneycroft Fowler, *Concerning Isabel Carnaby* (London: Hodder and Stoughton, 1898), pp. 219–20.
38 Le Gallienne, p. 38.
39 *Ibid.*, pp. 39–40.
40 *Ibid.*, pp. 40–42.

10

Fact and fiction in biography

PHYLLIS ROSE

Writing about innovation in the novel, Virginia Woolf noted the courage it took for a novelist to say that "what interests him is no longer 'this' but 'that.' " She expanded, "For the moderns 'that,' the point of interest, lies very likely in the dark places of psychology. At once, therefore, the accent falls a little differently ... The emphasis is laid in such unexpected places that at first it seems as if there were no emphasis at all; and then, as the eyes accustom themselves to twilight and discern the shape of things in a room we see how complete the story is, how profound." Woolf was showing people how to read the fiction of Chekhov, as well as her own fiction and that of Joyce and Proust. She was signaling a shift in the novel's representation of reality, and I suggest that biography has come to the same point and is about to make a similar mimetic shift. Because of its peculiar relationship to what we call "fact" – it seems to have an obligation to the empirical world that the novel does not have – biography is more conservative aesthetically than the novel. In elements of composition, such as plot, characterization, and point of view, biography follows where the novel leads. Biography – and I mean by that the highest reaches of biographic art, self-conscious, artful biography, composed and not compiled biography – aspires to the condition of the novel.

Of all ways of readjusting our sense of what is important, choice of subject is the most palpable. We can agree, I think, that biographies are being written about kinds of people they were not being written about twenty years ago. Women, for example. Women who are not movie stars, who are not Wallis Simpson, who are not Helen Keller or Eleanor Roosevelt. In the past twenty years we have had biographies of Edith Wharton, George Eliot, Virginia Woolf, and Willa Cather. We have had both "standard biographies" and interpretive biographies. Even though these women writers had to wait so much longer than their male contemporaries for biographical attention, there seems now to be a great deal to say about them. Why has it taken so long for women to be the subjects of biographies? Obviously, because they were not important. As Henry James put it in the preface to *The Portrait of a Lady*, "Millions of presumptuous girls, intelligent or not, daily affront their destiny, and what is it open to their destiny to be, at the most, that we should make an ado about it? . . . The novel is of its very nature an ado." A biography is as much or more of an ado. And what does a person have to do or be to merit one?

Until recently, one thing you had to be – whatever your calling – was successful. You had to be the Great Writer or the Famous Person. In the preface to her inventive biography of Mary Ellen Peacock Meredith, Diane Johnson wrote a kind of manifesto in favor of what she calls, in the title of the book, *Lesser Lives*:

Many people have described the Famous Writer presiding at his dinner table, in a clean neckcloth. He is famous; everybody remembers his remarks. He remembers his own remarks, being a writer, and notes them in his diary. We forget that there were other people at the table – a quiet person, now muffled by time, shadowy, whose heart pounded with love, perhaps, or rage, or fear when our writer shuffled in from his study . . . A lesser life does not seem lesser to the person who leads one. His life is very real to him; he is not a minor figure in it. He looks out of his eyes at our poet, our chronicled statesman . . . And he is our real brother.

Now Mary Ellen Peacock Meredith was a bad girl. She did not love her husband, the Famous Writer George Meredith, and she committed adultery with a painter named Henry Wallis, not nearly so famous. Meredith, unable to comprehend this offence, concluded she was mad, and it was with a reputation for insanity that Mary Ellen Peacock made her tangential way into posterity. Diane Johnson's revisionist book shows why Mary Ellen might have wanted to make love with a man who was not her husband and have believed herself justified in doing so; it does not require us to believe she was insane. Telling the story from her point of view inevitably changes the story told. In fact, I would argue that telling her story at all changes the story told. It is customary, says Johnson, to treat Mary Ellen in a paragraph or a page as an episode in the life of her husband or her father. Her life can, of course, be looked upon that way, "but it cannot have seemed that way to her."

Another example of the way in which a brilliant and daring choice of subject inevitably raises a whole new set of concerns was provided by Jean Strouse's *Alice James*. Alice was the sister of Henry and William James, the one known as a novelist, the other as a psychologist. Alice James was known as their sister, and an invalid. Yet she was a witty, talented woman, who left a considerable gift to posterity in the form of her letters and diary, a gift which, up to now, has been considered minor. Alice James herself acknowledged that in conventional terms her life had been a failure. No major work. No husband or children. No glory. Yet she did not quite accept conventional notions of success. In Jamesian terms success consisted of defining one's own uniqueness, and Alice James's uniqueness expressed itself in a mixture of invalidism and private writing. To quote Strouse, "Failure was a bedrock human experience she could claim as her own. An expert at suffering, she could *convert* the waste of her life into something more lasting than private unhappiness." Strouse's account of Alice James's life is virtually a meditation of the theme of failure, which is the lot, after all, of more of us than is the glory of her brothers.

The dream of writing "the lives of the obscure" is as old as biography. Dr. Johnson had it, on the grounds that "there is such an uniformity in the state of man ... that there is scarcely any possibility for good or ill, but is common to human kind." Virginia Woolf had it, on the grounds of distaste for the powerful. But neither Dr. Johnson nor Virginia Woolf made more than a beginning in this area whose time may have finally come.

One of the most vital and promising branches of biography at present is family biography, which is one way of writing the lives of the obscure. Whose imperfections, whose human inability to live up to an impossible ideal means more to us than our parents'? From Edmund Gosse's *Father and Son* to Geoffrey Wolff's

The Duke of Deception, parental biography consists in depicting – and in some way accepting – fallibility. Gosse's father was the laughingstock of the Victorian scientific establishment for trying to reconcile fundamentalist Christianity with the new science, which proved, through the fossil record, that life had evolved much more slowly than the Bible claimed. His ingenious idea was that God had planted misleading evidence in the rocks as a test of man's faith. But Edmund Gosse does not mock his father. His implicit point, like that of much family biography, is "He was a man, take him for all in all. We shall not look upon his like again." Because everybody is important at least to their children, family biography cuts across biography's bias in favor of the famous, the successful, the powerful, those whose ideas do not get laughed at and those whose books do get written, as it cuts across the genre's other great bias, the favoring of the individual over the group, so that even *Haywire* by Brooke Hayward, which comes so close to being conventional movie-star biography, seems to me, in its family orientation, exciting and innovative.

Everybody's biography – failed or successful, minor or major – is potentially worth writing. Critics may continue to judge biographies by some notion of the subject's intrinsic importance, but biographers should and will increasingly demand that the *donnée*, the given, the unquestioned premise, which Henry James argued for in the novel, be accorded them, too. It is a reviewer's cliché that a biographer is worthy of his subject, but I believe I have heard the bizarre opposite as well, that the subject was unworthy of his biographer. The subject was, if I recall correctly, neurotic, alcoholic, not a good enough poet, a flop. The biographer was criticized for not having chosen a fitter subject. But for a new generation of biographers it may be precisely such failures, insufficiencies, self-betrayals, self-erasures that make their subjects intriguing. Good biography depends, among other things, on a catalytic conjunction between subject and biographer. What is intriguing, what catalyzes the imagination, only the biographer himself or herself can determine. A personal validation on the part of the biographer is implicit: a "trust me; this will be important."

In starkly political terms, biography is a tool by which the dominant society reinforces its values. It has ignored women; it

ignores the poor and the working class; it ignores the unpriv-
ileged; it ignores noncelebrities. Such a formulation is useful
only up to a point, because in fact biography ignores almost
everyone. As a genre, it is much more elitist than the novel,
which has always taken middle-class and middling characters as
subjects. We welcome the attention that biography is now
paying to women, but the novel has been paying attention to
women for well over a century, showing a concern with the
everyday and unheroic which has nourished generations of
readers. To choose one of many possible examples, George
Eliot's portrait of Dorothea Brooke in *Middlemarch* was conceived
as a portrait of a Saint Theresa of the Midlands, a woman with the
passionate, ideal nature of a Saint Theresa, but no chance,
because of the pettiness of her circumstances, of matching Saint
Theresa's achievement. To write about women it was necessary
to write about compromise and failure and to acknowledge that
tragedy can be enacted in a bourgeois setting, when an individual's happiness and not kingdoms are at stake. Many of the
greatest novels of the nineteenth century – *Madame Bovary, Anna
Karenina, Tess of the d'Urbervilles,* and *The Portrait of a Lady* – are
based on that democratic assumption, and even as the novel
moves into the modernist period, with *Ulysses* and *Mrs. Dallo-
way,* it is still in pursuit of that elusive figure of Everyman or
Everywoman. But biography is still shaking off assumptions
about fit subjects closer to those of classical tragedy, which dealt
only with royalty and heroes, although, to satisfy our secular
sense of the sacred, it has traditionally added artists and writers.
In biography, the bourgeois–democratic revolution is just
beginning.

For, of course, what happens when you start writing biographies about the minor and failed is that they don't seem so
failed or minor anymore. When you write about the unfamous,
they become famous. About twenty years ago, for example,
Virginia Woolf was considered by the academic establishment a
quirky, secondary author. That she is now major has to do not
with any change in her intrinsic worth but with the spate of
publications, many inspired by the women's movement, which
has been devoted to her in the past years. And now that Woolf is
major, she is no longer, alas, minor. As a subject, she has lost her

subversive potential. We have gained a major writer but lost a semi-obscure life, which is as it should be. "Tomorrow to fresh woods and pastures new." Biography will find new candidates for obscurity and dominance.

I would like to turn now to another kind of innovation in biography subtler than innovation in subject matter but equally important – formal innovation, new ways of handling chronology, characterization, perspective. Every choice of form makes a statement about the way life is, changes the illusion of reality conveyed by a piece of writing. As much as his or her subject and theme, the ostensible content, an author's handling of formal variables affects what a biography says. It is because of formal innovation that contemporary biography gives the illusion of dealing more successfully and fully with the inner life than biography of the past.

Much more than the novel, which from its beginnings, in *Tristram Shandy*, has rebelled against chronology, biography has tended to begin placidly and obediently at the start of the subject's life, to proceed in an orderly and annual fashion, and to conclude with his death. If one volume concerns The Middle Years, you can be sure there will be others about The Early Years and The Later. In the great age of modernism, novelists like Joyce, Woolf, and Faulkner were fascinated by the distinction between external and internal time, between time measured by clocks and time as perceived by an individual, speeding up or slowing down in response to emotions, looping through past to future as memory and anticipation, those radical processes of the brain, destroyed the present and with it conventional chronology. A novel would seem wittily archaic if it began with its protagonist's birth and pretended to cover the activities of his or her life on an annual basis. But this is what biography generally does. Where novels routinely concentrate on the events of a brief period of time and get access to the past through memory, biography has largely denied itself this flexibility.

Along with conventional chronology goes an archetypical biographical plot: the subject is born, has a childhood full of latent talent; in early adulthood, the subject has troubles, but they are overcome; his talent, like a bulb pushing its stalk up through the ground, inevitably expresses itself. And, like a flower, his talent after a while withers, and the writer dies. Too many literary biographies still have as their guiding metaphor the organic image of the writer as a kind of plant, whose genius has a seed-time, an inevitable flowering, and a blowzy stage of decay. This image, and its correlative assumption that the child is the father of the man, dates back at least as far as Wordsworth. And it has been reinforced by Freudian psychology, which we must also hold responsible for the tedious way that most biographies begin with the least interesting part of a writer's life and seem, in some crucial ways, never to move beyond it.

It is possible to handle things differently. Justin Kaplan's *Walt Whitman* begins at the end of Whitman's life and eases artfully into a treatment of the years preceding *Leaves of Grass*, where a more conventional biography might have begun. Not only is this disruption of the usual pattern of biography refreshing aesthetically, it also seems to produce other formal changes with an impact on the biography's content. Instead of continuity of character, Kaplan emphasizes discontinuity. Whereas most biographies assume constant development and present later work as emerging from earlier, Kaplan insists there is no necessary connection between Walter Whitman, schoolteacher, printer, newspaper editor, idler about town, and hack writer of the 1840s and Walt Whitman, the author of *Leaves of Grass* and self-proclaimed "kosmos" of 1855. In Kaplan's handling of this life, there is nothing inevitable about the flowering of Whitman's genius. Instead there is a dialectic between the mundane and the miraculous – between lazy aimless hours spent riding the ferry between Brooklyn and Manhattan and the writing of the great poem *Crossing Brooklyn Ferry*. For the Freudian narrative, Kaplan substitutes the more dynamic Eriksonian paradigm of development, which presents adult life as a series of crucial adjustments and self-definitions. This Walt Whitman makes himself, unmakes himself, and remakes himself in the course of the years. "In what may have been his ultimate disguise," writes Kaplan, "he declared his belief in the existence of the real Me, the core Walt Whitman who stood apart from the pulling and hauling of events and relationships." Clearly Kaplan does not believe in "the real Me," that undissolved aspirin at the bottom of the cup of life. He believes in the partial, tentative, and temporary creation of selves. It is a more sophisticated handling of character than that usually found in biography, where the emphasis tends to be on the stable and unwavering portions of the ego. What Kaplan achieves is what Woolf called the dissolution of character and regarded as one of the modern novel's distinctive achievements. She was thinking of how character was becoming a fluid stream of consciousness, or a discontinuous series of gestures and structures, but not something that could be described in a paragraph and illustrated in a series of dramatic episodes.

Point of view is another fictional technique whose appearance in biography is recent. When it goes unconsidered, the point of view is usually that of the disciple or worshipper – the biographer, in short, who has a great deal invested in establishing his or her subject's stature. Occasionally the biographer will adopt the point of view of the detractor or deflator, but then, too, something is at stake: the subject must be special to merit taking down a peg or two. But point of view, as any fiction writer knows, can shift from scene to scene, and should, depending on what the author wants to convey.

The opening of Kaplan's life of Whitman is unusual not only for presenting the poet at the age of sixty-five, sleeping under his own roof for the first time in his life, but because it then shifts back suddenly to the situation he has just left, living with his brother, George Washington Whitman, "a blunt, practical man, inspector in a Camden pipe foundry," who does not see much difference between *Leaves of Grass* and *Hiawatha*. He is embarrassed by the impropriety of his brother's poems, by their insistent sexuality. Through the eyes of George and his wife Louisa, we see the poet initially as an exhibitionist, a misfit eccentric, a social embarrassment – an invigorating perspective with which to begin a biography of a man we too predictably defer to and whose genius, if anything, we romanticize.

Often the most radical perspective you can adopt on a person's experience is his or her own. I believe that life is as much a work of fiction – of guiding narrative structures – as novels and poems are. Each of us, influenced perhaps by one ideology or another, generates our own plot, our own symbolic landscape, a highly individual configuration of significance through which we view our own experience and which I call a personal mythology. Kaplan employs his best imaginative effort to delineate the structures of understanding and belief which Whitman himself imposed on his experience. A case in point is his handling of Whitman's homosexuality. There is no doubt that Whitman was homosexual, yet when certain English homosexuals tried to get him to declare himself publicly one of them, Whitman furiously rejected what he called their "morbid inferences." Does this mean that he had not, as we would put it, come to terms with his sexuality? Well, he had come to terms, but they were his terms, not ours. He thought of his own psychological make-up through the grid provided by phrenology, one of the ephemeral orthodoxies which filled his mind and significantly influenced the way he looked at his own life. And phrenology distinguished, naively, we might say, between love of comrades, which it called "adhesiveness," and sexual love, which it called "amativeness." Thus, when Whitman fell desperately in love with Peter Doyle, a trolley operator, and pursued him with an obsessiveness that appalled even himself, he could describe it in his diary as "diseased disproportionate feverish adhesiveness," and Kaplan does not presume to contradict him. He refrains from trying to prove conclusively things about Whitman which Whitman himself didn't know.

If you read Kaplan's biography of Whitman for information only, you may miss how much in it is new. To the extent that the way things are said changes what is said, much is new. But we have all long since learned how to handle complicated points of view, disrupted chronology, and discontinuous character in novels and films, so I think we do not appreciate how unusual such sophistication is in biography. In fact, if Kaplan's achievement as a biographer is understood, his work could help lead biography away from its stale Freudian and romantic assumptions, the increasingly sterile search for the hidden and unconscious, and towards a more invigorating presentation of the way a person wills himself into being within a vivid arena of time and place.

If artful biography follows, after a considerable time, where the novel leads, we might well ask, why the delay? Why is biography, aesthetically speaking, so conservative? The answer lies in the genre's relationship to what we trustingly call Fact. The antagonism between Fact and Art in biography is sufficiently worked over. Whether we call them history and literature or granite and rainbow, we are all aware that biography has two faces, looks in two directions. Those of us who are fond of the art of biography as opposed to the craft, who may respect compiled biography but are more interested in composed biography, sometimes regard Fact as a kind of sack of stones to be drawn behind us up the hill of literature. At the merely quantitative level, the problem is significant. Leon Edel, no mean rock piler, complained many years ago, before cassette recorders and Xerox machines, about "documentary surfeit." More recently, he has confessed to a sinking of the heart whenever he confronts another archive. The biographer of Shakespeare or Milton may yearn for more fact, but there can hardly be a biographer of any person since the middle of the last century who can wish more material available or his or her subject's life longer. I think it no accident that one of the most satisfying literary biographies ever written, Walter Jackson Bate's *John Keats*, has as its subject a writer dead by the age of twenty-six.

But if fact hampers, it also enables. The biographer, carrying a load (or working a lode) of information, cannot be so inventive as the novelist, true. The enabling part is that he *need* not be so inventive. Certain biographers – the ones who might, with a slightly different configuration of talents, have written fiction – turn to biography because they do not have to generate material from imagination. So while we may grumble about fact, we grumble as we would about a friend with a penchant for garrulousness. Fact itself is not the enemy. The enemy is an Anglo-American respect for fact which makes biographers timid and a naiveté about the nature of fact which guarantees that Standard Biographies will go on being written and being respected, if not for their readability (it has gotten quite acceptable to mock them on this score) then for their thoroughness and impartiality.

Standard biographies have been mocked for as long as people have talked about biography. Largely, the issue seems to be weight. Carlyle inveighed against valuing biographies by their heft, and there is a Greek proverb to the effect that a big book is a big pain, although whether a biography was specifically alluded to I do not know. In Strachey's preface to *Eminent Victorians*, the antagonist is Standard Biographies – "those two fat volumes with which it is our custom to commemorate the dead. Who does not know them, with their ill-digested masses of material, their slipshod style, their tone of tedious panegyric, their lamentable lack of selection, of detachment, of design?" Strachey claimed to have learned two lessons from these dreadful books: brevity and impartiality. The revolutionary principle was brevity, for it held up an aesthetic ideal. To aspire to brevity focuses attention on the act of choice in writing, on the leaving out as well as the putting in, on the fact that more is inevitably not said than said. The ideal of brevity forces you to confront the fact that in choosing to include this and not that, you have, at every moment, to invoke the authority of a chosen design, an intent to create such a portrait but not another.

What is puzzling in Strachey's preface is his idealization of impartiality. "It is [the biographer's] business to lay bare the facts of the case, as he understands them. That is what I have aimed at in this book – to lay bare the facts of some cases, as I understand them, dispassionately, impartially and without ulterior intentions." But anyone who has read so much as a paragraph of Strachey's masterpiece knows that what makes it the most delightful example of the biographer's art is precisely its "ulterior intentions," its deliciously wicked absence of impartiality. Of course he does not come right out and say that Thomas Arnold, for example, is a stuffy prig, with a tendency to mistake himself for God and his schoolboys for the Chosen People. This is what he says: "His congregation sat in fixed attention ... while he expounded the general principles both of his own conduct and that of the Almighty, or indicated the bearing of the incidents of Jewish history in the sixth century B.C. upon the conduct of English schoolboys in 1830." The ironic parallel ("both of his own conduct and that of the Almighty"), a technique learned from Gibbon and Pope, bears the burden of the critique. Now this is witty, elegant, inspired writing, but it is by no means a dispassionate laying down of the facts.

Strachey was willing to admit to an aesthetic design in his work, but not to an intellectual one. This was misleading of him, but I think very English, for the English at their best often pretend they haven't an idea in their heads. This they call objectivity. And so great is the prestige of objectivity in the Anglo-American tradition that even Strachey, Strachey with his French ways, chose to hoist that banner, when what he really practiced, generically speaking, was polemical biography, argumentative biography, biography in the service of idea.

Bloated compendiums of trivial information about famous people are too easy to attack. Why bother? What defines the genre of Standard Biography is not bloat or slipshod craftsmanship but an aspiration to comprehensiveness and impartiality. And what I hold against Standard Biographies is not that they are unreadable – the best of them are highly readable – but that they are not, as they pretend to be, impartial, any more than Strachey was. Let me give two examples which are among the most elegant and most readable modern literary biographies: Quentin Bell's *Virginia Woolf* and Gordon Haight's *George Eliot*. These are good books by any standards. Both are filled with invaluable information. Yet, full as they are, both inevitably leave things out. That is why this kind of biography, which purports to be so fair and objective, is more deceptive than the most flagrantly partisan biography. Quentin Bell leaves out a treatment of Woolf's writing, which is to say he omits much of her inner life apart from her madness, leaving us with the impression of a sick woman who depended extravagantly on a supportive husband. Gordon Haight does not omit accounts of George Eliot's writing to the extent Bell does, but he rarely speculates about her inner life, favoring the done, the said, the written. This gives all the more emphasis to the one theme he allows himself, his one speculation about George Eliot's emotional life, that she needed someone to lean on, that she was not fitted to stand alone.

Obviously I have not picked these two examples of the partiality of the impartial biography quite at random. Both Bell's biography of Woolf and Haight's of George Eliot are books about women writers by men whose assumptions about women are so deeply assimilated as to have for them the force of truth, self-evident truth. That George Eliot needed someone to lean on is supposed to be a neutral observation. But there is no neutrality. There is only greater or lesser awareness of one's bias.

And if you do not appreciate the force of what you're leaving out, you are not fully in command of what you're doing.

If artful biography follows where the novel leads, we could see even further into the future of biography by seeing where the novel is at present. And where is the novel? You could say it is heading towards biography, rushing to embrace fact. In various ways, contemporary novelists are seeking to break out of the box of subjectivity, of concern with perception and private experience, which writers like Woolf and Joyce led fiction into early in the century. In various ways contemporary novelists have been seeking to regain the amplitude and solidity of the Victorian novel. So, for example, E. L. Doctorow included in *Ragtime* historical figures – Emma Goldman, Evelyn Nesbit, J. P. Morgan, and Houdini – who are imagined as involving themselves in the lives of the fictional characters. V. S. Naipaul's novels *Guerrillas* and *A Bend in the River* were both based on nonfiction essays by Naipaul (one on Trinidad, the other on Zaïre) which to my mind surpassed the novels that followed them in aesthetic intensity. Yet the press rightly welcomed Naipaul's novels, so exotic in locale, so filled with information about the Third World, as Conradian, bringing into the novel a late-Victorian amplitude and concern with history. I would mention, finally, Norman Mailer, who has been aggressively blurring the line between nonfiction writing and fiction for many years.

His novel *The Executioner's Song* told the life story of Gary Gilmore, the condemned murderer who attracted nationwide attention in 1976 by demanding that his death sentence be enforced. The novel, which is massive – some thousand pages – covers in its vast extent only nine months or so, from the time Gilmore left prison, having spent eighteen of his thirty-five years there, until the time he was executed by a firing squad virtually before the eyes of the world. It is based on hundreds of hours of interviews with Gilmore and his friends, especially his girlfriend, Nicole Baker, and in some ways it is as much the story of these other people – Nicole, Gilmore's cousin Brenda, her shoemaker father Vern Damico, decent, kindly, well-intentioned people of no great means or figure in the world – as it is the story of Gilmore.

Fact and fiction in biography

Subtitled "A True-Life Novel," *The Executioner's Song* is so indistinguishable from a biography that the *New York Times* placed it on the fiction best-seller list only with the caveat that the book seemed like nonfiction to the editors. As a novel, it is unsettling. As a biography, the challenge it poses is awesome. The sheer mass of information Mailer inherited from Lawrence Schiller, who did the actual research, is terrifying – terrifying, too, its expense and the legal complexities involved. Yet all that information Mailer had to work with, in conjunction of course with his genius, gives the book its density, a narrative texture as complicated and full as in the greatest works of imagination. Shaking my belief that less is more, *The Executioner's Song* made me wonder if a satisfying account of anyone's life could be made out of less material or in briefer space. Massive fact clearly did not hobble Mailer. Indeed, it seems to have liberated him from the oppressive weight of his own personality. With true-life materials, he achieved the kind of intensity – like that of Boswell's *Life of Johnson* – biographers achieve only rarely.

All good biography, like all good art, depends upon a subversive effect: showing the truth, the beauty, the interest or importance of something which before would have seemed blank space, negative, trivial, something for the mind to skim rather than dwell upon in detail. The shocking effect wears off quickly. After looking at it for a decade or so, we begin to see in a Jackson Pollock painting more than the dribblings of a maniac. We begin to see the beauty almost too easily. That dreary salesman, Willy Loman, seems not an outrageous subject for a tragedy on the grand scale, but an inevitable one. The shock of the new becomes the shlock of the familiar. The innovative work becomes the standard against which another great artist must rebel, which explains why the activity of art never ceases and why biography, like the other arts, has a future.

The way people manage to live their lives without prior rehearsal is amazing and insufficiently wondered at. To provide such rehearsals vicariously, to extend one's range of lived experience, is one of literature's important functions, enabling us to live more fully because we have imagined more fully. That is true of biography and it is true of the novel. We may learn from Emma

Woodhouse's failure of insight and we may wish we had met her. We may learn from Alice James and regret or rejoice that we never met her. At some level we do not realize that Emma Woodhouse never lived and do not realize that Alice James did. While we are reading about them, the two women have the same ontological status. Both biographer and novelist deal in the selection and arrangement of detail so as to reproduce, for the reader, a certain vision of reality. Both are magicians, manipulators, creating the illusion of life and significance. But the biographer's greater feeling of obligation to some objective standard of reality – the prestige of fact – has tended to inhibit his imaginative intensity.

In the future, novelists seeking to escape from personality will discover, like Mailer, the solace of fact, and biographers will discover the truth of the imagination. The two will not, in fact, come together as seems theoretically possible because most novelists will not discover the solace of fact and most biographers will continue to write standard biographies. But it is always the exceptional case that makes the future worth looking towards.

NOTES

This article is reprinted from Rose's *Writing of Women: Essays in a Renaissance* by permission of Wesleyan University Press.

11

Jerome Hamilton Buckley: a bibliography

DAVID M. STAINES

1945

William Ernest Henley: A Study in the Counter-Decadence of the 'Nineties. Princeton: Princeton University Press, 1945; London: Oxford University Press, 1945; New York: Octagon Books, 1971.

1948

Review of *Forces in Modern British Literature, 1885–1946* by William York Tindall. *Modern Language Notes*, 63 (1948), 285–86.

1949

Twelve Hundred Years: The Literature of England, volume II. Edited by William G. Crane, Wilbur G. Gaffney, Don M. Wolfe, and Jerome H. Buckley. Harrisburg, PA: Stackpole and Heck, 1949.

1950

"The Revolt from 'Rationalism' in the Seventies and Some of its Literary Consequences." In *Booker Memorial Studies: Eight Essays on Victorian Literature in Memory of John Manning Booker, 1881–1948*. Edited by Hill Shine. Chapel Hill: University of North Carolina Press, 1950. 122–32.

"Pater and the Suppressed 'Conclusion'." *Modern Language Notes*, 65 (1950), 249–51.

1951

The Victorian Temper: A Study in Literary Culture. Cambridge, MA: Harvard University Press, 1951; London: George Allen and Unwin, 1951; London: Frank Cass, 1952; New York: Vantage Books, 1964. Reissued with a new preface, Cambridge, MA: Harvard University Press, 1969; Cambridge: Cambridge University Press, 1981.

1955

Poetry of the Victorian Period. Selected and edited with critical and explanatory notes, brief biographies, and bibliographies by Jerome Hamilton Buckley and George Benjamin Woods. Chicago: Scott, Foresman, 1955. Revised edition, Chicago: Scott, Foresman, 1965.

Review of *Walter Savage Landor: A Biography* by R. H. Super. *Journal of English and Germanic Philology,* 54 (1955), 285–87.

1956

"General Materials." In *The Victorian Poets: A Guide to Research.* Edited by Frederic E. Faverty. Cambridge, MA: Harvard University Press, 1956, 1–28. Revised edition, Cambridge, MA: Harvard University Press, 1968. 1–31.

Review of *La Poésie française en Angleterre, 1850–1890, sa fortune et son influence* by E. Hilda Dale. *Modern Language Notes,* 71 (1956), 54–56.

Review of *Le Roman et les idées en Angleterre, 1860–1914,* volume III by Madeleine L. Cazamian. *Modern Language Notes,* 71 (1956), 391–93.

"A Distrust of Voices." *New York Times Book Review,* August 5, 1956, 14. (Review of *The Hero in Eclipse in Victorian Fiction* by Mario Praz, translated by Angus Davidson.)

1957

Review of *Thackeray: The Uses of Adversity, 1811–1846* by Gordon N. Ray. *Modern Language Notes,* 72 (1957), 60–62.

1958

Poems of Tennyson. Selected with an introduction and notes by Jerome Hamilton Buckley. Boston: Houghton Mifflin, 1958.

Review of *The English Common Reader: A Social History of the Mass Reading Public 1800–1900* by Richard D. Altick. *Modern Language Notes*, 73 (1958), 132–33.

Review of *Thackeray: The Age of Wisdom* by Gordon N. Ray. *Journal of English and Germanic Philology*, 57 (1958), 823–25.

1959

Review of *A Book of Verses: FitzGerald's Rubáiyát*, edited by Carl J. Weber. *Victorian Newsletter*, 15 (1959), 20–21.

Review of *Caricatures by Max from the Collection in the Ashmolean Museum* and *Max's Nineties: Drawings 1892–1899* by Max Beerbohm. *Victorian Studies*, 2 (1959), 343–44.

1960

Tennyson: The Growth of a Poet. Cambridge, MA: Harvard University Press, 1960; London: Oxford University Press, 1961; Boston: Houghton Mifflin, 1965; Cambridge, MA: Harvard University Press, 1964.

Review of *Tennyson and The Princess: Reflections of an Age* by John Killham. *Journal of English and Germanic Philology*, 59 (1960), 164–65.

1962

Masters of British Literature, second edition, volume II. Edited by Robert A. Pratt, D. C. Allen, F. P. Wilson, James R. Sutherland, Carlos Baker, Jerome H. Buckley, Francis E. Mineka, and Richard Ellmann. Boston: Houghton Mifflin, 1962.

The Rubáiyát of Omar Khayyam. With Introduction by Jerome H. Buckley. New York: Collier Books, 1962. 9–18.

"The Fourth Dimension of Victorianism." *Victorian Newsletter*, 31 (1967), 7–10.

Review of *A Drama of Political Man: A Study in the Plays of Harley*

Granville Barker by Margery M. Morgan. *Modern Drama*, 5 (1962), 246–47.

Review of *Fathers of the Victorians: The Age of Wilberforce* by Ford K. Brown. *Journal of English and Germanic Philology*, 61 (1962), 935–37.

1963

Idylls of the King. Selected and introduced by Jerome H. Buckley. Boston: Houghton Mifflin, 1963.

1964

Review of *The Poetry of Clough: An Essay in Revaluation* by Walter E. Houghton. *Journal of English and Germanic Philology*, 63 (1964), 378–80.

Review of *Tennyson's Maud: The Biographical Genesis* by Ralph Wilson Rader. *Journal of English and Germanic Philology*, 63 (1964), 820–22.

1966

The Triumph of Time: A Study of the Victorian Concepts of Time, History, Progress, and Decadence. Cambridge, MA: Belknap Press of Harvard University Press, 1966; London: Oxford University Press, 1967.

Victorian Poets and Prose Writers. Compiled by Jerome H. Buckley. New York: Appleton-Century Crofts, 1966. Second edition, revised and enlarged, Arlington Heights, IL: AHM Publishing, 1977.

1967

"Symbols of Eternity: The Victorian Escape from Time." In *Victorian Essays: A Symposium*. Edited by Warren D. Anderson and Thomas D. Clareson. Kent, OH: Kent State University Press, 1967. 1–16.

"Tennyson's Irony." *Victorian Newsletter*, 31 (1967), 7–10.

1968

The Pre-Raphaelites. Edited with an Introduction by Jerome H. Buckley. New York: Modern Library, 1968. Revised edition with a new Bibliography, Chicago: Academy Chicago, 1986.
Review of *Shelleyan Ideas in Victorian Literature* by Roland A. Duerksen. *Keats-Shelley Journal*, 17 (1968), 126–28.

1969

"*The Victorian Temper* Revisited." *New Literary History*, 1 (1969), 69–73.
Review of *Tennysonian Love: The Strange Diagonal* by Gerhard J. Joseph. *Modern Language Quarterly*, 30 (1969), 618–20.

1970

"Autobiography in the English *Bildungsroman*." In *The Interpretation of Narrative: Theory and Practice*. Edited by Morton W. Bloomfield. Cambridge, MA: Harvard University Press, 1970. 93–104.

1972

"Pre-Raphaelite Past and Present: The Poetry of the Rossettis." In *Victorian Poetry*. Edited by Malcolm Bradbury and David Palmer. London: Edward Arnold, 1972. 123–37.

1974

Season of Youth: The Bildungsroman from Dickens to Golding. Cambridge, MA and London: Harvard University Press, 1974.

1975

The Worlds of Victorian Fiction. Edited by Jerome H. Buckley. Cambridge, MA and London: Harvard University Press, 1975.
"A World of Literature: Gissing's *New Grub Street*." In *The Worlds of Victorian Fiction*. 223–34.

1976

"Victorian England: The Self-Conscious Society." In *The Mind and Art of Victorian England*. Edited by Josef L. Altholz. Minneapolis: University of Minnesota Press, 1974. 3–15.
Review of *Victorian Conventions* by John R. Reed. *Nineteenth Century Fiction*, 31 (1976), 114–18.
Review of *Tennyson's Major Poems: The Comic and Ironic Patterns* by James R. Kincaid. *Journal of English and Germanic Philology*, 75 (1976), 450–53.

1979

Review of *A View of Victorian Literature* by Geoffrey Tillotson. *Western Humanities Review*, 33 (1979), 167–69.
Review of *The Confessional Fictions of Charles Dickens* by Barry Westburg. *Nineteenth Century Fiction*, 33 (1979), 508–12.

1980

"Howard Mumford Jones." *American Philosophical Society Year Book 1980*. 595–98.

1981

"George Eliot's Double Life: *The Mill on the Floss* as a Bildungsroman." In *From Smollett to James: Studies in the Novel Presented to Edgar Johnson*. Edited by Samuel I. Mintz, Alice Chandler, and Christopher Mulvey. Charlottesville: University Press of Virginia, 1981. 211–36.
"Constructing and Deconstructing Autobiography." *Review*, 3 (1981), 95–102.
Review of *David Copperfield*, edited by Nina Burgis. *The Dickensian*, 77 (1981), 172–73.
Review of *The Tennyson Album: A Biography in Original Photographs*, compiled by Andrew Wheatcroft, and *Tennyson: The Unquiet Heart* by Robert Bernard Martin. *Victorian Studies*, 24 (1981), 511–13.

Jerome Hamilton Buckley: a bibliography

Review of *The Forms of Autobiography: Episodes in the History of a Literary Genre* by William C. Spengemann, and *Approaches to Victorian Autobiography*, edited by George P. Landow. *Nineteenth Century Fiction*, 36 (1981), 79–83.

1982

"The Persistence of Tennyson." In *The Victorian Experience: The Poets*. Edited by Richard A. Levine. Athens, OH: Ohio University Press, 1982. 1–12.
"Well-Brokered Talents: The Victorian Profession of Authorship." *Victorians Institute Journal*, 11 (1982), 117–28.

1983

"Towards Early-Modern Autobiography: The Roles of Oscar Wilde, George Moore, Edmund Gosse, and Henry Adams." In *Modernism Revisited*. Edited by Robert Kiely. Cambridge, MA: Harvard University Press, 1983. 1–15.
Review of *Dickens and Women* by Michael Slater, *Charles Dickens: Resurrectionist* by Andrew Sanders, and *Dickens and the Short Story* by Deborah A. Thomas. *Nineteenth Century Fiction*, 38 (1983), 334–37.
Review of *Figures of Autobiography: The Language of Self-Writing in Victorian and Modern England* by Avrom Fleishman. *Modern Language Quarterly*, 44 (1983), 325–27.

1984

The Turning Key: Autobiography and the Subjective Impulse since 1800. Cambridge, MA and London: Harvard University Press, 1984.
"The Identity of David Copperfield." In *Victorian Literature and Society: Essays Presented to Richard D. Altick*. Edited by James R. Kincaid and Albert J. Kuhn. Columbus, OH: Ohio State University Press, 1984. 225–39.
"Looking Backward: Victorian Poetry and Prose." *Victorian Newsletter*, 65 (1984), 1–3.

1985

"The Jekyll–Hyde Life of a Man of Letters." *Boston Sunday Globe*, January 20, 1985, 87, 89. (Review of *The Memoirs of John Addington Symonds*, edited by Phyllis Grosskurth.)
"A Life behind a Screen." *Times Literary Supplement*, March 15, 1985, 275–76. (Review of *With Friends Possessed: A Life of Edward FitzGerald*, by Robert Bernard Martin.)

1986

Review of *E. J. Pratt: The Truant Years 1882–1927* by David G. Pitt. *Journal of Canadian Poetry*, 1 (1986), 138–40.
Review of *The Sense of the Past in Victorian Literature* by Raymond Chapman. *Clio*, 16 (1986), 81–84.

1987

Review of *Memory and Writing: From Wordsworth to Lawrence* by Philip Davis. *Victorian Studies*, 30 (1987), 423–24.
Review of *The Inner I: British Literary Autobiography of the Twentieth Century* by Brian Finney, and *Victorian Autobiography: The Tradition of Self-Interpretation* by Linda H. Peterson. *Journal of English and Germanic Philology*, 86 (1987), 461–64.

Index